Caribbean Time Bomb

CARIBBEAN TIME BOMB

The United States' Complicity in the Corruption of Antigua

Robert Coram

PUBLISHED BY ROBERT CORAM

Published by Robert Coram, 2007

ISBN 978-0-615-16996-5

First published in 1993

Book design by Bernie Klein

Printed in the United States of America

For all my students

Acknowledgments

Many people contributed to this project.

In Atlanta, Linda Matthews, head of Special Collections in the Woodruff Library of Emory University, pointed me toward valuable reference works. In New York, George Wade has been of immense and continuing help. In Vermont, retired U.S. Customs agent Larry Curtis provided highly significant and heretofore unpublished information. In England, Robert and Alison Spendelow shopped for various books not available in America; they also tracked down King Juan II.

Numerous people in Antigua opened their homes and their hearts. They wish to remain anonymous. I hope that one day the mood of their country will change and that they will not fear to have their names associated with a project such as this.

A special thanks to Harvey Ginsberg, an alchemist of an editor.

Finally, Jeannine Addams, more than anyone else, made it happen.

Contents

Book Two

EACH ENDEAVORING, ALL ACHIEVING

Book Three

"ANTIGUA ME COME FROM"

Caribbean Time Bomb

Prologue

From Jamaica east to Puerto Rico and down through the southward plunge of sun-splashed islands that constitute the Leewards and the Windwards and stretch all the way to South America, there is no country so corrupt as Antigua. The modern history of Antigua is chronicled in the recurring scandals that have distressed the nation since 1978. Facts of the corruption and details of the scandals are well-known to most Antiguans. The names of the knaves and the future plans of the con men who slouch through Antigua also are recognized. But because all of this malfeasance radiates from one of the great heroes of the Caribbean—Prime Minister Vere Cornwall Bird—nothing is done. No punishment is meted out. And today the carnival of corruption continues.

The story of Antigua is more than a simple story of moral decline. It is the story of how something noble was wrecked. The most enduring and the most uplifting dream in the hearts of men, especially in the hearts of former slaves and former colonial subjects in the Caribbean, has been the dream of freedom. Antigua was lifted to freedom in the great arms of Vere Cornwall Bird. He made the dream come true. But extortion, rapacity, and an insatiable greed destroyed the dream. The moment was lost. And that is the melancholy story of Antigua.

Vere Cornwall Bird is the last surviving member of that group of grand old men who leaped from the trade union movement of the 1930s and 1940s to become political leaders who carried their countries from the servitude of colonialism to the glory of independence. They were men who, within the brief span of a single generation, lifted their people from the hell of the canefields to full equality in the family of nations. Because Bird fills a unique niche in the history of Antigua, he is in fact, if not in title, Prime Minister for Life. Bird became Antigua's first national hero at a time when Antiguans yearned for such an individual. He was all they had. And because heroes are few on Antigua, there is a compulsion to hold onto and to venerate Vere Cornwall Bird.

V. C. Bird, as he is commonly known, is to Antigua what George Washington was to America. Because Antigua is so small and because there are so many islands in the Caribbean, Bird is not well known to the outside world. But inside the region his aura shines brightly—or at least it did until the late 1980s. Now tragedy is tied to the name.

The story of how a national hero became a figure of ridicule and of how his tightly knit family disintegrated is a warning to everyone about the perils of money and power and success. And the story of how Antigua was brought to the precipice of collapse can serve as a signpost for small countries around the world.

V. C. Bird has dominated the Antiguan trade union movement and Antiguan politics for more than a half century. He is called "Papa" and "The Father of the Nation." Only one man, a lonely and often-ridiculed newspaperman named Tim Leonard Hector, has loudly and consistently raised his voice against V. C. Bird. And Hector has been arrested eleven times for his temerity. Twice he was jailed and denied habeas corpus hearings—once for nine days and once for nineteen days—before being released.

Antiguans read but did not react to much of what Tim Hector wrote. They forgave Bird's every offense, and at each election but one they returned him to office. They watched impassively as V. C. Bird turned Antigua into a virtual totalitarian state and became the undisputed sole ruler who suppressed almost every form of opposition. On no other island in the Caribbean has so much political power been concentrated for so long in the hands of one man.

Had Bird retired after leading his country to independence, he would be recognized as the greatest of all Antiguans and the most noble of Caribbean men. But now he has a dual legacy.

On one hand he will forever be remembered as the man who fought and prevailed against the horrors of British colonialism; the visionary who shook off centuries of slavery and servitude on the great sugar estates; the bold leader who used a fledgling trade union to achieve political power and to found a new nation. But he also will be remembered for the corruption that he first condoned, then sponsored, and finally participated in. His face has appeared on the label of beer bottles and casino chips, his name on the international airport, and his hands in everything. Under V. C Bird, Antigua has become not only a sanctuary but a spawning ground for crooks and scoundrels, a place where, for the right price, one can buy everything from a diplomatic passport to a government minister, an island where all of one's schemes, no matter how illegitimate, can find official sanction. No other Caribbean nation, not even Haiti under the Duvaliers, has been plundered and mismanaged for so long in so public a fashion by a single family and with such devasting results.

Members of the Bird family have long believed that because of V. C. Bird's early years, they have almost a divine right to rule Antigua. When I first met members of this extraordinary clan more than a decade ago, they were united against political pretenders. But now the two oldest brothers are engaged in a bitter battle to succeed their father. I have talked with both brothers about their bitter strife, and I have watched the family become fragmented, as members shift their allegiance from one brother to the other.

Antigua may be the last country in the Caribbean in which a head of state employs totalitarian tactics to ensure that a political dynasty is established and that one of his sons succeeds him in office. V. C. Bird has used tear gas and armed riot police to break up peaceful gatherings of the opposition, and he often denies opposition politicians vital access to government-owned radio and television.

The prime minister's oldest son, Vere Bird, Jr., is a man in whom the farcical and the dangerous commingle. Tall, stooped, bright-eyed and anxious, Vere junior is extraordinarily devoted to his father. For years he was a member of the Cabinet; and if constituent services can be a criterion, he may be the best pure politician on Antigua. But like the firstborn son of many great men, Vere junior has had considerable difficulty fulfilling his potential. Vere junior turns up at the center of almost every money-grubbing plot in Antigua, everything from an $11 million airport scandal to gunrunning for Colombian drug smugglers.

Lester, the second son, is considered brilliant and charismatic, an inspired orator, and by far the most intellectually gifted of the prime minister's children. Massive, defensive, hedonistic, and a man of overweening ambition, Lester had the opportunity and the ability to continue his father's political leadership and to become the hope of Antigua and a spokesman for the Caribbean. He might have brought this oft-neglected region the recognition it so badly needs and the respect it so desperately craves. But today Lester Bird is among the most tragic figures of the Caribbean. He traded his birthright for a bowl of porridge.

A third son, Ivor, operates the family-owned radio station. Angry, dull, loutish, and avaricious, Ivor, like many dull-witted men with borrowed power, confines his actions within a very narrow range—usually between ludicrous and absurd. He once tried to sell one of the most historic spots on Antigua to a New York organized crime family, but he is best known for his excessive drinking, bar fights, and general dissolution. Roswald, a fourth son, is a college teacher and something of a mystic who surfaces from time to time to remind Antigua that his family is "destined" to govern the nation. As if to balance the scales, a daughter, Hazel, is a radio evangelist who inveighs against the wages of sin.

She has much to preach against, since under her father, Antigua, which once was among the wealthiest islands in the West Indies, has become a supplicant in the community of nations, a worst-case scenario of what can happen to a former colony after independence: pandemic corruption, a country tottering on the edge of bankruptcy with an infrastructure that is falling apart.

Outside of Antigua and beyond the confines of the U.S. State Department, it is not generally known that for more than a decade Antigua and America have had an extraordinarily close relationship. No other English-speaking island in the eastern Caribbean has had a greater U.S. presence or received more

U.S. dollars than Antigua. What most Americans do not know, and what the United States government would like to keep secret, is that America has spent almost two hundred million dollars since 1979 to support and perpetuate the government of V. C. Bird.

The United States displays such avuncular political closeness and such financial benevolence because Antigua has virtually abandoned its sovereignty where the giant to the north is concerned. The Bird government has granted concessions to the U.S. government that America gets nowhere else in the world. For example, any aircraft belonging to the U.S. government can land on Antigua any time of the day or night, without prior notice, and without anyone on board having to go through Customs or Immigration. This gives the U.S. military, the CIA, and a half-dozen other government agencies carte blanche to use Antigua for whatever secret training exercises, enforcement efforts, or clandestine operations military men or government agents can devise. Plausible denial can be maintained because there is no record of the U.S. presence. And it is doubtful that any other small island nation anywhere in the world would allow the U.S. military, on a regular and consistent basis, to blow up its coral reefs as part of underwater demolition training. But until 1991, once or twice each week, big hunks of Antigua's reefs were blasted out of the sea by America's underwater warriors.

In return for such privileges, America has propped up Bird's government with numerous grants from the Agency for International Development. Two U.S. military bases—an air force tracking station and a naval support facility—are second only to tourism in their economic impact. While these two bases are cash cows for Antigua, they contribute virtually nothing to America's national defense. In the late 1980s, Antigua increased the annual rent for the outposts by two thirds—the fee was raised from $750,000 each to $1.25 million each. (All currency references are to U.S. dollars unless identified as East Caribbean dollars [EC$].) Various attempts have been made to close the bases—their functions could easily be duplicated elsewhere—but Bird's entreaties to the State Department kept them open. In 1990 the Pentagon began multimillion-dollar expansion programs at both bases. Without this enormous and continuing

U.S. financial support, it is likely the Bird government would have collapsed years ago.

Nevertheless, the Bird government, time after time, has defied, provoked, and antagonized the United States. Because Bird is considered a friend and because America needs a Caribbean playpen, the United States ignores all but the most egregious confrontation and goes to extraordinary lengths to avoid confronting what the State Department privately describes as "the most corrupt government in the Caribbean."

Consider a few incidents from the past:

- When Robert Vesco, who had defrauded American investors of $224 million and who was wanted by the U.S. Department of Justice for an illegal campaign contribution to Richard Nixon, was discovered hiding on Antigua, Lester Bird deceived and misled State Department officials until Vesco escaped. Yet a few years later, the U.S. government stopped an Internal Revenue Service investigation of Lester Bird. Lester was born in New York and is a U.S. citizen—a multimillionaire U.S. citizen who pays no taxes. Lester was so emboldened by United States malleability that he forced the State Department to change its official records so that "four of his legitimate children" might be declared U.S. citizens.
- U.S. Navy vessels, on at least three occasions, smuggled 155-millimeter howitzers into Antigua for transshipment to South Africa—actions that violated a United Nations embargo.
- After America'a primary interest in the Caribbean shifted from curtailing the spread of communism to curtailing the spread of illegal narcotics, the U.S. government did nothing and said nothing when Vere Bird, Jr., was caught moonlighting as a gunrunner to a Colombian drug cartel. The British jurist who conducted an inquiry into the affair made a pointed reference to the refusal of the U.S. government to provide information crucial to the inquiry.
- Land under long-term lease to the U.S. government was, on at least two occasions, leased again to third parties by the Antiguan government, in one instance to an American organized-crime group. The Antiguan government also

pressured the State Department into returning part of the land leased for the U.S. Air Force tracking station. And when an Antiguan businessman appropriated and fenced in a section of the Air Force base, the Bird government refused to intercede.

- Antigua is considered a significant nexus in the narcotics trafficking business. But for years Antigua was the only country in the eastern Caribbean that refused to share information about narcotics trafficking and money laundering with the U.S. government. Antigua relented in 1991 after being promised substantial financial grants under a U.S. narcotics assistance program.
- Antigua is an annual destination for some 200,000 tourists, 47 percent of whom are from America. These tourists fly into what is advertised as a tropical paradise and the premier "up market" in the Caribbean. But the Bird government allows many hotels to pump raw sewage into the sea only a few yards off the most popular tourist beaches. No island in the Caribbean is more of a public health hazard to tourists than Antigua.
- The U.S. government gave green cards to Vere Bird, Jr.; to Cutie Francis, who until 1992 was the prime minister's longtime mistress and a woman of great political influence; and to almost every official in the Bird government. If a shift in Antiguan politics should threaten any of these Antiguans, their green cards will allow them to flee to America.

Today the flawed relationship between America and Antigua continues. Like a bumbling giant courting a diseased tropical princess, America continues to shower Antigua with money, attention, and protection. Without America's continuing intervention and support, the history of Antigua could well have taken an altogether different course.

Antigua is a three-island nation located about twelve hundred miles southeast of Miami and a little more than two hundred miles east-southeast of Puerto Rico. Antigua and Barbuda, along with the uninhabited island of Redonda, are three of the quirkiest and most disparate islands in the Caribbean. That they compose one country is proof either of God's sense of humor or of English bureaucracy run amuck. Antigua (pronounced *An-TEE-ga*) is oval-shaped and measures roughly nine miles by twelve miles. The eastern coast faces the blue waters of the Atlantic Ocean, and the beaches—except in a few protected coves—are too rough and wave-pounded for hotels. The western shore faces the tranquil Caribbean Sea and is the location for most of the island's forty-odd hotels. The population of Antigua is about sixty-two thousand.

Antigua is physically different from many of its Caribbean neighbors in that it is relatively flat. Only in the southwest corner of the island can a few small mountains be found. Boggy Peak is the tallest, at 1,330 feet. Tourists always want to go to the tallest peak, but to reach Boggy Peak requires a taxi ride up a rough unpaved road and then a half-hour walk. Taxi drivers do not like to drive up unpaved mountain roads, they do not like to walk, and they do not like to wait when they could be carrying another fare. So most taxi drivers rarely mention Boggy Peak. Rather, they tell visitors that Shirley Heights, which is on the distant southern coast and can be reached by paved road, is the highest peak.

Like much of the Caribbean, Antigua suffers from occasional hurricanes, storm surges, wave action, landslides, and, less frequently, earthquakes. But it is the lack of mountains that causes perhaps the most serious of regularly recurring disasters. Because there is no landmass tall enough to break moisture-bearing clouds, Antigua has an annual rainfall of only about forty inches, most of which occurs in the summer months and is, as one seventeenth-century writer said, of such "prodigious impetuosity" that much of the water runs into the sea. Droughts of Old Testament dimensions occur every few years, and water must be imported from Dominica at about $20,000 per bargeload. The lack of fresh water remains an expensive and unresolved problem for hotels.

English Harbour—one of the best-known hurricane holes in the Caribbean—and Nelson's Dockyard, both on the south side of Antigua, are reminders that Captain Horatio Nelson served here from 1784 until 1787. English Harbour is one of the world's premier yachting centers; and each year the winter tourist season officially ends in April with Antigua Sailing Week, an event that attracts some of the grandest yachts in the world.

Rising above English Harbour, Nelson's Dockyard, Falmouth, and much of the southern part of the island is Shirley Heights. Hundreds of Antiguans and tourists congregate here each Sunday afternoon for one of the best long-running parties in the Caribbean. Tourism-conscious Antiguans sponsor the party. Buses jammed with hotel guests and cruise ship visitors haul tourists to the mountaintop, where they congregate around what once were gun emplacements that guarded the harbor. Men and women stationed at the U.S. military bases are there. Antiguans are there. In fact, this is the only place on the island where tourists and Antiguans socialize together in any appreciable numbers. They drink beer, eat barbecued chicken, listen to calypso bands, and, as they look out over the sea and the mountains, understand what the poet meant with the phrase "where every prospect pleases."

Tourists are often disappointed with much of what they find on Antigua. At many hotels, making an overseas telephone call is a laborious process that requires giving the number to an operator, then waiting ten or fifteen minutes. If the telephone operator is taking a break or if it is mealtime, the call might not be made for an hour. On most days, the electricity goes off several times, sometimes for minutes and sometimes for hours. During summer months the government desalinization plant provides water only one or two days each week, and homeowners who turn on their kitchen faucets often get nothing but sludge and rust. As for the famous sights of Antigua, English Harbour, which is filled with white faces and "yachties," offers little and charges much. Fig Tree Drive, a narrow and tortuous road lined with a few banana trees, is mentioned in all the tourist literature. This "rain forest," as some tourism literature calls it, is much touted by cab drivers, almost certainly because it is a long ride from the capital city and not because of any inherent attractiveness. A visit there invariably leaves the tourist asking, "Is that all there is?"

What does stick in the mind of the tourists is the roads. They are narrow and have potholes large enough to qualify as landmarks. Speed limits are not enforced and local vehicles usually operate only at top speed. There appear to be no rules of the road. Antiguans pass each other on blind curves and over the crest of hills with such reckless abandon that the sides of many cars are dented and scraped and manifest a national rust rash. Even normally circumspect State Department literature cautions government employees about the hazards of driving in Antigua. The situation is aggravated by the unfettered cattle and donkeys that roam the island. There are few road signs, and an attempt to drive around the island can result in hours of wandering.

From the air, Antigua seems green and lush and covered with thick forests. But in truth the island is almost devoid of trees. The greenery comes from bushes and from the scraggly, thorn-covered acacia shrub that Antiguans call "cassy." A visitor finds that here a banana is called a fig, an avocado is called a pear, and that this island, once world famous for its sugarcane, today grows so little cane that the molasses to make Cavalier rum—Antigua's national product—must be imported.

Even though there are few road signs on Antigua, eventually all roads lead to the capital city, St. John's. Half the population of Antigua lives in St. John's, a city pushed into and overflowing from a declivity high on a ridge on the northwestern flank of the island. The city is dominated by a cathedral at the top of the hill and a casino at the bottom. In between is a rabbit warren of brightly painted chockablock buildings that tumble down the hill and sprawl in a tangled hodgepodge at the edge of one of the loveliest harbors in all the Caribbean. Chickens and goats and spavined dogs roam the narrow streets. Cars park at various angles, and the jammed thoroughfares must be negotiated slowly and with great care. Old men sit in the shade and play a board game called warri. Raw sewage flows into many of the open gutters. Near the top of the ridge, along Independence Avenue, the flow is minimal and the odor barely noticeable. But as one saunters from the cathedral down toward the harbor and the casino and the expensive stores of Heritage Quay and Redcliffe Quay where cruise ship visitors congregate, the volume grows and so does the aroma. In the most heavily traveled portion of St. John's, the olid air wraps the visitor in a hot and oppressive blanket; the greatest danger in crossing a street is not that of being run over but that of stepping ankle-deep into a camarine sludge of human waste.

Today the young people of Antigua and the thousands of Antiguans who have emigrated to England, Canada, or America are restive. CNN has shown those left behind that there is another world out there, and they crave to be part of that world. They are ardent consumers who want to forget the poverty-racked years of colonialism. They desire the latest cars, the newest television sets, and all the gadgets the Americans take for granted. These Antiguans know more about the corruption of V. C. Bird than about his historical legacy. They know the Bird government has pushed Antigua into a slough of failure and corruption from which it will take years to emerge.

But it has not always been this way. There was a time when Antiguans looked toward the future as a united and committed people. There was a time when Antiguans had an unshakable confidence in V. C. Bird and felt that this great bear of a man, this former Salvation Army captain, would lead them to the promised land. His shoulders were broad enough to carry his people, and his stern visage was a symbol of probity and rectitude. V. C. Bird would show them what freedom and self-determination were all about.

There was a time when Antiguans had hope.

CODRINGTON LAGOON
Codrington
The Highlands
BARBUDA
Sand Ground
The River
Palmetto Point
Cocoa Point
Antigua approximately
28 miles, S.W.

DICKINSON BAY
McKINNON'S SWAMP
RUNAWAY BAY
DEEP BAY
U.S. Naval Facility
Antigua Air Station
Antigua International Airport
St. John's
Crabbs Peninsula
ANTIGUA
MILL REEF
Bethesda
English Harbour
WILLOUGHBY BAY
Shirley Heights

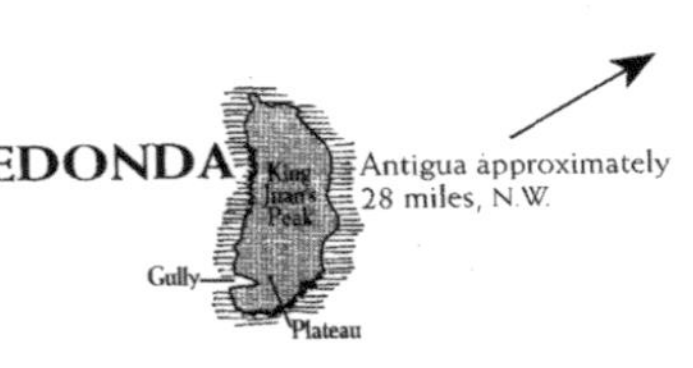
REDONDA
King Juan's Peak
Gully
Plateau
Antigua approximately
28 miles, N.W.

Book One

UNDER THE TAMARIND TREE

1

Cockles and Widdy Widdy Bushes

The pivotal event in the history of Antigua occurred under a tamarind tree near the remote village of Bethesda on the south-eastern side of the island. In January 1951, Bird stood in front of several hundred poor and hunger-wracked canefield workers and looked at Alexander Moody-Stuart, who, as managing director of the Antigua Sugar Estates, Ltd., controlled the syndicate that represented the political and economic power of Great Britain. Moody-Stuart was a man considered almost omnipotent by those who worked in the canefields. But Bird stared Moody-Stuart in the eye and said his people no longer would toil in the canefields for a shilling a day; that they would strike until they were given an honest day's pay for an honest day's work. And then, like an Old Testament prophet, he raised his great arm and thundered that until better wages came, "We will eat cockles and the widdy widdy bush. We will drink pond water."

Moody-Stuart laughed. He was straight and crisp and natty in his white drills. He almost sparkled in the sunshine, and he was a jarring counterpoint to the work-bent Antiguans, whose gaunt bodies were covered with little more than rags. He stared up at Bird in disbelief. Then he threatened Bird. One old man who was there recalls that Moody-Stuart said, "I will crush you into subjection. I will beat your head against a wall."

V. C. Bird remained calm. "We will eat cockles and the widdy widdy bush," he repeated. The message was clear: Do what you must; use every weapon at your disposal, but we will not work until you increase our pay. Moody-Stuart climbed atop his great white horse and rode away. And Vere Cornwall Bird rode into the pantheon of Caribbean heroes.

There is no historic marker at the tamarind tree. The solitary tree stands by the side of a little-traveled road, and the tourists who occasionally pass do not give it a second glance. But if an older Antiguan mentions "the tamarind tree," most other Antiguans know the place of which he speaks. In a swale, isolated and alone, the tree stands about forty feet tall. Its trunk is twisted and its bark is dull gray. Surrounding fields are covered with weeds and "cassy" bushes. Off toward the south, perhaps a mile away, the pale emerald expanse of Willoughby Bay sparkles in the sun. The bay is backed by Horseshoe Reef and the great blue Atlantic; and strong easterlies, after racing unfettered all the way from Africa, cross Willoughby Bay and the weed-covered fields and rustle the leaves of the tamarind tree. One can stand in its shade and listen to the leaves sigh and moan in the wind from Africa.

The account of what took place here in January 1951 comes from Bird, from union loyalists, and from a few old people who were there when it happened. Some people who lived in Antigua at the time recall neither the event nor the speech. But this doesn't matter; it is not important. The history of Antigua—that is, the history of Antiguans as a people free from colonialism—is brief, and there is not much in that short span of years to engender a stirring in the national bosom.

And history, the oral history as remembered by V. C. Bird and recorded by his trade union, is clear and unequivocal. For as long as there is an Antigua, what Bird said at Bethesda will be remembered and invoked whenever an Antiguan wishes to show determination and willingness to sacrifice for the cause of freedom.

One of the many ironies of Antiguan history is that Bethesda, named for the biblical city and meaning "place of healing," was the location for such a tumultuous event. Bird knew when he made his speech that his words would unleash the full fury of the British sugar plantocracy upon Antiguans. Not only the workers but their children would suffer. If Bird did not prevail against Moody-Stuart, Antiguans would remain in a condition barely distinguishable from that of the years of slavery that officially had ended with emancipation in 1834. The canefields were infernal regions from which there was no surcease. Salaries differed only by a few pence from what had been paid to slaves a hundred years earlier. And now the Antigua Trades and Labour Union, of which Bird was president, was demanding a more equitable system.

In 1951, in most countries where there was an organized labor force, this would have been a basic, simple, and legitimate request. But in colonial Antigua it was also revolutionary. The trade union had been formed in 1939, about the same time Moody-Stuart organized Antigua plantations into a syndicate; and from the beginning Moody-Stuart had decided if there would be a raise—usually there was not—and then passed his decision down to the union. There was no appeal.

Bird and Moody-Stuart remembered their previous confrontation. It had happened several months earlier when Bird told the Englishman, "We will not plant this year's crop until we know the amount of our wages." Moody-Stuart refused to name a figure and the union voted to strike.

Moody-Stuart went to see the governor. A young Englishman on his first important appointment, he was intimidated by Moody-Stuart and was well aware of the deference other planters afforded the man. So the governor readily agreed when Moody-Stuart asked him to declare martial law. By January 1951, when Bird and Moody-Stuart met under the tamarind tree, the strike had been in force for several months and union members were in desperate straits. The tourism industry was still unknown, there were few manufacturing facilities, and for most Antiguans the canefields were their only source of money. Their plight was aggravated by two devastating hurricanes that had struck the island within ten days of each other the previous September. Many homes had been leveled and gardens destroyed. Moody-Stuart was convinced that with no money and no food the families of union members would pressure them to return to the fields. The strike, which many workers felt was an obligatory and necessary part of every negotiation, had lasted long enough for them to believe the point had been made. It was time to return to work. Perhaps next year the union would win.

But every time Bird had fought Moody-Stuart in the past, he had come away with far less than he wanted. This time he must win. Before Moody-Stuart's arrival at the tamarind tree, Bird had beseeched the workers to continue the strike, promising that this time there would be no compromise.

Bird and the workers had nothing to lose. The land was covered, as Bird still reminds Antiguans in his speeches, "with cattle, horse, and donkey mess," and stagnant ponds were the only source of drinking water. Bird convinced Antiguans to make whatever sacrifices were necessary to improve their lot. The basic concern was food. If the workers continued to strike, what would their wives and children eat? Bird gazed across the canefields at Bethesda, at the place where the four great sugar estates of Blakes, Ffryes, Delaps, and Long Lane came together, and he saw a roadside patch of wildbush, a sort of broomweed that Antiguans call the widdy widdy bush; he looked across the emerald serenity of Willoughby Bay, from whose beaches hungry Antiguans sometimes dug cockles to boil and eat; and he knew what he would say to Moody-Stuart.

As Moody-Stuart rode away that day, he must have thought that this was his chance to break the union. From his point of view there was nothing in Bird's background to cause alarm. Bird had been born December 7, 1910, on New Street, one of the most brutal slums in St. John's. He was the illegitimate son of a destitute father who later had committed suicide. Because the island's Anglican-run secondary school did not accept illegitimate children, Bird had only an elementary school education. He had spent two years in the Salvation Army and, during the past decade, had gained a reputation as a man who used physical means to solve disagreements. In the eyes of Moody-Stuart, Bird was little more than a semiliterate union leader, a union leader who, oddly enough, was known as the first strikebreaker on Antigua. During World War II, Bird had worked at Coolidge Field, the U.S. Army Corps base, as a timekeeper. When his fellow workers voted to strike, Bird came to work before the strikers could set up a picket line and, by so doing, broke the strike before it began.

But the Antiguans who toiled in the canefields had an entirely different view of Bird. Antiguans are a deeply religious people, and Bird's service in the Salvation Army made him someone special. Antiguans considered Bird a mystic, a towering man of religious certitude and trade union zeal. Already they were beginning to call him "Papa."

The Antigua Trades and Labour Union had been formed in 1939, and Bird became president in 1943. He energized the union, moving tirelessly about the island "organizing the unorganized," in the phrase of the day.

Throughout the region, charismatic labor leaders were emerging as political leaders: Robert Bradshaw of St. Kitts, William Bramble of Montserrat, Grantley Adams of Barbados, Ebenezer Joshua of St. Vincent, Eric Gairy and T. A. Marryshow of Grenada, and Alexander Bustamante and Norman Manley of Jamaica. These men were turning union strength into political strength. Bird was pursuing the same path to power. He had already been elected by Antiguans to serve on the island's legislative council and was also on the executive board of the council.

Bird remembers exhorting the assembled caneworkers after Moody-Stuart rode away; he evoked Antigua's failed march from slavery, and he reminded his listeners of their emancipation in name only and of their colonial subjection. Even today, more than forty years after the confrontation at the tamarind tree, these highly emotional topics remain Bird's political touchstone.

So come with me now back through those melancholy years. Because unless one understands slavery and sugar, unless one can feel the heat of the canefields and the burden of colonialism, there is no understanding of how V. C. Bird was able to take his people from the edge of the abyss into the sunlight, and then from the sunlight to the edge of another abyss.

2

Sugar and Slaves and Everything Bad

When V. C. Bird stood under the tamarind tree and angrily said that Antiguans would eat cockles and widdy widdy bushes before submitting to further mistreatment from British colonial masters, he was giving voice to a people who had forever been disenfranchised. With his speech, he uncapped a deep and roiling well of animosity that had bubbled in the Antiguan heart for more than three hundred years, a well whose water remained bitter through the generations.

The Africans who were brought to Antigua as slaves were as isolated and remote as the island upon which they lived. Antigua has always been set apart from its Caribbean neighbors. Located on the outer northeast corner of the Leewards as they begin their precipitous plunge to the south, it hangs off to the side as if flung there by centrifugal force.

Columbus discovered Antigua. On November 11, 1493, he sighted it from a distance but did not come ashore. He paused long enough to name it Santa María de la Antigua after a cathedral in Seville before sailing away. Because Antigua had no fresh water, it was disregarded for more than a century.

Those were years of intrigue and war in which Spain was decimating the indigenous Amerindian population and Holland, England, and France were increasing their possessions throughout the region. Wars of colonial rivalry used the islands of the West Indies as pawns. St. Lucia changed hands fourteen times. But no one wanted Antigua. The Spanish tried to settle the island in 1520, but it was too dry and they moved on. In 1629 the French tried, but they also abandoned the island.

It was not until 1632 that a group of English settlers sailed down from St. Kitts and claimed the island for the British crown. Within days this remote outpost of empire was attacked by Indians, who kidnapped several of the settlers' wives before the attack was repulsed. The Indians returned many times over the years, presumably more to harass the settlers and plunder their supplies than to take Englishwomen. But the English had an amazing tenacity when it came to holding on to land that was not really theirs, and each time the Indians were defeated. However, in 1666, the French seized the island and retained possession until it was returned to England the next year by the Treaty of Breda. Occasional Indian attacks continued until the turn of the century, but by then the little English outpost had become a bastion of empire and was far too strong for marauding Indians.

Sugar was the source of Antigua's strength. King Sugar. The most significant aspect of Columbus's second voyage was not the discovery of Antigua or any other island, but rather that he brought sugarcane to the New World. Dr. Eric Williams, a former prime minister of Trinidad and Tobago and the Caribbean's premier historian, said sugarcane was "the greatest gift of the Old World to the New." Even though Columbus brought sugarcane in 1493, it was almost two hundred years later that Antigua began producing sugar. By then, production had spread from Hispaniola to Jamaica, Puerto Rico, Cuba, and throughout the Caribbean. Sugar plantations existed on Antigua, but not until 1674 did Christopher Codrington, an Englishman with a sugar plantation in Barbados, bring modern planting, harvesting, and processing technology to the island.

In a region where there is no winter and life is a long stretch of bright, sun-blasted days, sugarcane can grow as it will grow nowhere else in the world. Only days after planting, the cane bursts through the soil and stretches upward. Canny planters early on saw the potential for enormous profits if one problem could be overcome: labor. The planting, growing, and harvesting of sugarcane and the processing of the cane to sugar is extraordinarily labor-intensive, a never-ending toil of Sisyphean proportions. It is work that no indentured bondsman from England or Ireland could perform, and the work was too hot and too tough even for convicts who were provided an unwelcome detour on their route from England to the colonies. The English and the French would have enslaved the indigenous Indians, but by that time most of them were dead.

So the English planters of Antigua, as did planters throughout the Caribbean, and as did cotton planters in the colonies of the American South, turned to the slave trade. The slave trade had begun about 1515 with the Spanish and was adopted by the Portuguese, the Genoese, the Dutch, and—in 1564—by the English.

Historians call the combination of slavery and sugar the Great Triangular Trade: ships left Europe or America with goods to be exchanged on the west coast of Africa for slaves. This was the first side of the triangle. The second side, called the Middle Passage, was the voyage from Africa to the West Indies or America of boats packed with slaves. (Mortality rates aboard the slave ships were as high as 34 percent, and in the waiting furnaces of the canefields it was even worse: Eric Williams says that for every fifty-six blacks still alive on a plantation at the end of three years, forty-four had perished.) The third side of the triangle was the voyage from the West Indies to Europe or America with sugar or rum.

This practice was of such deep and heinous dimensions that it has become almost genetically imprinted on people of the Caribbean. Just as Jews will remember the death camps of World War II for a thousand years, so today, centuries later, slavery and colonialism remain as fresh in the mind of Caribbean people as if they happened yesterday. This evil matrix dominates almost every aspect of Caribbean life, a still-festering historic burden that bows the psychological back of virtually every black person in the region.

But the English, like other colonial powers, never realized—and there is no evidence they cared about—the legacy that slavery, sugar, and colonialism would leave in the Caribbean. The English were interested only in the almost incalculable wealth being brought from there. This subjugation of an entire race is the reason that today, on English-speaking Caribbean islands, there remains such a dichotomy of feeling toward the English. Although Antiguan society was founded upon the cultural and economic exploitation of black people by the English, the only system Antiguans had to emulate was that of their oppressors. Their government, their heritage, their speech, the everyday minutiae of living—all came from the English, the people who raped their women, humiliated their men, and ignored their children. As a result, the values of many middle-class Antiguans today are the values of the English. But other Antiguans find anathema anything and everything to do with England.

"Betty's Hope" was the first modern sugar plantation on Antigua. Only two years after Christopher Codrington brought in the new technology, so many planters had followed his lead that sugar had become the most important crop on the island. By 1706 the island was almost 100 percent committed to sugar; twenty-seven sugar mills were located there.

In 1710 a group of assemblymen, representatives of government elected by white planters, attacked and killed the governor of Antigua. The incident must have served as an example to the slaves, because a generation later a group of them plotted to revolt and seize control of Antigua. They were to strike during a party attended by the planters; and had not the date of the party been changed, and had not the conspirators fallen to arguing among themselves, thus allowing the plot to be discovered, in all likelihood the plan would have succeeded. And had the conspiracy of 1736 been successful, Antigua would have been the first island in the heart of the Caribbean in which slaves took control. The origin of the scheme, unlike the successful plot that resulted in establishing the black Republic of Haiti a half century later, was strictly internal: Antiguan slaves were revolting against their treatment by British sugar planters.

By 1748 the number of sugar plantations on Antigua had risen to 175. What had been a densely forested island became a denuded land. By 1764 Antigua had 300 sugar plantations and a population of about thirty-seven thousand, of which twenty-five thousand were slaves. In the Caribbean, its wealth was surpassed only by Hispaniola and Barbados. For the next two hundred years Antigua's economic strength was to remain almost exclusively in sugar, a dependency that, in good times, brought Croesean riches to sugar planters, but one that in bad times brought devastation to planters and slaves alike.

Codrington achieved prosperity beyond calculation. The

expression "wealthy as a West Indian planter" was coined because of men like him. In 1685, eleven years after he opened Betty's Hope, he leased the nearby island of Barbuda from the British crown to be used as a provisioning station for his plantation. The lease would pass down through various generations of Codringtons for the next century and a half, and the results of Barbuda's being a privately held fief outside the mainstream of Caribbean development was to cause unique and still-continuing problems for that tiny island.

When Antigua's newfound wealth made it attractive to other European nations, the English raised protective forts around the island, spacing them so cannon could provide overlapping fields of fire. Since cannonballs then carried as far as a mile, the English constructed more than three dozen such forts. The largest was Shirley Heights, which remained the most important even after England's military bases in the Caribbean were drastically reduced.

The presence of the British military was comforting to Antiguan sugar planters, for the fear of slave uprising was pervasive and enduring.

By the mid-1700s, slaves were the economic foundation of Caribbean life. The quarrelsome countries of Europe have seldom been as unanimous on any issue as they were on the value of slave labor in the Caribbean. And West Indian planters exercised vast influence in European affairs, particularly in England, where they were the most powerful group in Parliament.

One of the quirky little footnotes to Antiguan history, and also a comment on how the impact of slavery remains a factor in everyday Antiguan life, is the presence of mongooses on the island. They were brought to Antigua in the 1800s to clear the canefields of rats. Even though the rats, fat and slow from gorging on the sweet sugarcane, were a staple in the diet of Antiguans, they multiplied in such numbers that they became pests and health hazards. The mongooses not only ate the rats, they ate just about everything else they could find on the ground, including snakes and a burrowing owl, both of which are now extinct on Antigua, replaced by the bright-eyed mongooses. The sleak little creatures slither from the shrubbery at every hotel, pop their quivering noses out of the tall grass, and frolic along the edges of the beach. They have no natural predators; their life is a Valhalla of eating and breeding.

The influence of sugar planters continued unabated until the latter part of the eighteenth century, when whispers of abolition escalated into a thunder of public sentiment. Abolition, to most sugar planters, was anathema. And planters were supported in this by the British Navy, especially its senior officers: that is why planters erected statues of British naval heroes throughout the Caribbean; that is why Nelson's Dockyard in Antigua is preserved.

Nelson sailed to Antigua in 1784 as a twenty-nine-year-old captain. His billet was as temporary commander in chief at English Harbour. He was vigorous in enforcing the Navigation Acts, which prevented foreign ships—particularly those from the newly independent United States—from trading with British islands. Eric Williams says the Navigation Acts also "sacrificed" the West Indies to British commercial interests. Nelson was not a popular man on Antigua, and his letters and records of the time show the dislike was returned. He often complained of the heat and the bugs and the weather, and he called Antigua a "vile spot" and "this infernal hole."

By the beginning of the nineteenth century, two factors were working against the continued success of the sugar plantations. First, protective laws and tariffs kept the price of sugar high even while the demand for free trade in sugar was growing. Second, Antiguan sugar planters and their protectors in the British Navy ignored the growing antislavery movement. By 1807 the revulsion against the slave trade resulted in a law that made the importing or trading of slaves illegal. Sugar planters ignored the law, and slave trading continued until emancipation was enacted in 1834.

As emancipation approached, Great Britain suggested that its colonies in the West Indies take four years to make the shattering transition from slavery. In turn, Antiguan sugar planters met to discuss how they might oppose this threat to their business. To the consternation of those present, Samuel O. Baijer, a planter and leader of those who opposed abolition, stood up and said, "I have been making calculations with regard to the probable results of emancipation, and I have ascertained beyond a doubt, that I can cultivate my estate at least one third cheaper by free labor than by slave labor."

He convinced his fellow planters. And Antigua, alone in the English-speaking Caribbean, and purely for the economic benefit of planters, went from slavery to emancipation overnight. Emancipation was to become effective at midnight on a Saturday. Late that afternoon slaves from all over the island began walking toward their churches; they wanted to be worshipping when the hour of freedom came.

Nicholas Nugent, speaker of the House of Assembly, told a group from the American Anti-Slavery Society in 1837: "There never was so sudden a transition from one state to another by so large a body of people. When the clock began to strike the hour of twelve on the last night of July, 1834, the Negroes of Antigua were slaves—when it ceased they were all free men! It was a stupendous change and it was one of the sublimest spectacles ever witnessed, to see the subjects of the change engaged at the very moment it occurred, in worshipping God."

In the years after emancipation, some sixty-seven villages were established around the island as Antiguans moved away from the plantations and sought their own destiny. The villages had names such as Liberta, Freetown, and Freemansville.

But with emancipation came a harsh reality. Baijer had been right—emancipation was an economic boon to planters: it was far cheaper for British planters to pay wages to free men than it was to feed and support slaves. Antiguans had to work on the plantations—there were no other jobs—but now the planters could pay whatever they wanted. They did not want to pay much. The former slaves had no choice but to stay in the canefields, working from dawn to dusk for a shilling a day. As free men in a British colony, Antiguans knew even greater deprivation than they had as slaves.

The latter part of the nineteenth century was bitter as gall for Antiguans. Novelle Richards, the poet who also chronicled the history of the Antigua trade union movement, wrote that these years were the burning crucible in which Antigua's determination was forged. The sugar industry continued its decline, as European sugar beet growers realized their product could supplant sugar. As a result, all Antiguans suffered. They lived in rickety and leaky homes built of woven sticks plastered with mud—the infamous "wattle and daub" houses whose dirt floors were home to vicious, biting "jiggers." Antiguans wore clothes of burlap, and their houshold utensils were pottery and hollowed gourds. Light came from a flambeau, a rag stuffed into a bottle of kerosene, and the only source of water was the same pond from which animals drank. Diseases ravaged the people. Epidemics were common.

Novelle Richards wrote that rarely have a free people been beset with so many reasons to long for the security of those colonial times when medical attention, hospitals, and food were provided, when all the needs of the people were attended to by the famed British civil servants who ran the country smoothly and with an efficiency that only the British, the world's greatest natural corps of civil servants, could master.

Riots broke out as Antiguans demanded higher wages and an education that would enable them to compete both in the emerging Caribbean and in the outside world. They wanted to be represented in the political process. But the British sugar barons were so concerned about their crumbling economic empire that they failed to realize Antigua was becoming a boiling pressure cooker. They screwed down the lid of control even more tightly.

In 1918, when a group of angry Antiguans burned several plantations and attacked St. John's, V. C. Bird was eight years old. One of his earliest memories is how, in the ensuing riot, the police shot and killed several people. The riots were quelled and the British colonial system remained unchanged.

On January 13, 1928—shortly after he turned eighteen—V. C. Bird entered the Salvation Army. Six months later he was appointed a cadet sergeant on the Salvation Army Training College staff in Trinidad. On August 12, 1929, he was promoted to captain and assigned to Grenada. Four months later, on December 5, he was granted homeland furlough. He went to Antigua and never returned to the Salvation Army. Then, as now, it was assumed that when people joined the Army they would remain for life. Bird never gave the Salvation Army a reason for his not returning. His service officially ended in December 1929, although the Army waited until July 30, 1930, to close his records.

For the remainder of his life Bird would hark back to his two years in the Salvation Army. In many trade union speeches he would draw upon the cachet of his captaincy, realizing that the trade union, when sanctified by the Almighty, translated into powerful politics.

Bird has said many times that he left the Salvation Army because of racial discrimination; that the Army then did not allow its black officers to sleep in the same bunkhouse with white officers. However, there is no record of any complaint from Bird or any letter of his resignation in any Salvation Army records. I pursued this question from the regional headquarters in Atlanta to the national headquarters in Virginia to international headquarters in London and finally back to the Caribbean. The territorial commander of the Salvation Army in Jamaica wrote and said, "Whether he left the Army because of racial discrimination or not, I do not know. It would however be unfair to print such information unless there was solid proof to suggest his contention that he suffered racial discrimination."

Bird's political opponents have long maintained the true reason he abruptly left the Army was that he had been accused of misappropriating Army funds. The territorial commander again denies this. His letter said, "There is *No* [his emphasis] indication in our records to show that the then Captain was guilty of any form of dishonesty, or to show that he was dismissed for dishonesty. If he had been . . . I am sure that this would have been so stated in our records."

The time between Bird's leaving the Salvation Army in December 1929 and his emergence as a leader in the trade union movement in 1939 is a missing decade in his life. In his speeches, he rarely mentions these years. And beyond the writings of union supporters, there is no credible history of that decade. However, the controversy that surrounded Bird's Salvation Army career continued. For a while Bird worked as a bookkeeper for the largest baker on Antigua. In her book *A Small Place,* Antiguan writer Jamaica Kincaid says that Bird seemed unusually prosperous for a young bookkeeper, and that when the baker wanted to see the financial records, Bird tossed them into a furnace.

Westindian Digest, a magazine published in England that is effusive in its praise of everything Caribbean, has another perspective on the missing decade in Bird's life. In the issue of

November 1988, the magazine's publisher wrote, "Bird had his own business, established a few years before. He was doing quite well and could have sat on the sidelines, earning a good income and leading a comfortable life. But the need to change the society, to improve the lot of the poor, raged within him. It was a fire he could not extinquish, a thirst he could not quench. Bird turned his back on a life of comfort and assumed the workers' cause as his personal crusade."

During the 1930s, the Caribbean was a cauldron of discontent: strikes on St. Kitts, a revolt against paying customs duties on St. Vincent, strikes on St. Lucia, labor disputes in British Guiana, a general strike in Trinidad, a strike in Barbados, and labor problems on sugar plantations and the docks in Jamaica.

Sugar prices continued to fall, plantations went broke, and mass unemployment was the rule. Every British governor in the West Indies called for ships and troops to quell disturbances. In the British colonies, more than three dozen people were killed and more than one hundred were wounded.

During the early 1930s V. C. Bird fathered an illegitimate daughter, Hazel. Then in October 1936, his wife gave birth to their first son, Vere Cornwall Bird, Jr. On February 21, 1938, came a second son, Lester Bryant Bird, and Roswald and Ivor followed. Bird's home was so small that Vere junior and Lester slept in the same bed. A few years later, after V. C. Bird and his wife separated, and V. C. became engrossed in trade union activities, Vere junior became a father substitute for his siblings, a paternal older brother responsible for their safety, meals, and well-being. It was a role he would cherish all his life; and when the family became fragmented, he turned those powerful paternal instincts toward his constituents.

In 1939, V. C. Bird emerged from the historical shadows as a founding member of the Antigua Trades and Labour Union. It was his first step in becoming a national figure. By then, law and order were threatened throughout the Caribbean. A Ulotrichian Lodge had begun on Antigua wherein workers were secretly taught their rights. Anger over the conditions in the canefields caused riots, and sugar workers were fired upon by agents of Moody-Stuart. Two people were killed and thirteen were injured. But when it was all over, not a penny more was being paid to workers. Discontent grew.

A royal commission from Great Britain came to Antigua to investigate; and one of the commission members, Sir Walter Citrine, a trade unionist, called for a public meeting in the schoolroom of the cathedral in St. John's. At the meeting he urged Antigua sugar workers to form a trade union and fight for better working conditions and more money.

Two weeks later the Antigua Trades and Labour Union was organized with Reginald St. Clair Stevens as the first president. V. C. Bird was a member of the board, a group referred to as "the Executive." Reginald Stevens was a jeweler, a very conservative businessman who is remembered as honest and straightforward in his dealings both with Moody-Stuart and with union members. But there were some who thought he proceeded too slowly. In September 1943, Stevens was forced out and V. C. Bird was elected president. Stevens, like several other early trade union leaders, died under mysterious circumstances a few years later. Jamaica Kincaid says Antiguans link the allegation that V. C. Bird burned his employer's books to the replacing of the original honest members of the union.

With a new and growing trade union as his power base, the career of V. C. Bird was launched. This illegitimate and uneducated young man from the slums of St. John's was about to confront Moody-Stuart and the sugar syndicate. He was also about to do battle with the economic and colonial power of Great Britain.

3

The Birds Flock . . . and Meet a Newspaperman

One hot afternoon in the summer of 1992, I stopped by the side of the road near Bethesda and talked with an old woman who was cutting grass from a ditch. Her body was stooped and most of her teeth were gone, but her eyes revealed a fiercely independent spirit. When I asked her about the tamarind tree, her eyes widened and she said she had been there; that she was among the workers standing behind V. C. Bird when he confronted Moody-Stuart. She picked up the front of her long skirt to show me how she had carried widdy widdy bushes, and she told me how she had plucked fruit from the guinnip tree and crushed and boiled it and then mixed it with fish to make stew for her family. She said her family had drunk pond water and that often they were sick. The times were so hard that five or six adults would sit in a tight circle and share a single cigarette.

Then I asked her about the prime minister, about Mr. Bird. She stood a bit taller. Her eyes flashed as if daring me to disagree. "V. C. Bird, he put shoes on our feet," she said. "Radio. He bring radio to us. V. C. Bird and Labour. They do it."

"Is he a good man?" I asked.

"After God, come V. C. Bird."

Events unfolded in a predictable fashion following the confrontation at the tamarind tree. Moody-Stewart cracked down harder, and the suffering of Antiguans became greater. Cockles and widdy widdy bushes, washed down with stagnant pond water, became their regular fare.

The temptation to end the strike and go back to work was

strong. To make sure the workers remained resolute, Bird sent union men to the various estates. Moody-Stuart charged those men with attempting to incite a riot and sent them to jail. Others were banished to jails in England, and it is only in recent years that some of them were released and returned to Antigua.

But the workers stood fast; they did not return to the cane-fields. Bird filled them with hope, a hope born of desperation. They hoped for fair wages. They hoped for political strength. They hoped for a better life for their children. They hoped for decent homes and enough food. They hoped for better educational opportunities. And while they hoped, they fought the English colonial masters. A rash of fires swept Antigua. The Globe Hotel and the office of the colonial secretary were burned, as were barges along the waterfront. Other boats were sunk. The British sent in the Welsh Fusiliers to quell the disturbances. Then came a commission of inquiry. The commission wanted to talk to V. C. Bird, who clearly was the moral force behind the strike. But Bird refused to appear until British troops were removed. He had begun to think of Antigua as "my island." The British agreed with his demands and packed up. An election was held that year for the Legislative Council, the island's governing body, and V. C. Bird and the trade union won an overwhelming victory.

But Bird also had a major setback in 1951. The battle with Moody-Stuart turned so vicious that he was afraid he would be jailed; he traveled to the U.S. embassy on Barbados, where he applied for a visa to America. He remembers that the visa was refused and that he came back to Antigua to carry on the battle. There is no doubt that the United States had reservations about granting Bird a visa. Those were the days when Bird was flirting with communism, a time when he picked the first Monday in May, a date very close to May 1—the great holiday of communism—as Labor Day on Antigua. Even today, trade union men from the old days call each other "comrade." Whether or not Bird was refused a visa is not known. What is more probable is that the process became so protracted that Bird grew impatient and returned to Antigua.

Bird's recollection is that the strike lasted a full year before Moody-Stuart capitulated and the trade union realized its first great victory. Workers received a 25 percent pay increase, a large percentage, but because the salary was so small, not much additional money.

As is always the case on Antigua, history has at least two diametrically opposed versions. The sons of planters or estate managers dismiss the incident at the tamarind tree. They say the strike lasted about three months and that the crop for that year was lost. Then there was a period of about six months before the next crop and in the interim the strike was settled. They say the old ways continued; that, in fact, Bird cut a deal with Moody-Stuart not to call any more major strikes in the canefields, and that Bird agreed to focus trade union attention on small businesses. These sons of estate managers contend Bird's victory has assumed a symbolic importance far out of proportion to its actual impact.

Symbolic or not, the victory was the foundation for a series of advances for the ATLU. And even if the victory was symbolic, it nevertheless was a victory. And for people who had never won in their dealings with the British, symbols were important. The victory also marked the beginning of the end for both the sugar syndicate and colonialism.

Bird takes full credit for what happened after the confrontation at the tamarind tree and for the advances that followed. And he deserves credit. But the early 1950s were tumultuous and pivotal years throughout the Caribbean. Sugar planters knew the days of King Sugar were numbered. And Great Britain knew that once the great sugar estates were gone, the Crown would have little reason for being in the Caribbean. Throughout the islands, people were increasingly demanding proper roads, better schools, modern medical facilities, access to higher education, and not only a seat at the political table, but a place at its head. The time was coming when the islands no longer would be the British West Indies, but simply the West Indies.

In many ways, the most important factor for change had been World War II. While the people of the Caribbean were beginning to form trade unions, Franklin Delano Roosevelt and Winston Churchill had met in 1940 to do a little horse trading. Churchill came out of the deal with fifty destroyers and Roosevelt wound up with ninety-nine-year leases for military bases in Trinidad, Guyana, Antigua, St. Lucia, Jamaica, and the Bahamas, as well as in Newfoundland and Bermuda.

No money changed hands. It was a clean swap—boats for real estate.

On Antigua, the United States controlled the northern third of the island. Today, of all the islands involved in the Roosevelt-Churchill trading, Antigua is the only one on which America still has a presence. The other bases either reverted to Great Britain after World War II, or, when the individual islands became independent, to the local governments.

World War II brought an American presence throughout the Caribbean. And on Antigua, America did what Great Britain had never done: trained Antiguans in semitechnical and technical jobs, paid them fair salaries, and—most important of all—turned their heads away from England and toward the north, toward America.

The attraction was mutual. American soldiers stationed on Antigua saw an idyllic island whose numerous picture-book beaches were devoid of hotels. The soldiers began to talk of the potential in tourism and of what would happen when the world heard of this wondrous place.

One of the first developments after the war was Mill Reef, a residential community on the southeast coast where some of the wealthiest families in America, among them the Mellons and Harrimans, built million-dollar homes with spectacular views of the sea. Because Mill Reef was the first and because it was so rarefied, Antigua thought of itself as "upmarket"—a place that catered to the wealthy. It was a belief that, some four decades later, would lead to a potential catastrophe.

Mill Reef was as quiet, remote and insular as it was exclusive. The millionaires there supported Holberton Hospital and provided scholarship money for promising young Antiguans, but the dollars were not as widespread as Antiguans had hoped. As they waited for the surge in tourism, they became impatient. They knew there was a country besides Great Britain whose people had money to spend. But Antigua continued to depend on sugar—an industry that by then was gasping for life.

In 1956 the ministerial system of government was introduced and V. C. Bird was appointed minister of trade and production. And in 1961, when trade union representatives formed a majority in the legislature, he became chief minister, controlling both the ATLU and the government.

In the late 1950s and early 1960s, the long-awaited surge in tourism finally began. Today Bird takes credit for moving his country from sugar to tourism. Again he deserves credit, for he was in a position of leadership when the change happened. But tourism was the only choice open to Antigua, just as it was the only choice of other Caribbean islands.

In 1965 the sugar industry was in such serious trouble that Moody-Stuart said the syndicate would close down the estates unless the British government provided financial assistance. Confronted with the prospect of thousands of Antiguans losing their jobs, the British government provided the equivalent of about $1 million to bail out the syndicate. Then George Walter, the popular general secretary of the ATLU, demanded higher wages. Moody-Stuart knew the bailout was only a stopgap and that within a year or two the declining sugar market would force the syndicate to close the estates. He was incredulous that a union, which in effect was also the government, was making demands that the government itself would have to satisfy. So he granted the wage increase. Walter was a hero to those who worked in the canefields—they got the raises—but he created a financial nightmare for his union colleagues in government who had to find the money to pay for the raises. Not long after granting the wage increase, Moody-Stuart left his palatial hilltop home and quietly returned to England.

The trade union, which from the beginning was Bird's base of support, demanded as much of his attention as did his government post. Personality clashes and political animosities frequently led Bird to expel senior union members. George Walter was one of those expelled, ostensibly because he had organized an unauthorized strike but more likely because of his popularity. Walter formed his own union, the Antigua Workers Union, and, as its political arm, the Progressive Labour Movement (PLM). Bird's opposition to the Antigua Workers Union was as personal as it was bitter. Many members of the AWU were former members of Bird's ATLU. His power was diminished each time a disgruntled member left to join the AWU, and it was not long before the new trade union had almost as many members as Bird's.

In 1966, a constitutional conference was held in London, with Chief Minister V. C. Bird representing the crown colony of

Antigua and Barbuda. It was agreed that Antigua, Barbuda, and Redonda would become an associated state of Great Britain, one of the first colonies in the eastern Caribbean to achieve associated statehood.

Associated statehood is rather like independence with training wheels; the mother country takes care of serious matters while the fledgling state handles the housekeeping. Antigua conducted its internal affairs while Great Britain remained in charge of national defense and foreign affairs. Because an associated state is led by a premier rather than a chief minister, V. C. Bird became the first premier of Antigua.

By then the members of Bird's Antigua Labor party were easy to identify. Red and white were their colors, and party loyalists wore the colors every day: red shirts, red pants, red belts, and red socks. Some even wore red shoes and drove red cars.

In 1967, Bird's government, aided by a loan from Great Britain, took over thirteen thousand acres of sugar lands, putting much of the island, the sugar industry, a powerful trade union, and the government itself in the control of one man—V. C. Bird.

In 1968 Bird exercised his power in a way that astonished his countrymen and provided a profound insight into his character and into how he would respond to political opposition. It was the first step in his transformation from Caribbean hero to despot. The Antigua Workers Union under George Walter had grown to the point that it was demanding official recognition. On February 12, 1968, a crowd estimated at more than ten thousand marched to insist on union recognition. Bird remembered how Moody-Stuart dealt with labor problems; and before the strike could be called, he declared a state of emergency and implemented martial law. No more than two people could walk abreast down the street. When another crowd formed to insist on union recognition, Bird ordered the police to disperse it with tear gas.

Perhaps the most significant thing about the protest, even beyond Bird's use of tear gas, was that it marked the political debut of Tim Hector, a man who, for the next quarter century, would fail in his pursuit of political power but who would become one of the most fearless journalists in the Caribbean.

Hector had recently returned from more than a decade in Canada, where he had been an avid follower of America's civil rights moment. When Bird's policemen tossed tear gas into the crowd—Hector says they "lobbed the canisters in a gentle parabola"—it was Tim Hector who showed the crowd how to catch the canisters and toss them back at the police. When the police set up barricades and organized phalanxes of riot-gear-equipped men to charge into the crowd, it was Tim Hector who told the crowd to take to the rooftops and stone the police. Bird's attempt to suppress the new union failed, in part because enough civil servants cast their lots with it to almost paralyze the government, but also because of Tim Hector. The government was forced to recognize and to negotiate with the new union.

In 1971 George Walter won the general election and became premier. Papa Bird, the man who had energized the trade union movement and who had confronted Moody-Stuart at the tamarind tree and who had won major concessions from the sugar syndicate and who had been the first premier of Antigua, was tossed aside.

During the next few years Antigua would face strife and tension. And V. C. Bird would be at the center of the conflict, reprising his role as an outsider fighting established authority. Bird, who attended conferences with Norman Manley of Jamaica, Eric Williams of Trinidad, and Grantley Adams of Barbados, all of whom were graduates of Oxford University, liked to present himself as a man of statecraft, great intelligence and considerable negotiating ability. But being rejected by the people whom he had led for so long was a devastating blow, and he reacted as would anyone who had learned his political lessons in the give-no-quarter world of a union organizer.

In 1970 Bird had opened ZDK, a new, family-owned radio station. During the years when he was out of power he used the radio station, along with some dubious political techniques, to create fear throughout the island. Explosive devices were set off, and, while no one was killed, the bombs created great tension and anxiety. It is widely suspected that Bird ordered the bomb campaign in order to undermine the Walter government. No one else had any reason to undertake such systematic terror. ZDK regularly reported—sometimes truthfully and sometimes not—that bombs had been planted in various schools. Each broadcast forced the schools to close and send the students home. Bird's union followers were suspected of burning several boats and of assaulting Walter's supporters.

The early 1970s were the low point in the life of Lester Bird. The prime minister's second son had left Antigua in 1957 to attend the University of Michigan and then law school in London. After living abroad for more than a decade, he came home shortly before his father was defeated as premier. After the election, Lester was heckled and ridiculed on the streets of St. John's. A proud man, Lester did not take the abuse kindly. The overnight transition from being the son of Antigua's most prominent union and government official to being the son of a defeated politician was mortifying and painful. Lester's wife is from St. Lucia and she had never liked Antigua. So in 1971 Lester packed his bags and planned to return to London. He was never coming back to Antigua.

Tim Hector intervened. Lester and Tim had been boyhood friends. Both had left Antigua about the same time to attend college. During their years abroad they had frequently corresponded. Now they were home as part of Antigua's intellectual elite. Hector, wanting Lester to stay, managed to have him appointed head of a local cricket association. The game of cricket is to Antigua what baseball is in America, and to be head of the cricket association was enough of an honor to keep Lester on the island. Hector asked Lester to be the godfather of his son Rohan, who was born in 1972. Lester and his older brother, Vere junior, who was also a London-educated lawyer, opened the law firm of Bird and Bird. Then Hector saw to it that Lester was hired as the attorney for his newly formed political party, called the Antigua Caribbean Liberation Movement (ACLM).

The brothers who had slept together as small boys now worked in the same office, and their law practice thrived. They saw each other socially and visited often with their father and helped plan his return to political power. Both Vere junior and Lester announced they would be candidates for Parliament in the next general election. The two young men had never been closer to each other or to their father.

The recession of the early 1970s sent out shock waves that overwhelmed Antigua. Walter was forced to shut down the last vestiges of the sugar industry. Antigua's oil refinery was closed. And tourism, which had begun with such promise, almost disappeared. Unemployment was high. Shortly before the next general election, Rowan Henry, a popular lawyer, and his wife were murdered. Bird publicly hinted that someone in Walter's political party had killed Henry.

It was almost as if the historical wave that Bird had ridden to such advantage had pushed him aside long enough for another person to take the blame for Antigua's problems. Then the wave picked up Bird again. After five years on the beach, he returned to the premier's office in 1976. Vere junior and Lester were elected and became part of his government. One of V. C. Bird's first actions was to file charges against George Walter for profiteering while in office. Walter went to jail for several months. He appealed and his conviction was overturned, in part because of evidence that V. C. Bird had tampered with the jury.

By all accounts, Bird's time out of office was the most searing experience of his life. After he returned, it was as if he had realized the fragility and ephemeral nature of political power. He formed a new government that was devoid of even the appearance of restraint. And his two sons were about to become embroiled in a series of scandals. During the next few years, Antiguans were to learn a great deal about Vere junior and Lester.

Vere junior is a thin man with a cervine quality to his long limbs. He has the anxious smile of a puppy that wants badly to be liked, and he can be diffident to the point of fawning. But there is something in his eyes that cautions people not to take him lightly. Those who know him say he is not very bright, that he is an opportunist who would crawl into bed with the Devil. His behavior after becoming a minister did not belie that assessment. Vere junior is a complex person whose character is paradoxical. He describes himself as a "down-home man of the people," and throughout Antigua, even among his enemies, he is known as someone whose word can be depended upon. Unlike many Antiguan officials, he is approachable; and his constituents often call him by his first name. When Vere junior entered government, he asked for and was given the portfolio of minister of public works, aviation, and communications, a ministerial post with the most patronage to dispense, and he worked it with consummate skill. He is a paternal sort, the ultimate ward-heeling machine politician who engenders an almost fanatical devotion. Although he soon became a multimillionaire, Vere junior continued to live simply.

Not long after becoming minister, Vere junior managed to obtain the first and only license granted for cable TV on Antigua. He got the idea when Dr. Percival Perry, a prominent Antiguan scientist and businessman who once had worked for IBM, presented a highly detailed plan to Parliament and asked for approval to create a cable TV system. The presentation was so detailed that it even included the number, placement, and cost of poles to carry the heavy cables to all parts of the island. Vere junior appropriated the plan and, as minister of communications, granted himself the right to install the system. One of his few modifications was to install the cables atop existing utility poles; after all, he was minister of public works. Today there are few places in the world where rickety utility poles are as cluttered and overburdened as they are on Antigua.

Vere junior is married, but his wife and children have lived in Brooklyn, New York, for many years.

Then there is Lester, whose nickname as a boy was "Giant Malt" because he was the biggest, slickest, and smoothest kid on the island. Lester, an all-American broad jumper at the University of Michigan, has always been a bit distant and aloof. Although he is two years younger than Vere junior, he has always overshadowed his older brother, and it was assumed that one day he would take over as prime minister. Lester is an urbane man, a brilliant and eloquent orator who speaks in stone tablets. He is also six feet four with a heavy frame that gives him an intimidating physical presence. Aside from his sheer bulk, his most impressive physical attribute is his feet. They are enormous. But big as they are, they rarely get him anywhere on time. Lester is famous for scheduling meetings and not showing up; he even schedules meetings when he knows he will be out of the country. The feeling of power Lester exudes is emphasized by his close-cropped hair, full face, and a mustache that curves down the sides of his mouth. As self-indulgent as Vere junior is ascetic, he wears a gold chain around his neck, a big gold ring on his finger, and he drives a BMW (formerly he drove a Lamborghini). He lives in a new, palatial home overlooking the sea.

Like his older brother, he is said to be a millionaire with several fortunes stashed away in Swiss, Bahamian, and American banks. From the time he returned to Antigua to practice law, he made no secret of his desire to become prime minister. Many Antiguans believe that Lester prefers the company of foreigners, particularly wealthy white foreigners, to that of Antiguans.

Lester's wife and children have lived in Connecticut for many years.

Antigua writer Jamaica Kincaid compares the Birds with the Duvaliers of Haiti. She says that Vere junior is the Papa Doc figure, brooding and melancholy with a mean streak that no one wants to awaken, and that Lester is like Baby Doc—a big, fleshy man who enjoys fast cars and faster women.

4

"I Would Do It Again"

In the late 1970s, in a spectacular debut, the Birds of Antigua introduced themselves to the world. An unknown family on an obscure island suddenly was at the center of an international scandal. The other party in the scandal was Gerald Bull, who owned a Canadian-American company called Space Research Corporation. Bull was the greatest artillery-building genius in history. He designed the most powerful and most accurate artillery weapons in the world.

Bull came to Antigua in 1977. Since 1961 Bull's Caribbean operations had been located in a remote section of Barbados, where he was conducting research on HARP, the High Altitude Research Project, whose goal was to accomplish what Jules Verne had fantasized about: developing a weapon powerful enough to launch an artillery shell into space. Bull believed it was not necessary to spend billions of dollars accomplishing the feat; it could be done with his guns for a fraction of that cost. Part of Bull's expenses were borne by Canadian scientists who were interested in using HARP for weather research and communications. But the U.S. Army was paying half the bill; and it was the military applications that the Army found most compelling. As HARP research became increasingly expensive, Bull depended more and more heavily on the Pentagon for funds.

During the 1976 elections on Barbados, Prime Minister Errol Barrow was defeated by Tom Adams, who ordered Bull to pack up his guns and move them elsewhere. After looking around the Caribbean, Bull decided Antigua was the place for him.

Errol Barrows introduced him to V. C. Bird, who had recently been returned to office, and to Lester Bird and his impressive set of portfolios, including minister of foreign affairs and minister of economic development. In 1977 the triumvirate of Bird, Bird, and Bull was formed, a secret agreement was reached, and Bull moved the Caribbean branch of Space Research Corporation from Barbados to Crabbs Peninsula, on the northeast corner of Antigua. There the HARP research resumed. As on Barbados, the U.S. Army continued to be the major source of money for Bull's research, and U.S. Army officers constantly monitored Bull's experiments. Weather and communication uses for HARP were forgotten in the rush to develop more powerful and more accurate artillery weapons.

The arrangement between Bull and the Birds granted Space Research an exemption from customs and immigration laws and said the company could bring in both equipment and military observers from foreign countries without records being kept. This meant that military officers from around the world could come to Antigua to evaluate Bull's weapons, and there would be no way to trace their comings and goings. It is not known how many countries took advantage of this arrangement, but it is known that high officials in the apartheid government of South Africa came, saw, and bought.

V. C. Bird, with the advice of his son Lester, found in Space Research a way to quell any potential demonstrations by political opponents. The two Birds asked Bull to outfit and train an existing but moribund organization known as the Antigua and Barbuda Defense Force. The Defense Force could suppress the marches and demonstrations that are so much a part of Antiguan political life. Bull agreed and the training was conducted by Gordon Dewey, a retired U.S. Army Special Forces sergeant. One of the first duties of the newly trained group was to act as a private security force for Space Research.

The arrangement between V. C. Bird and Gerald Bull remained a secret until 1978, when longshoremen on the docks at St. John's were loading Space Research containers onto a vessel named the *Tugelaland* and a crane collapsed, causing a container to break open. Artillery shells and barrels for 155-millimeter howitzers spilled across the dock.

The Tugela is a river in South Africa. The *Tugelaland* was registered in West Germany to a company that was controlled by the government of South Africa.

Once again Tim Hector found himself deeply involved with the Birds, but this time as a newspaperman. Hector's political frustrations had caused him to turn his attention and his intensity toward journalism. He published *Outlet,* a weekly newspaper, and wrote a column called *Fan the Flame.* Only a few hours after the artillery shells and howitzer barrels rolled across the dock, Tim Hector had been alerted. Hector knew that since 1963 there had been a U.N. embargo against shipping weapons to South Africa. His front-page stories caused local longshoremen to refuse to handle any more shipments from Space Research. Demonstrators took to the streets, chanting, "Space Research must go."

The SRC site at Crabbs Peninsula and the offshore waters were part of a restricted area patrolled by armed guards of the Defense Force. Antiguans could not see what was going on, but they could hear. The noise of 155-millimeter howitzers being fired echoed across the island. There were even stories that SRC was testing large bombs for the U. S. Army. Many people on the island were singing a new calypso song:

The U. S. have this new bomb,
Somebody jokin',
To kill people thousands of miles around,
Is joke they're makin',
Now is one thing I fear, is jokin' they're jokin',
Suppose they want to test it right here,
They have to be jokin'. . . .

The Bird government banned the song from being played on the government-owned ABS Radio and on the family-owned ZDK Radio.

Lester Bird was the government spokesman for everything relating to Space Research. He attacked Hector, saying the newspaper stories were incorrect, that no artillery shells or weapons were being shipped through Antigua, and that the longshoremen who reported the broken containers had seen nothing more than telemetry devices and high-speed-photography equipment. Space Research was supporting the Defense Force and providing money to the government to pay its civil servants, Lester said. And since some one hundred Antiguans worked for SRC, to kick the company off the island would be the same as kicking Antiguans out of Antigua.

Hector wrote that officials at the highest levels of the Bird government were being paid substantial amounts of money to allow Space Research to operate on Antigua. And he printed copies of Space Research checks cashed by the Bank of Toronto and made out to Lester Bird's top aide.

V. C. Bird called a Cabinet meeting, during which his government ministers confronted Tim Hector. The publisher may have lacked proper training as a journalist and he may have been emotional in his writing, but he knew the fundamental principle of investigative reporting: have irrefutable proof of all allegations. Hector marched out a shipping agent and several dockworkers who told the Cabinet they had seen the howitzer barrels and the artillery shells spilled on the dock. He produced copies of freight bills showing how the *Tugelaland* departed Antigua, made a call in Spain, and then continued to South Africa.

Lester Bird dismissed all this. In the orotund speaking manner he favors, Lester said Hector's evidence was "neither irresistible nor compelling," and he told Parliament that Hector should be charged with treason. He organized marches where people wore T-shirts imprinted with the slogan SPACE RESEARCH MUST STAY. And he allowed the shipments of weapons through Antigua to South Africa to continue.

The headquarters of Space Research was a ten-thousand-acre site straddling the U.S.-Canadian border south of Montreal and in the mountains of Vermont. The company was far better known in Canada than in America, and word of what was happening with SRC in Antigua caused a Canadian television crew to fly down and investigate. The Canadians, as do most reporters who come to Antigua, went to the publisher of *Outlet,* the man who had broken the story. Hector learned a valuable lesson in working with the Canadians. He had found that even if he broke a story and hammered the Birds for weeks, little would change. The Birds dismissed him as a frustrated politician and rode out whatever storm he kicked up with his little weekly newspaper. But working with the Canadians taught Hector that he was part of the international fraternity of newspeople. If his articles could seize the attention of the international press, then the international press could publish or broadcast stories that guaranteed a reaction from the Birds. After all, Antigua depended a great deal upon the Canadian and American governments for loans, grants, and gifts. It was embarrassing to the Birds when they were exposed in the international press.

Hector gave the Canadian television crew everything they wanted. He showed them records and he turned over sources. He even called officials in the Bird government and told them the Canadians were on the island to do a tourism documentary. He convinced them to talk to the Canadian reporter. After a few innocuous tourism questions, the reporter turned to the subject of Space Research. The local officials were open and candid. Later they boasted of having been on international television, ignoring the fact their statements about Space Research were creating an international media-storm.

The Canadian report was aired in Great Britain as well as in Canada. Both the United States and Canada then annouced they were opening an investigation into Gerald Bull, his company, and the role of Antigua in what appeared to be a violation of a U.N. embargo against arms-trading with South Africa.

The Bird government was beginning to feel the heat. Premier Bird learned that the BBC World Service was about to air a lengthy story about Antigua and Space Research. He ordered ABS Radio and ZDK Radio to suppress the program.

Antiguans wanted Space Research off the island. More demonstrations took place. For the second time, V. C. Bird teargassed his people.

In the meantime, a federal grand jury was convened in Vermont. The U. S. Customs Service was the lead agency in the investigation, and the special agent in charge was Larry Curtis, a senior agent with considerable experience in investigating international conspiracies. His work on behalf of the grand jury began in 1978 and continued through part of 1980. One of his first duties was to fly to Antigua and determine if 155-millimeter howitzers shipped from Space Research headquarters had stayed on the island as V. C. Bird contended, or if, as the U.S. government suspected, the weapons had been transshipped to South Africa.

Curtis was briefed by the senior State Department official in the eastern Caribbean, the U.S. ambassador in Barbados. The ambassador then called V. C. Bird to advise him that Curtis was arriving and that he was traveling under U.S. government authority.

To this day, Curtis does not know how he was recognized when he stepped off the crowded commercial flight at Antigua's international airport. But a young Antiguan woman representing Premier Bird identified him, escorted him around local customs officials, then showed him where to hire a taxi that would take him to his hotel. "I protested," Curtis remembered. "I told her I was to meet a port official. She said he was not available but that he would contact me."

So Curtis went to the hotel the young woman recommended, a remote hotel on the distant south side of the island. He was not the type to sit around waiting, so once he was in his room he picked up the phone to track down the Antiguan official. The telephone was inoperative. After numerous attempts from a pay phone in the lobby, Curtis finally reached someone in the government who said the port official would contact him the following day.

"The next morning I took a taxi and went to the government center in St. John's," Curtis told me. "The port official was not available. However, he would be soon." In the interim, Curtis was given a tour of the government center. He was escorted from room to room and introduced to various ministers, the last of whom was in a corner office overlooking Independence Avenue. Protesters were chanting and marching outside the office. They carried placards that stated SPACE RESEARCH MUST GO. At one point the chanting reached such a high volume that Curtis grew alarmed.

The minister, whose name Curtis does not remember, smiled and said, "You don't have to worry. These Antiguans make a lot of noise but they won't hurt you." Then the minister smiled, pointed his finger at Curtis, paused a moment and said, "But there is always a first time."

Later that day the port official showed up and escorted Curtis to his office, where he was to present documents that would prove the 155-millimeter howitzers and the radar vans shipped by Space Research had stayed on Antigua. But he could not find the records. And when the port director called other offices, the records were not there either. After a half day of dragging Curtis from office to office, the port official said the records were in Parliament, where the Space Research issue was being debated. The records "might be available tomorrow," Curtis was told.

The next day Curtis met Colonel Rogers Gregory, a vice president of Space Research, and the two men jumped into a taxi and drove out to Crabbs Peninsula. Curtis remembers what happened as the taxi approached the gate that sealed off the peninsula: "A half-dozen guys came running out pointing weapons at me. The cab was surrounded." Even Colonel Gregory was unnerved. He stuck his head out the window and anxiously said, "It's okay. It's Colonel Gregory."

Gregory then summoned Sergeant Dewey from a trailer that served as a command headquarters, and the two men escorted Curtis through the Space Research property. The first stop was at a wooden building constructed from SRC shipping crates—an indication of the volume of equipment that had arrived on Antigua. As he approached the door, Curtis heard what sounded like chanting. Inside were about forty young Antiguans, members of the Defense Force, singing "Space Research must stay. Space Research must stay." As they sang, they applied the same slogan to T-shirts.

Curtis knew that dozens of howitzers had been shipped from SRC headquarters to Antigua. But when he was shown the test-firing area, he saw that "only a few of the 155-millimeter howitzers were there. Radar vans and related range equipment known to have been shipped to Antigua were not there."

Later, when Curtis and the Antiguan port official were having a quiet cup of coffee away from SRC executives, the port official apologized to Curtis for the runaround he was being given. The port official's job was at stake. After a third day of unsuccessful efforts to see records proving the artillery weapons remained on Antigua, Curtis was facing a weekend on the island. And Monday was a holiday. "Maybe you can see the documents Tuesday," he was told. But Curtis doubted he ever would see the papers. And he was tired of being followed everywhere by a government security agent. So he took the next flight out.

However, his investigation for the federal grand jury continued. Lester Bird's training as a lawyer and his years in America had taught him about the long arm of federal grand juries. He was threatened by the investigation and the media attention that could come as a result of the grand jury's work. As would many lawyers under similar circumstances, he launched a preemptive strike and announced that he may have been wrong in his earlier support of Space Research. In November 1978, the Birds formally asked Space Research Corporation to close the Antigua firing range. But the shipments of weapons to Antigua continued. And the U.S. Army remained a close partner with Gerald Bull in developing what was coming to be known as the "Supergun."

South Africa, despite the arms embargo, was building its army into the most powerful military force on the African continent and one of the world's top ten strike forces. But there remained a shortage of heavy artillery ammunition, particularly 155-millimeter howitzer shells. A former CIA agent named John Stockwell told a Canadian television program called *The Fifth Estate* that the CIA wanted to supply the shells to South Africa. The idea was to order an ammunition-laden vessel to South Africa. The cargo ostensibly would be for distribution into Angola, but the South Africans would divert the howitzer shells for their own use. Even though the idea was vetoed by the State Department, Stockwell said the CIA continued to seek ways to assist South Africa.

Whether the CIA used Gerald Bull's company as a conduit to ship heavy artillery and ammunition and portable radar vans to South Africa is not known. What is known is that the weapons and the shells continued to flow to Antigua. Curtis suspects that Bull went to his friends at the Aberdeen Proving Grounds, where the U.S. Army conducts artillery tests, and asked for help. The Army then went to the U.S. Navy for assistance. Curtis says that at least three, perhaps four, loads of shells, gun barrels, and sophisticated radar equipment were shipped aboard Navy LSTs from Cape Canaveral, Florida, down through the Caribbean to Antigua—an extremely dangerous voyage for craft designed for storming enemy beaches rather than traveling on the high seas.

The U.S. Navy shipments were of a clandestine nature from start to finish; the LSTs did not go through the port at St. John's, but rather entered the coral-studded entrance to Crabbs Peninsula and unloaded their illegal cargo in the restricted area guarded by the Defense Force. Curtis believes the shipments then were loaded into sea containers and sent to South Africa.

Several months later, the South African prime minister, P. W. Botha, announced that his country had developed a new long-range 155-millimeter artillery piece of extraordinary accuracy.

It was clear from the information Larry Curtis turned over to the federal grand jury that Antigua was the nexus that made the South African connection possible. As a result of the investigation, Gerald Bull was indicted for and subsequently pleaded guilty to selling more than $30 million worth of howitzers, shells, and radar tracking systems to South Africa. He was sentenced to a year in jail but was released after four months. He went to Belgium. By the mid-1980s Iraq's Saddam Hussein had become his best customer for the latest model of the Supergun.

After the brief Persian Gulf War, U.N. inspectors used oxy-acetylene torches to dismember two Superguns that Baghdad could have used to attack targets more than 150 miles away. These were the follow-on weapons of artillery pieces tested in Antigua. But Gerald Bull was not aware that the culmination of his life's work was being cut to pieces; he had been assassinated in Brussels, killed with a pistol shot to the back of the head as he entered his apartment. His killer was never identified. But because Hussein was a bitter enemy of Israel, it was publicly speculated that the assassin was a Mossad agent.

Most of this Tim Hector was not able to report. The shop where his newspaper was printed was owned in part by a government minister. After Hector published several Space Research stories, his business no longer was wanted. And no other shop would take on the work. *Outlet* closed in mid-1978.

No one on Antigua was charged with any crime in connection with Space Research. In fact, there was no inquiry into the matter.

Larry Curtis, now retired and living in Vermont, has vivid

memories of Space Research. It was his biggest case in a twenty-seven-year career with U.S. Customs, and several things still trouble him. Evidence presented to the grand jury indicated that $200,000 was passed from Space Research to top Antiguan officials. But Gerald Bull was the target of the grand jury, not corrupt Antigua officials, and the information was never made public. And in all the excitement over Bull's indictment and guilty plea, newspaper and television reporters ignored the vital role played by the U.S. Navy in the clandestine artillery shipments.

"I don't know why no one ever picked up on that," Curtis said.

In 1979, when a reference was made in the Antiguan Parliament to lingering problems caused by Space Research, Premier Bird took offense. He stood up and reminded everyone how Gerald Bull had bought uniforms, then equipped and trained the Antigua and Barbuda Defense Force. He reminded Parliment how Gerald Bull provided money to pay government workers. "Space Research was not a mistake," he said. "I would do it again."

5

Firebrand

Tim Hector once wrote that under slavery he would have been a "field nigger," but that is almost impossible to imagine. It is equally difficult to imagine this militant idealist growing up in the dehumanizing conditions of a colony in the British West Indies and then squaring off against the almost-omnipotent Bird family.

One day I went to his home to talk to him about his boyhood, about newspapering, and particularly about how he returned to the business after the Space Research stories, a tale of such a serendipitous turn that even today he shakes his head in amazement when he recalls it.

Hector lives in a small home on Fitzroy Pestaina Street in the northern suburbs of St. John's. As with most roads in the capital city, there are no signs to indicate the name of Hector's street. The long straight thoroughfare runs east and west, and when I wondered how I would recognize the house he told me: "Look for the mango tree in the front yard." The tree is by far the largest in the neighborhood and an easy landmark. Heavy drapes over the sliding glass doors blocked the slight breeze and the inside of the house was oppressively hot.

Tim Hector emerged from somewhere in the rear, wearing only a pair of shorts. As is true with many Antiguan men, his skin is tight, and, were it not for the aldermanic girth of middle age, he might have passed for being in his thirties. His eyes are the eyes of a young and idealistic poet. He is a virtual anablepid, who sees both above and below the surface of things. His speech is that of a man of intellect and passion, intense, driven, and uncompromising. As usual, he was smoking. Through an open door I saw two of Hector's four children and several older people, all part of his extended family. The children are named Che, Indira, Rohan, and Amilcar.

Hector sank into a chair and waved for me to sit on the sofa. He lit another cigarette and nodded attentively when I asked him about growing up in a British colony.

"You must remember that my middle name is Leonard," Hector said."When I was a boy I read of Leonardo da Vinci. Cats like that fascinated me. My name was Leonard and his was Leonardo." Hector's eyes widened and he waved his arms and smiled as he remembered his epiphany. "A man with my name was a sculptor, painter, and one of the great artists of the world. The Renaissance and the Greeks and Romans also fascinated me. And I realized that these islands were capable of producing men like that. We are capable of those things."

Tim Hector was born in 1942. He did not know his father, and he was raised in a strict fashion by his mother, an aunt, and by the extended family that is common on Antigua. Hector's boyhood was different from that of his friends. While buddies like Lester Bird were allowed to play after school, Hector had to come home and read to his grandfather. The most vivid memories of his youth concern those long sultry afternoons spent reading to the old man, who had suffered a stroke. Hector read from newspapers: from *The Worker's Voice,* the ATLU paper; from *The Antigua Star* and from *The Trinidad Guardian.* He also read from books, one of which was a biography of Leonardo da Vinci.

Hector's aunt worked as a typesetter at *The Worker's Voice.* The newspaper was a block from his house, and after he was about ten years old, on the afternoons he did not read to his grandfather, he was at the paper. Novelle Richards, the poet and chronicler of Antigua's trade union movement, then worked there and served as a mentor to young Hector. Together they listened to the *BBC World News,* and Richards would talk to Hector of what was going on globally and how it influenced what was happening in Antigua. One day Richards asked Hector to write a news brief about a story on the BBC, and soon Hector was writing the briefs on a regular basis.

When he was fifteen, Hector wrote a long letter to the editor regarding a near riot that occurred at a local soccer game. The letter presaged what was to become Hector's highly individualistic style of journalism. Deeply personal and politically intense, it was filled with a wide range of historical and literary allusions. He called it an "alternative" sort of newspapering. His letter to the editor did not simply report the events at the soccer game; it compared the disturbance with similar riots on Trinidad and other Caribbean islands, and it raised questions about issues that might have prompted the disturbance. Hector had listened to Eric Williams, the charismatic Trinidadian politician and brilliant historian. He had read Williams's book *Capitalism and Slavery* before it was banned in Antigua. And he had read of Leonardo da Vinci and come to believe he could do anything. All these elements came together in the letter to the editor, which prompted an enormous reader response and set the first dreams of being a journalist dancing in young Hector's head.

Under colonialism, there were only two high schools on Antigua—one for girls and one for boys. The British denied a high school education to most Antiguans because the colonial system needed a large class of laborers to work in the canefields. The few allowed to attend were expected to become civil servants. In the year Hector finished his elementary school education, he was one of five boys to win a high school scholarship; but when he finished high school, he did not enter the civil service. Instead he received a Commonwealth scholarship and went to a university in Nova Scotia in which he majored in history and philosophy.

Hector attended college during the tumultuous 1960s and, like most people in college during those years, was forever changed by the experience. For a naive young man from a tiny colonial island to be tossed into the upheaval of the civil rights movement was a momentous awakening. He heard the speeches of Martin Luther King, Jr., and Andrew Young and Stokely Carmichael and Malcolm X, and his life would never be the same. Feelings and emotions and ideas that few Antiguans his age could imagine were tossed about in his head, and he exploded with the knowledge of what he could accomplish in life. He was overflowing with thoughts that could not be suppressed, and he became a debater of formidable dimensions and the

Canadian spokesman for all matters regarding black West Indians.

All the time he was at the university, Hector was sending articles back home to *The Antigua Star* and *The Worker's Voice*. Articulate and wide-ranging, they created much talk on Antigua. Young West Indian men such as Hector occupied a peculiar place in America's civil rights movement. It did not matter how forceful or how persuasive they might be, their credibility was limited because they came from a country that remained a colony, or, like Hector, had been educated in a former British colony. On the other hand, people who lived in the subjection of a colony had even more to fight for than did American blacks.

West Indians in Canada had little if any influence on the American civil rights leaders who occasionally journeyed there to make speeches. Whatever influence these young people might have, it could be exercised only back home.

In 1967 Hector was doing postgraduate work when V. C. Bird threw George Walter out of the ATLU. Hector rushed home in November and easily found work as a high school teacher. But he was politically awakened, a throbbing, pulsating, would-be agent of change who was determined to take a leadership role in ridding Antigua of the effects of colonialism. He craved to be one of the political leaders who would seize power in the aftermath of colonialism. And the route to political power was through a trade union.

Hector was too much of a firebrand to be at home in Bird's labor union, so he joined in the planning for George Walter's new Antigua Workers Union. He demonstrated such eloquence and powers of persuasion that, once the union was formed, he became chairman of its political party, the new Progressive Labour Movement (PLM). The PLM published a newsletter called *The Trumpet,* and Hector was the only person considered as editor. The format of the paper was simple: a front page taken up with a single story in which Hector attacked the Bird government, and a collection of smaller stories on the inside. Every week the pressrun sold out. It was the first time any newspaper had attacked V. C. Bird, and the newspaper did much to increase the stature and popularity of young Tim Hector. High office and great political power seemed almost a certainty.

Then came the battle with V. C. Bird over union recognition, followed by the march of ten thousand people and the demonstration in which V. C. Bird's police used tear gas. Hector's role in showing Antiguans how to toss the tear gas back at the police is remembered bitterly by V. C. Bird. Because Hector was a bright and promising politician, and because he was largely responsible for rendering Bird's martial law ineffective, Bird had to neutralize him. So Bird called Hector a communist. It was a label that was to trouble Hector for decades.

George Walter was wary of Hector, not because he thought Hector had leftist leanings but because Hector was too messianic, too intense, and too strong-willed—qualities that make for a great journalist but a poor politician. Walter used Hector and then forced him out of the party. When Walter became premier, there was no room in his government for Hector.

To this day Hector remains bitter about how Walter treated him. "The king who can ultimately decide such things is not yet born," Hector said. "And his mother is dead."

Hector did what a defeated politician often does in the Caribbean; he formed another party, the new Antigua Caribbean Liberation Movement (ACLM). He also began writing for *Outlet*, the party's newspaper. It was the year that black American athletes at the Olympics in Mexico City stood atop the awards platform and raised their fists in protest, and that image of a black fist raised on high became the logo of *Outlet*. Many of Hector's articles were highly critical of George Walter's government.

Hector had remained a teacher and was promoted to headmaster of a local school. But many times between 1971 and 1976—V. C. Bird's exile years—he had to close school and send his students home because of what he calls the "bomb scares."

In an effort to control the unrest created by V. C. Bird, premier George Walter issued a Public Order Act, which said anyone desiring to hold a public meeting must first have police approval. Then came the Newspaper Act, which said newspapers had to be licensed and had to pay an annual fee of almost EC$4,000.

Hector could not afford such a fee. He would have to shut down the *Outlet* unless he came up with a solution. In studying the Newspaper Act he found that a newspaper was defined as a "for-sale product." Hector saw this as a loophole and jumped through it—he gave away copies of *Outlet.* Naturally, any contributions were not refused. Even so, Hector was hauled off to jail. He was released after six hours because no one could determine what the charge should be. The government quickly tightened the Newspaper Act to the point that it covered even interoffice memos.

V. C. Bird was fighting to make a political comeback and he liked the way Hector was attacking Walter. He had never read Machiavelli's *The Prince,* but he was enough of a political pragmatist to know that the enemy of his enemy was his friend. Bird forgot Hector's involvement in forcing him to recognize the AWU. He forgot he called hector a Communist. Bird challenged the Newspaper Act, won, and the act was ruled unconstitutional. Bird was delighted when Hector cranked up publication of *Outlet* and continued his attacks on George Walter. Bird and Hector found themselves in a marriage of convenience. But Hector published only a few issues before Walter appealed the decision and won. Again, Hector was out of the newspaper business.

V. C. Bird made speeches promising that, if he were reelected, one of his first priorities would be to repeal the oppressive Newspaper Act. When he returned to office in 1976, he did just that, and Hector was yo-yoed back into the newspaper business. There is little doubt that Bird must have later regretted his repeal of the Newspaper Act, because by unleashing Tim Hector he created a monster.

About this time V. C. Bird took another action that was then little noticed but that would have a marked effect on Antigua in the late 1980s and early 1990s. Bird had not lived with his wife since the early 1950s, and in the interim he had fathered numerous illegitimate children. No one seems to know the exact number, but an even dozen is the accepted figure. Then Bird judged a school beauty contest and was so taken with the thirteen-year-old winner—a wide-eyed and bathukolpic beauty with the improbable name of Cutie Francis—that he moved her into the prime minister's official residence. Soon afterwards Bird quietly sponsored a law lowering the age of consent from sixteen to thirteen. From the prime minister's residence, which was the old Moody-Stuart house, Cutie quickly evolved into a precocious political operative and a shrewd businesswoman. She presided over an era of *Fotzepolitik* that would last until 1992.

Tim Hector had been back in the newspaper business less than two years when he broke the Space Research story. To Hector, this was more than a story; it offended him both on a personal and a philosophical basis that Antigua was involved in the clandestine shipment of artillery weapons to South Africa. George Walter had used him and tossed him aside. And now the Birds were shipping guns to South Africa. Hector wondered if he would always be betrayed by his friends. He wondered why black people in Antigua were sending guns to an apartheid government that would use the guns to kill other black people. He pursued the story with an angry zeal.

Fueled by the same zeal, he went on to attack V. C. Bird at every opportunity. And Bird, a wily old union organizer, was not one to sit and take it.

The government canceled Hector's newspaper registration, then arrested and convicted him for publishing an unregistered newspaper—a criminal charge. Hector paid a small fine. This did not teach him the intended lesson. Hector's journalistic sails have no reefing points. He began a series of stories that exposed the Birds to ridicule among their Caribbean neighbors. So the Bird government passed a Public Order Act, making it a criminal offense for a reporter to probe into the conduct of government affairs, to publish an article that might undermine confidence in a public official, or to criticize public officials. The act also said that the truth of the articles might not necessarily constitute a defense.

The inevitable confrontation came soon after Hector's sources told him of a warehouse on Antigua filled with beer, the label of which carried the prime minister's photograph. Hector sneaked into the warehouse—which he called "a secret place"—and took pictures of the enormous beer inventory. He carried away a few bottles of "Antigua Gold Beer" and "Antigua Malt." Then he put on his political hat and told an ACLM rally that no beer carrying the image of the prime minister could be sold on Antigua without the full cooperation of the prime minister. He showed the crowd the bottles he had found in the warehouse and said the beer would be sold as Antiguan beer when in fact it had been brewed in New Jersey.

The Birds charged Hector with violating the Public Order Act. A magistrate ruled that, even though the prime minister's picture was on the beer bottles, Hector had failed to connect the prime minister with any plan to distribute the beer. Hector was found guilty and fined EC$5,000. He appealed, but when he lost the appeal, he paid the fine.

Then he wrote that a minister who handled many of the private business affairs for both Lester and the prime minister had been stopped by U.S. Customs in Miami and found to be carrying a suitcase filled with $2.5 million in cash. Hector had been tipped off to the story by the U.S. embassy. But the truth did not matter. Again Hector was charged with violating the Public Order Act. The prime minister's entire Cabinet, fourteen ministers of government, testified at the trial that the prime minister had nothing to do with the money his friend was carrying. The prime minister did not appear, but he sent his bodyguard to testify that he knew nothing about the incident.

An overloaded calendar caused the magistrate to call a recess in the trial. For weeks Hector stood by to return to court. But he, like the magistrate, had other commitments and he flew to Jamaica on business. While there, his case was suddenly scheduled for the next day. Hector could not be reached by telephone and, when he did not appear in court, a bench warrant was issued for his arrest. Hector rushed back to Antigua, where he was arrested at the airport and carted off to jail. It was nineteen days before his writ of habeas corpus was heard.

When Hector walked out of the habeas corpus hearing, he found his case had been rescheduled and was about to begin. He ran from jail to the trial and had barely sat down before he was convicted and sentenced to serve six months. He filed an immediate appeal, but it was nine days before he was released from jail. As he walked home, people on the street waved and applauded. A few days later he appealed. The judge upheld the decision but reduced the sentence to three months. Hector again appealed, this time to a higher court, which agreed with him that the Public Order Act was unconstitutional. But then the Bird government appealed and the decision was reversed. So Hector appealed to the Privy Council in London, the highest and last court of appeals for legal matters in Antigua.

The legal process was not to be resolved until 1989. And by

then Hector's lonely battles with the Birds had become the stuff of which movies are made.

But even so, Space Research remained his lodestone. More than a decade later, as we sat in his house and talked, I said to him that his was the single most impressive body of newspaper work I had ever known. For his part, he dwelled at length on Space Research. After a while he paused, sighed, and shook his head in fond remembrance of the old days. Then he said, "Of all the stories I ever published, I still believe Space Research was my best work."

6

"My People, We Are Free This Night"

Tim Hector's newspaper stories have resulted in his being arrested eleven times on criminal charges. He says he paid fines on several of the charges and that he won all the others. His boyhood friend Lester Bird has sued him for libel three times. On each occasion, Lester dropped the charges. All of this has made Tim Hector a tortured man. Although he is now in his fifties, he is a child of the sixties, and at bottom, a person whose philosophy was formed in the crucible of the American civil rights movement. His world view is that of a man who sees black people as brothers who are oppressed by whites. He finds it painful in the extreme that black Antiguans commit egregious crimes against each other and that most of his journalistic battles have been with fellow blacks.

The first example he always invokes is Space Research. And he particularly relishes the tale of how he returned to the newspaper business after the Space Research stories when no one on Antigua would print his newspaper. That day as we sat in his house, he lit another cigarette, looked at the ceiling for a moment as he gathered his thoughts, and then began.

After the shop that printed *Outlet* dropped Hector's business, he realized he must have his own "printery," to use the Antiguan word. The best price he could find for a press was around $30,000—an amount far out of his reach.

However, Hector's wife Arah firmly believed he should continue in the newspaper business. The task of raising $30,000 was not as daunting to her as it was to her husband. She launched a money-raising campaign: dances, cake sales, flea markets, she did them all. Hector shakes his head and smiles in pride when he recalls her labors. He thought the campaign was "utterly foolhardy." By late 1979 Arah had collected about $7,000, less than one fourth of the money needed. At this rate, even if the price of a press remained constant, it would have been the middle 1980s before he could buy his printery. Hector was not optimistic about returning to the newspaper business, and most of his energies were devoted to leading the ACLM.

"Then I ran into this long-haired fellow," Hector recalled. He took a deep puff from his cigarette and laughed. "He was a hippie bouncing around the world. Pete Mateka was his name. He said he could go back to the States and find a printing press for a lot cheaper than thirty thousand dollars. So I told him if he found a press to let me know and I'd send him the money."

For a moment Hector was silent. He shrugged as if still amazed by what later happened. "He found it," he said. "Everything I needed for under ten thousand dollars. A branch of the National Council of Churches threw in a few thousand dollars. And all at once I had a printing press."

Hector kept the news of his purchase quiet. He planned to install the press in an old building near Independence Avenue where his office was then located. The bulky printing press was quietly removed from the docks to the building in St. John's. There, Hector was dismayed to discover that the press would not go through the doors. Hector was told he would have to remove the roof, hire a construction crane to lower the press into the building, then replace the roof. In the meantime the enormous shipping crate sat in front of the building.

It was only a matter of days before the crate was drawing a great deal of attention. Friends of the Birds said the reason Hector had scuttled Space Research and the big guns of Gerald Bull was so he could import his own guns—proof positive was the enormous package in front of his building. Hector laughed and said the crate contained something even more powerful than a 155-millimeter howitzer: a printing press.

The Bird government checked with Customs and found that Hector indeed had managed to buy and import a printery.

"As of February 15, 1980, I was back in business," Hector recalled with a triumphant laugh.

The *Outlet* resumed publication at a time that was fortuitous in both a journalistic and historic sense. V. C. Bird was campaigning for reelection, and the main plank in his platform was independence. The country had been an associated state longer than any other island in the eastern Caribbean. Other islands had gone on to independence, and it was time for Antigua to do the same. When the election was over, Bird's Antigua Labour Party had won all but one seat in Parliament, and Bird began planning his trip to London so he could carry out his campaign pledge.

In December 1980, V. C. Bird departed the warm and humid air of Antigua for the bitter cold of London, where he entered into final constitutional negotiations with Great Britain. November 1, 1981, was set as the date when Antigua and Barbuda, along with Redonda, would become a new nation.

But before then, Tim Hector would again be fighting with the Birds. And again he would pay dearly. In 1981 one of Antigua's many Rastafarians was jailed on charges of smoking marijuana in public. While in jail the young Rastafarian was beaten to death. Hector wrote a slashing and emotional story of the beating.

"People have read of the Biko trial in South Africa," Hector said. "This incident was exactly the same. But in South Africa it was white people doing it to a black person. It was done here by black people against a black person."

Antiguan law decreed it an act of contempt for a newspaper to publish details of a case before the case went to trial. The Bird government contended that the Rastafarian was in jail because he had committed an offense and that the offense had not been adjudicated. Therefore, when Hector wrote about the Rastafarian's death, he was, in effect, writing about the case. He was charged with contempt, found guilty, and ordered to pay an EC$2,500 fine. He paid.

"The whole thing had a Kafkaesque ring," Hector remembered. "What got the govenment was a quote I used in the story." Here Hector tilted his head, flicked his wrist, and quoted with pride: "'A man died. A dog died. And that is the end of the matter.'" He laughed. "They did not like that."

"Why did you pay?" I asked. "Why didn't you fight?"

"That was one of those instances where it was easier to pay and to get on with business," Hector said.

The telephone on the table in front of Hector rang. He ignored it. The phone rang again and from somewhere in the rear of the house I heard a conversation. Hector's daughter Indira was being asked to call her father to the telephone. She was reluctant, but after a few more exchanges she appeared in the door and looked at her father. He grimaced in annoyance, quickly picked up the telephone and leaned forward, clearly prepared to make the conversation brief. After a few seconds his eyes widened and he bent forward even more, almost huddled over the telephone. His firm and authoritative voice turned soft and inquisitive. Then he issued a few instructions, replaced the receiver, closed his eyes and sighed.

I waited.

"An odd phone call, considering our conversation," he said.

"Anything you want to talk about?"

"That was my office at *Outlet.* The Antigua Public Utilities Authority has cut off my electricity. They say I owe them five thousand [East Caribbean] dollars and until I pay there will be no electricity."

Hector did not need to explain further. Like many Antiguans he sometimes falls behind in paying the high fees of the APUA. Usually this is not a problem. But for weeks Hector had been hammering the government minister who was responsible for the APUA, accusing him of what could charitably be termed incompetence. A few days earlier the minister had publicly threatened to shoot Hector. Now it appeared he had settled for cutting off the electricity at Hector's newspaper—an act perhaps even more painful than bullet wounds.

"If he said I owed"—Hector rolled his eyes and searched for a figure—"three thousand twenty-six dollars and fifteen cents, I might not quibble. But five thousand dollars? Exactly five thousand dollars? And they have no bills or documents to substantiate this. It is harassment because of what I've written." Hector snorted.

"Are you going to pay it?"

(Five thousand East Caribbean dollars is $1,923 in U.S. currency.)

Hector shrugged. "I told my secretary to write them a check."

"Why don't you fight it?"

Hector smiled. "It would languish in the courts for months.

I have to have electricity to put out my newspaper." He paused, took a deep puff from his cigarette and snorted in disgust. The smoke blasted from his nostrils and caused him to look for all the world like an angry bull. He shrugged. "Another example of an instance where it is easier to pay and get on with business."

Then, having headed off still another effort to stop publication of *Outlet,* Hector continued talking of his favorite subject: how the Birds have ignored the rule of law and treated Antigua as a private fief in which they are invincible and invulnerable.

In 1981 Hector found that Premier Bird had allowed his face to be engraved on gambling chips at the Castle Harbour Casino. He wrote that this proved the premier "publicly and personally endorsed gambling." He added insult by saying the tables at Castle Harbour were so crooked that American gamblers refused to play there when they came to Antigua on gambling junkets.

For Antigua, the year 1981 was as pivotal as 1951, the year V. C. Bird confronted Moody-Stuart. With independence, the stability and continuity of colonialism would end and Bird would step into the vacuum. A constitution was being prepared, the omissions in which would—a decade later—shake Antigua to the core and resound around the world. Two months before independence, the Parliament of Antigua passed the Defense Act of 1981. The first part of the act codified an existing fact by formally establishing the Antigua and Barbuda Defense Force. The second part of the act set up a National Security Council and said the NSC must be consulted before any decision of a military or paramilitary nature was taken by the prime minister or the Cabinet. The Parliament also decided that, once Antigua became independent, the country should establish the job of ombudsman to investigate and report on complaints from citizens who may have evidence of maladministration of government.

Antigua was in a euphoric mood as summer ended and independence approached. More than $3 million was set aside to celebrate what was being viewed as another emancipation day. At long last, the country whose wealth had been built on the backs of slaves and exploited by colonialism would become a free and independent nation.

The government began constructing an Independence Arch

across Independence Avenue. But the arch collapsed. Repairs, along with significant overruns, brought the cost of the arch to around $200,000.

On November 1, 1981, a few minutes after midnight, V. C. Bird watched a contingent of British sailors lower the Union Jack for the last time. It had waved over Antigua more than three hundred years. Members of the Antigua and Barbuda Defense Force hoisted the new flag of the new nation. V. C. Bird recognized his guest, Princess Margaret, who represented her sister, the queen of England, and presented an emotional speech in which he said, "My people, we are free this night. But freedom cannot exist without responsibility. The full burden of our freedom now rests upon our shoulders. What we do with that freedom is our own responsibility. We can blame no other."

V. C. Bird was no longer premier. After having been a central figure in Antiguan politics for four decades, the seventy-year-old, semiliterate man was prime minister. The septuagenarian who, when he became angry, lapsed into dialect, and whose recurring speech for the past thirty years had been of cockles, widdy widdy bushes, and pond water, was the leader of a new country, the motto of which was Each Endeavoring, All Achieving.

The British sailors who lowered the Union Jack and participated in the ceremonies enjoyed several days of revelry, then returned to their warship and sailed away.

The independence celebrations lasted more than a week, and part of the festivities included opening the new Parliment Building, which was built and paid for by Canada. It was a small white structure that Antiguans called "The Doll House."

After independence Antigua began flexing its newly discovered muscle. Foreign Minister Lester Bird flew to New York and gave a speech before the United Nations, a speech afforded each new member. The most memorable part of his address, which, like most of Lester's orations, was written by a Guyanese adviser, was its vehemence against the apartheid government of South Africa—the government to which Lester had shipped the big guns of Gerald Bull.

Antigua found quickly that some of the painful realities of independence were a far cry from the glorious celebrations.

Trouble was about to erupt on two fronts: one local and one international. Locally, Antigua faced serious problems with its sister island of Barbuda. Internationally, a scandal of unprecedented proportions was about to be revealed concerning Robert Vesco, a millionaire fugitive from American justice. In the coming months, both the prime minister and Lester Bird would defy the United States in order to protect Vesco, from whom, evidence indicates, Lester spent a great deal of time trying to extort money.

Vesco's appearance and the circumstances surrounding his presence on Antigua were international news. But the Vesco affair was only the first of a series of scandals that would bubble forth from Antigua during coming years. Few countries anywhere had such a tumultuous and corruption-riddled decade as did Antigua in the 1980s after Vesco proved that for the right price, anyone can buy anything on Antigua.

Antigua was independent. Bird had led his people to the realization of their dream. But soon the dream would turn into a nightmare; it would fall apart because the center—V. C. Bird—could not hold.

7

Lester and the Golden Goose

The conversation took place in the spring of 1982. In Antigua there was Jeff Hawley, Lester Bird's personal aide-cum-bagman; and in Atlanta there was a man who had served time in the federal penitentiary for bank robbery. The conversation revolved around how Lester was allowing Robert Vesco to hide on Antigua but was not receiving enough money in return. Lester was impatient.

"Number Two has ordered me to put pressure on Vesco," Hawley said. "Number Two" was his transparent way of describing Lester, the deputy prime minister.

"Number Two tells me there has been too much talking, and it is time he [Vesco] produces something," Hawley said. Vesco "has been given new documents" and new registration for his boat but in return was paying only $2,000 each month. "Number Two is concerned that he is promising a lot but producing little."

Vesco was a bird of such magnificent plumage that the Antiguans were awed. They also were in a dilemma. They had provided sanctuary for this golden goose and did not want to frighten him away. But they also wanted more of his largesse. Now Vesco's boat had been at English Harbour for six months and the Antiguans were growing bold.

Hawley said he had been counseled by the manager of a local casino "to get the smart boys in, take a knife and open up and put the liver on the plate." Hawley said Vesco kept about $4 million in cash on his boat, but that the problem with violence against Vesco is "there will be a hell of a lot of repercussions."

"He has been very nice to me," Hawley said of Vesco. "I can go on board and eat night and day. Twenty years ago that might have impressed me, but today that shit don't cut it."

Then Hawley bounced an idea off his ex-con friend. "Let me ask you a terrible thought," he said. "The key to pressure is the little fellow"—a reference to Vesco's young son. Hawley talked at length of kidnapping the boy and holding him for ransom.

Lester's personal aide was ready to play hardball.

Robert Vesco had been a fugitive for ten years when he surfaced on Antigua. He was an American financier who controlled Investors Overseas, Ltd., what had once been a go-go mutual fund. After defrauding investors of more than $224 million he fled to the Bahamas. Vesco also faced criminal charges in connection with an illegal $200,000 donation to the 1972 reelection campaign of President Richard Nixon. Vesco used the Bahamas as a base for his unrelenting efforts to buy his way out of trouble. In October 1980, a lawyer from a small town in southwest Georgia testified before a congressional subcommittee that he had been paid $10,000 and promised $1 million if he would use his friendship with Hamilton Jordan, President Jimmy Carter's chief of staff, to set up a meeting between Vesco and administration officials. The next month, while the U.S. government was pressuring Bahamian officials to deport Vesco, FBI agent Arthur Nehrbass said, "We gave the Bahamian government information on Vesco's drug-smuggling ties, money-laundering schemes, and the bribing of Bahamian officials." Nehrbass, who then was in charge of the Miami FBI office, said, "Vesco is a corrupter."

In the fall of 1981 Vesco's private jet suddenly departed from the Nassau airport and his yacht upped anchor and disappeared. It was assumed that U.S. pressure had forced his deportation and that he was out there somewhere in the Caribbean looking for a home. What no one knew was that he had made arrangements with the Birds and was en route to Antigua.

At the time I was a reporter for *The Atlanta Constitution,* where I wrote almost exclusively about narcotics trafficking, an assignment that brought me into contact not only with federal agents but with drug smugglers and hoodlums. In February

1982, one of those hoodlums told me Vesco was hiding on Antigua. I was given a copy of the tape-recorded conversation between Jeff Hawley and the ex-convict in Atlanta.

In March 1982, I made the first of what, over the next decade, would become numerous trips to Antigua. All of the visits were for more than a week, and one lasted more than a month. It was on the 1982 trip that I met Vere junior, Lester—and Tim Hector.

My first stop in Antigua was the U.S. embassy, then a rented storefront operation in downtown St. John's. Paul Byrnes was the chargé d'affaires. Short, owlish, and reserved were my initial impressions of Byrnes. I told him that Vesco was on the island and I asked if the U.S. government really wanted to arrest him; after all, if ever a man knew too much about too many prominent American politicians, it was Robert Vesco. And Antigua is a small place—surely the U.S. embassy was aware that Vesco was on the island.

Byrnes's reaction showed that my initial impression of him did not go far enough. Underneath that calm State Department exterior beat the heart of a persistent and determined man. Byrnes was a former FBI agent, a cop to the bone, and he quickly made it clear that if Vesco were on the island, it was news to him. He said he would demand a full accounting from Antiguan officials and that every effort would be made to capture Vesco. I revealed everything my source in Atlanta had told me, including the contents of the tape-recorded conversation, and told Byrnes how Vesco, using an assumed name, was living aboard a yacht in English Harbour.

Byrnes was visibly angry. Vesco could not be on the island without the knowledge of the prime minister. Even though the taped conversation made it clear that Lester was dealing with Vesco, Byrnes knew the prime minister was the only person who could provide the protection Vesco had to have.

Byrnes informed his boss, Ambassador Milan Bish, who coincidentally had left the embassy in Barbados several days earlier and was visiting Antigua. An urgent cable was dispatched to the State Department concerning Vesco's presence. I drove to Prime Minister Bird's office, where the permanent secretary, when I told him the reason I wanted to talk with the prime minister, shrugged and said, "You'll have to talk about that with one of his sons."

So I called Lester, who asked me to meet him at his large home overlooking the sea. By then the Vesco affair was causing such shock waves at the highest levels of the Antiguan government, and so much was at stake, that Paul Byrnes asked the commander of the U.S. Navy base on Antigua to send an armed escort with me. I went to Lester's home accompanied by a U.S. sailor carrrying a loaded M16. A half-mile away a shotgun-toting sailor waited in a truck; his job was to make sure I was not followed upon leaving Lester's house. And a flying squad of armed sailors was on alert at the Navy base and needed only a radio call to be racing out the gate.

When I arrived at Lester's, he invited me inside. But the Navy man had insisted I stay outside and in his view at all times. Lester's eyebrows rose at the sight of the Navy vehicle and the staring sailor behind the wheel. But we sat down on his patio and talked for almost an hour. Lester then was quite different, both in appearance and in substance, than he is today. He wore the polyester shirts, ties, and suits, all with the miniature lightning bolt pattern, favored by many Caribbean men. He was inexperienced in dealing with the American press corps. But the boldness, the arrogance, and the disingenuousness that were later to dominate his personality were in evidence.

"Mr. Vesco has been here," he said. "I will not deny that. It is my understanding he uses different names."

Lester took much the same line with the U. S. embassy. "Yes, he is here," he told Byrnes. "But why is it that anytime something happens on this island, it is laid at my doorstep? Are you sure the U.S. really wants to capture him?"

Byrnes was not dissuaded. He knew Lester well enough that the two could talk frankly outside official channels. Theirs was not a conversation couched in the gentlemanly locutions of diplomacy, it was an exchange between two men who knew each other well.

"Lester, this is a chance for Antigua to stand tall and gain international recognition," Byrnes said. "Turn him over to us."

But Lester would make no promises. Even as the U.S. embassy was clearing with the State Department an official request that

Vesco be arrested for the purpose of extradition, and while FBI agents were being dispatched from Puerto Rico, Lester stalled while the prime minister repeatedly promised that he would apprehend Vesco. In one-on-one talks with Byrnes, he said he had issued instructions that Vesco be arrested and turned over to U.S. authorities. But it never happened.

Even though V. C. Bird, as prime minister, was head of government, the head of state was Sir Wilfred Ebenezer Jacobs, who occupied the post of governor-general. While this job is largely ceremonial, nevertheless the man who holds it is Queen Elizabeth's representative and is higher in the diplomatic pecking order than is the prime minister. Sir Wilfred was kept fully informed by the U.S. embassy of every step the State Department was taking. In fact, it was in the governor-general's office that the official request for the arrest of Vesco was typed and presented to Sir Wilfred for transmittal to the prime minister.

Ambassador Bish and the chargé exchanged a series of cables with the State Department, and then a strong note was sent to the government of Antigua asking that the "highest consideration" be given to the immediate arrest and extradition of Vesco.

But rather than ordering authorities to English Harbour, Lester dispatched the commissioner of police to Barbuda and warned Vesco that the U.S. government was in hot pursuit. Vesco raced to his office in St. John's and frantically began making a series of phone calls to America. Several days later his boat suddenly upped anchor and departed English Harbour. However, it lingered in Antiguan waters for a few more days, apparently while Vesco waited to see if his last-ditch efforts to foil the hunt would be successful. Jeff Hawley, in a state of extreme agitation, showed up at the airport and, while talking with a departure lounge agent, watched in horror as one of his suitcases fell open and revealed stacks of large-denomination U.S. currency. He was so flustered that he grabbed the money, abandoned his luggage, and scurried from the airport.

Vesco escaped. When the FBI later contacted his oldest son, who lived in Miami, and gave him a copy of the tape recording revealing how his Antiguan hosts planned either to steal his money or kidnap his son, Vesco was so concerned that he put into St. Martin, climbed aboard his jet (which had been ferried from Antigua), and flew to his heavily fortified compound in

Costa Rica. There, he and his family went to ground. A few months later he flew to Cuba, where he remains today.

The aftershocks of the Vesco affair were numerous.

Tim Hector revealed that Vesco had been hiding on Antigua for six months. The Birds secretly had given him sanctuary before independence. Vesco rented two apartments and an office on Redcliffe Street in the heart of St. John's and was accompainied by armed guards as he freely moved about the island. The Antiguan government had isssued him a passport in the name of Rob Mezler. He lived in English Harbour aboard a new sixty-two-foot boat name *Halcyon.* He was looked upon with much affection there because he installed power lines in the yacht basin and had made arrangements to provide water and telephone lines.

Even after Vesco fled, his power and his ties to Antiguan officials confounded the U.S. embassy. During his last desperate days on Antigua, Vesco telephoned more than two dozen different numbers in America, mostly in the Southeast. Those telephone numbers were turned over to the FBI. But nothing happened. The embassy could not find out who Vesco called in America during a time of great personal crisis. Were they friends of the Birds? Were they people well-known in Washington?

The U.S. embassy sent the Immigration and Naturalization Service offices in San Juan and Miami a strongly worded memo saying that Jeff Hawley had been instrumental in the escape of Vesco and that he should be considered as suspicious on any future U.S. visit. Even though he was on the INS Watch List, Hawley never was stopped when running errands for the Birds. In the months after the Vesco affair, a young consular officer in the U.S. embassy named Bryant Salter became one of Jeff Hawley's closest friends.

Before leaving Antigua, I called on Vere junior and asked for a reaction to the Vesco affair. Like Lester, Vere junior was new in dealing with the press. He was candid and curiously diffident toward the United States—a mood that was to undergo a marked change in coming years. Vere junior took notice of the strong U.S. presence on Antigua—the embassy, air base, naval base, numerous AID projects, large Peace Corps contingent—and said, "We would not do anything to bring on the wrath of the United Staes." The Vesco matter "will make us a laughingstock to the world."

He was right. But the laughter was directed at how Lester, who was adding to his reputation as a smooth and sophisticated man, had protected Vesco for such a paltry sum.

Following hard on the heels of the Vesco affair were revelations about a bizarre group called the Sovereign Order of New Aragon. Even in the Caribbean, which is known as the crossroads of skulduggery and intrigue and a place where con men and soldiers of fortune wash up like flotsam on the beaches, there has rarely been a saga so comedic, so unbelievable, and with the potential for such mischief.

Tim Hector's revelations about the duplicity of the Antiguan government in the New Aragon affair would once again find him the object of the Birds' wrath.

8

Rossano Brazzi Is Enchanted

One day shortly after the Vesco imbroglio, Paul Byrnes's telephone rang and Rossano Brazzi was on the line. Brazzi was an Italian movie star of the 1950s whose most famous film role was as a planter on a remote island in *South Pacific*. During the movie he sang "Some Enchanted Evening," the highlight both of the film and of his career.

Brazzi told Byrnes that he was calling to answer whatever questions the chargé might have about the Sovereign Order of New Aragon, a mysterious group desiring to create a principality on Barbuda. But before Byrnes could ask any questions, Brazzi was off on a cadenza saying he was a knight in New Aragon, that Shirley Temple would be a knight, "and you might even be a knight." Brazzi sprinkled stardust through every sentence. He dropped the names of numerous celebrities and, with the patronizing arrogance that is the refuge of fading movie stars, he told Byrnes how those people sought protection and anonymity on Barbuda.

Byrnes was not dazzled. He was a pragmatist who took his job seriously, and he wanted to know the names of the principals behind New Aragon and how the United States would be affected by the presence of a new sovereign principality in the Caribbean. Brazzi did not want to answer questions. "Do you know Ronnie?" he suddenly asked.

Byrnes, who is retired today and living in Florida, confirmed the conversation. He said he responded by saying, "Mr. Brazzi, do you mean the president of United States?"

"Yes."

"No, I don't know the president."

"Well, I'm having dinner with him in a few days at the White House and I'll mention your name."

"I appreciate that, Mr. Brazzi. But don't be surprised if he doesn't know me."

Brazzi signed off, confident he had calmed down the chargé.

When a prince without a principality finds an undeveloped Caribbean island, all sorts of possibilities rear their heads. And when a multimillionaire American fugitive, who wants a place to hang his hat, discovers the same island, the scenario grows even more murky. Today, not even the people who were there can agree on who was involved or exactly what happened when the Sovereign Order of New Aragon wanted to create a principality in Barbuda, the sparsely populated sister island of Antigua controlled by the Bird government.

Those behind the Sovereign Order of New Aragon—whether Robert Vesco or an obscure collection of down-at-the-heels European royalty—looked the world over before they settled on Antigua as the location where the government would be most receptive to their ideas. A proposal submitted to the Bird government said the primary aims of the Sovereign Order of New Aragon were to "maintain the peace in the modern world, propagating the tradition of chivalry and charity and engaging in charitable works." Aragon's first proposal called for land on Antigua to be developed as a principality. Then the location was shifted to Barbuda. A palace was to be erected for Prince Joseph Gregorio, the leader of New Aragon. Port facilities, banks and commercial areas, as well as "residential areas for the knights," also would be built. The knights would come from "all over the world, and are persons of high finance and well educated."

The first rumblings about the Sovereign Order of New Aragon arose in the days after Vesco fled Antigua. Tim Hector revealed that Vesco had a proposal before the Bird government for a project whose boundaries and facilities, as well as goals, seemed to have been taken from an overlay of a proposal by New Aragon. Both the Vesco and the New Aragon plans envisioned an international airport, the runway of which would serve as a boundary between the Vesco or New Aragon property and the remainder of Barbuda. Knights and princes would land at the airport and go through Aragon's—not Barbuda's—customs and immigration facilities. The sovereign principality would—among other things—issue its own passports.

The American embassy wanted to know if the shadowy group was simply a shield for Vesco. If Vesco set up a principality and issued himself a diplomatic passport, he conceivably would be beyond the reach of American law-enforcement officials. And if he had the authority to operate banks, casinos, and another mutual fund, it could become another financial nightmare, not only for Americans, but for people around the world. And what if the new principality issued diplomatic passports to fugitives? Barbuda could become a sanctuary for the felons and con artists of the world. Although the New Aragon plan was easy to dismiss as a comedic or bizarre scheme, Byrnes was alarmed at the idea of a sovereign territory so close to America's back door, especially if the Birds granted everything Aragon was asking.

To quell the growing number of questions, New Aragon sent in its biggest gun—Prince Gregorio of Italy. He met with the Antiguan Cabinet and told the awed group that the Sovereign Order of New Aragon was founded in A.D. 718 and that his title could be traced to the time of the Visigoths. What he did not explain was why an organization that had been around for more than twelve hundred years had suddenly decided to go into real estate development. Prince Gregorio also paid a courtesy call on the U.S. embassy and left a thick, leather-bound book that was covered with red ribbons and wax seals. Prince Gregorio said the book would answer whatever questions the United States might have about New Aragon. But the book raised more questions than it answered.

The Barbuda property was not the only common denominator between Vesco and New Aragon. Lester Bird was dealing with both parties. A U.S. embassy investigation revealed that in addition to Prince Gregorio, whom few people had ever heard of, the front man for New Aragon was Rosanno Brazzi. Byrnes wondered what sort of mischief the Birds were up to, and he began making inquiries.

A few days later Lester telephoned Byrnes. Still smarting

from the Vesco fiasco, he wasted no time on diplomatic niceties. "Why are you asking questions about New Aragon?" he demanded.

"Lester, I represent the interests of the United States. My job is to ask questions. Now tell me what's going on."

"Paul, you are causing me a lot of trouble."

"Tell me what's going on and that will end the questions."

"I'll get back to you."

Within hours Byrnes received the telephone call from Rossano Brazzi. Some of those close to the affair say that Byrnes took the leather-bound book Prince Gregorio had given him, copied all the information contained inside, and sent cables to U.S. embassies in Milan and Rome, as well as to the CIA, the FBI, and a secret investigative office the State Department maintains in Miami. After a few months of silence, follow-up cables were sent. But someone or some agency had placed a veil of secrecy over the inquiries. For some still-unknown reason, no replies ever were received. It was as if the queries had disappeared into a black hole.

When I called Byrnes to ask about this, he said too much time had elapsed for him to recall the details. But he did remember that the leather-bound book had raised a lot of questions and that inquiries had been sent to a number of people. "It was an official inquiry from a U.S. embassy and it was ignored," Byrnes said. "No one responded. They all refused to answer my inquiries."

The Atlanta connection to New Aragon was intriguing. When I began asking questions, I was referred to Hurt, Richardson, Garner, Todd and Cadenhead, one of the most prestigious law firms in Atlanta. Then a man who said he represented New Aragon showed up at the Atlanta office of Carl Byoir and Associates, an international public relations firm. Jeannine Addams, a vice president of Carl Byoir, was given a tape recording of a wavery rendition of the national anthem of New Aragon, the first verse of which went as follows:

From the beaches by the seashore,
Where the pink sand meets the sun,
We shall raise our voice proudly,
Carry on, New Aragon."

As Barbuda is thought to be the only island in the Caribbean whose beaches are pink—because of wave-crashed shells—it was obvious that whatever musical merits the anthem might have lacked, it was founded on solid research.

Addams also was given a thick, leather-bound book covered with red ribbons and wax seals—apparently a copy of the same book Byrnes had been given. She showed the book to a friend who was a lawyer. After consulting with other lawyers, her friend said the book was gibberish; that it meant nothing and signified nothing.

Nevertheless, there were those who were anxious to receive the red sash of New Aragon to wear with their tuxedos. One was John Tipton, the former vice president of Tiffany's Atlanta store. He received an engraved document emblazoned with the seal of His Serene Highness, Prince Joseph Gregorio, which said, "Following review of your past humanitarian and charitable activities and your belief in the betterment of the human race, H.S.H. Prince Joseph Gregorio has accepted and approved your candidacy, and will graciously bestow upon you the Commandery Cross of the Sovereign Order of New Aragon. H.S.H. Prince Joseph Gregorio is pleased to bestow this high honour on you, and in His name we send you greetings and compliments."

The document was signed by Count Augusto Giuseppe M. Agazzi, grand chancellor of New Aragon.

I tracked Tipton down in Atlanta and asked him how he came to receive the Commandery Cross. He laughed. "I paid them five thousand dollars for the beer and wine franchise on New Aragon," he said. He showed me a letter saying that he had an exclusive beer and wine license for five years. The letter was signed by Grand Chancellor Agazzi. In return for the exclusive license, he was to kick back 40 percent of his profits to New Aragon.

It seemed that the people who had the most to lose if a principality were created on Barbuda—the Barbudans—knew the least about what was going on. Barbudans had heard nothing about Aragon until Tim Hector's newspaper stories were published. The Barbudans immediately dispatched a delegation to appeal for help from Prime Minister Bird. The delegation was led by Hilbourne Frank, a member of the Barbuda Council, who expressed fear of both Vesco and New Aragon. "The prime minister told us to keep it all quiet and see what happened," Frank said. "In the end we saw the government itself was wrapped up with the Sovereign Order of New Aragon."

Even though it had the full support of the Bird government, New Aragon fell apart—first, because Vesco was on the run; second, because Rossano Brazzi was arrested in Italy and charged with arms trafficking; and third, because of Hector's newspaper stories.

Even today, it is not clear if Vesco and the Sovereign Order of New Aragon were allied, or if it was simply coincidence they arrived at the same time with the same idea.

Morley Safer of *60 Minutes* showed up on Barbuda and did a tongue-in-cheek piece called "The Return of the Visigoths." To Safer, it was all a comedy. What Safer did not understand, and what so many others failed to see, was that while Aragon itself may have been a comedy, there was nothing funny about a sovereign principality being created in the permissive atmosphere of Antigua, one that could have become a Caribbean refuge where fugitives and scoundrels could buy diplomatic immunity. Events of the next few years would prove in a fashion most undeniable that Antigua welcomed and cooperated with such people. Aragon was not a comedy; it was a narrowly averted diplomatic disaster.

However, even today it is the comedic that still surfaces in dealing with Aragon. In 1992 I called John Tipton, who introduced me to Count Augusto Agazzi, the grand chancellor of New Aragon. The three of us went to lunch to reminisce about how Aragon had almost come to Barbuda. Count Agazzi is unemployed. His wife is a seamstress. Count Agazzi told Tipton and me in great detail about his recent trip to Europe as a guest of Prince Gregorio, and pulled out a brochure to show pictures of the hotel suite where he had stayed for a month. "Not one person in Atlanta knew I was in Europe," he said, a remark I found impossible to fathom.

When the topic shifted to New Aragon, Count Agazzi became somewhat formal. He said Vesco had no part of New Aragon. After his fourth glass of wine, he turned to me and said, "You may call me Augusto. Forget the bool-sheet."

Augusto clasped his hands, pursed his lips, studied the ceiling, and said, "Our mistake was Rossano Brazzi."

"How so?"

"We were going to have either Luciano Pavarotti or Rossano Brazzi be our front man. We decided on Brazzi because he was friends with Reagan and because Pavarotti was"—he waved his hand over his head—"too much up there." He shook his head in despair. "It was a mistake." He gave a Continental shrug, and smiled. "You know, every time I went to Antigua I took Lester a pair of shoes. He has very large feet, I don't remember what size, but it is difficult for him to find shoes. I took him shoes." A sip of wine. "I took him lots of others things, too."

9

Guano and Literature

At eight-thirty A.M. on June 13, 1992, a fifty-foot open boat called *Extender* departed from the Jolly Bay Harbour on the west side of Antigua. Two dozen people were aboard. The boat was bound for Redonda, twenty-eight miles to the southwest, on an expedition sponsored by the Museum of Antigua and Barbuda. It was the first expedition to the remote island in more than a decade. An hour after the lines were cast off, *Extender* slid from the lee of Antigua and began to roll, pitch, and wiggle under the influence of powerful seas pushed by twenty-knot easterlies. Every few minutes the bow smashed into the sea and flushed a school of flying fish. The sun was hot, the sky was clear, and the ride was exhilarating.

Shortly before noon *Extender* approached Redonda, a sharp-peaked brown and black island. It is the cone of an extinct volcano, part of which has collapsed, with dark cliffs rising 971 feet from the turbulent ocean. Old lava flows are clearly visible. From the sea the island appears most inhospitable, and the vertical slopes discourage anyone from wanting to land. Nevertheless, the boat moved into the lee of Redonda, anchored fifty yards off a narrow, boulder-strewn ledge that serves as the island's only beach, and passengers began going ashore in a small rubber boat. Some of the passengers sat on the rocks and watched seabirds, some went scuba diving, and about a dozen elected to climb Redonda. From the landing site the climbers slowly picked their way across the boulder field for about a hundred yards. Many of the boulders shifted and rolled underfoot. Then those of us who wanted to climb to the peak stood atop an enormous, fifty-foot-high colluvium and gazed up the grimpen—a sixty-degree gully that is the only means of ascent—and wondered if we had taken leave of our senses. The gully looked as if it had been dug by a giant ice cream scoop. It led from the pile of boulders at the edge of the sea to a plateau about five hundred feet above. The gully was straight, the bottom was covered with scree, and the sides were vertical. Much of the climb would be on hands and knees and we were cautioned at length about not causing a landslide—those below would have no avenue of escape. The gully was airless and still and the temperature was in the high nineties.

An hour and a half later the climbers were atop the plateau with no mishaps. An astonishing revelation had come twenty feet below, where the gully makes a sharp switchback. Here lay the rotting carcasses of two wild goats. And here, sweating, panting, and exhausted, we realized we had climbed a mountain so treacherous that even the wild goats could not always maintain their legendary surefootedness. And then came our blessed moment when a beneficent wind, moist and cool, blew with such strength it billowed our dirty clothes and refreshed our sweat-soaked brows.

The second part of the ascent was relatively easy. It wandered across a meadow-like area covered with nesting seabirds and along the edge of a cliff that plunged into the sea. The birds were quite close to the trail. It was obvious they had never before seen humans. They simply glanced at us and went back to their nesting duties. Thousands of seabirds live on Redonda, and many of them soared below us. The sea stretched out endlessly into the haze, and we looked down at the countless birds circling the upper slopes of Redonda and heard their cries snatched away by the wind.

Nine of us made the final assault on the peak, and it was good there were so few of us. At the top there was little room for more. We rested, stared over the sea, drank in the sweet wind, and listened once more to the mournful cries of the seabirds. Desmond Nicholson, director of the Museum of Antigua and Barbuda, planted the flag of Redonda, a tricolor of blue (for the sea), brown (for the earth), and green (for the vegetation). Then he pulled a flute from his daypack and passed out a half-dozen pages of sheet music. The first few notes, like the cries of the seabirds, were lost on the wind. We all leaned closer and began to sing the sweet and melancholy words of the Redonda national anthem, the first verse of which goes:

God who gave our island soil
In trust for evermore,
Grant grace that by our faith and toil
We hold our heirloom pure.

Soon it was time to go. We traversed the upper meadows and hastened across the plateau. We peered down the treacherous gully, took a deep breath, and began the final descent. A single misstep could have pitched one of us barrel-assing down the gully, creating a landslide. But except for bruises and a few cuts from the abrasive basaltic rocks, the descent was without incident. At the bottom, the heat was so oppressive, the dirt and grime was so pervasive, and we were so hot and exhilarated that several people staggered into the cooling sea, sat down, and let the gentle surf wash over them.

We rowed back to *Extender* and wearily climbed aboard. The captain took a head count and turned on the engine. We motored slowly around the leeward side of the island, all of us looking up toward the peak and shaking our heads in disbelief. Then our attention was drawn to the sea. The wind had risen and the waves were ten and twelve feet tall. Already we could feel the spume blowing from the tops of the waves. "Okay, people," the captain shouted. "Hold on tight and get ready to rock and roll."

We rounded the cliffs and plowed into the marching waves. Redonda was not through with us. It was as if the lonely and forbidding peak had lashed out a final time, chastising us for our temerity. One moment the bow of the boat pitched skyward at what seemed an impossible angle, and the next moment it pointed down as if ready to plunge into the depths. And in between it rolled and twisted and shook. The moan of the wind was unrelenting. Many of us sensed an onslaught of the collywobbles. Within a half hour, most of us were violently seasick. The gunwales of *Extender* were so high and so broad that many could not lean over the side, and their vomit was blown over the other passengers. It did not matter, because water was roaring on board in great sheets and washing everyone. The afternoon wore on. As always in these latitudes, there was no dusk. One moment it was afternoon and the next moment we were in darkness. The temperature dropped. The wind did not abate and the waves continued to tumble aboard. Many people, clad only in shorts and T-shirts, were shaking uncontrollably from the cold. Five and a half hours later we tied up to the dock at Jolly Bay Harbour; and chilled and exhausted, we disembarked.

The first organized expedition to Redonda in more than a decade was safely home. It was unlikely any of the participants would want to return.

Antigua is referred to as the "twin-island nation of Antigua and Barbuda," and both countries are included on government letterheads and tourist brochures, though even a casual glance shows that "Antigua" usually is of a much larger and bolder typeface than "Barbuda." Rarely is Redonda mentioned. In fact, most visitors to Antigua never hear of Redonda. But if they stay in a hotel on the southwest corner of Antigua they can look across the Caribbean and, on a clear day, see the island looming in the distance.

Isolated, precipitous, and harsh, Redonda presents a face of murderous innocence. It may be the only island in the Caribbean to treat every visitor as a trespasser. While this barren and wind-whipped island may seem an unimportant sidebar to the story of Antigua, Redonda is important for several reasons, among them its being part of the Birds' kingdom, and its symbolizing the tragedy that seems to befall virtually everything under the Birds' control.

This island, although it is not shown on most tourist maps of the Caribbean, has its own aristocracy; a king, dozens of dukes, and an unknown number blessed by royal "orders." Some of the best-known literary lights of both Great Britain and America have become part of Redondan royalty. The story of Redondan royalty is a story that, in the words of one English writer, "has been told and retold wherever London's lesser literati gather to damn their publishers, abuse their agents, and drown each other's sorrows in lesser-quality wines."

Columbus, during the Saint Mary phase of his second voyage, went on a spree of naming every island he saw after the virgin

Mary: Santa María de la Galante, Santa María de la Montserrat, Santa María de la Antigua, and, finally, Santa María de la Redonda—Saint Mary the Round.

The high, barren, haycock of an island is about a mile long and about one third of a mile wide. Lying between Montserrat and Nevis, it was little more than a navigational landmark until the 1860s. At that time, the centuries-old deposits of bird guano, which in some places were perhaps a dozen feet thick, were found to be of such high quality that they could be commercially mined. A conveyor belt with large buckets to haul the manure reached from the plateau to the sea. And, perhaps not unrelated to the prodigious amounts of manure, the literary kingdom of Redonda was created.

In 1865 the Irish trader Matthew Dowdy Shiell was en route to Montserrat. Shiell had his pregnant wife and eight daughters aboard, and, so the story goes, his wife gave birth to a son as the boat passed Redonda. Shiell, like most Irishmen, imagined he was descended from the ancient kings of Ireland. Mysticism and madness waged war in his soul. It is not clear which was in ascendancy when he saw in the birth of his son a way to resurrect the royal line. He declared his son the king of Redonda. And fifteen years later the young Matthew Phipps Shiel (he dropped the final *l*) was crowned atop the precipitous and wind-blown summit by the bishop of Antigua. The party was carried from the sea to the plateau in the buckets of the conveyor belts before hiking the remainder of the way.

Only an Irishman could convince a priest to climb a near-vertical, manure-covered remote island to officiate over a ceremony involving a boy king. Shiell the elder now had a king in the family, and—at least in his mind—the link with the ancient kings of Ireland had been restored.

Shiel the younger moved to England to study. Eventually he began writing science fiction articles for British newspapers, achieving such stature that for a while he and Jules Verne were considered literary peers. Then Shiel went on to write rambling, tempestuous, and undisciplined novels that even today have a devoted following. The best-known is *The Purple Cloud,* which was later made into a movie called *The World, the Flesh and the Devil,* starring Harry Belafonte.

Matthew Phipps Shiel wrote twenty-three books. One reviewer said all of Shiel's characters seemed intoxicated. But Hugh Walpole wrote, "A flaming genius, Shiel is just about the best romantic writer we have alive in England today. At his best he is not to be touched, because really there is no one else like him." And Jules Claretie said, " 'The Purple Cloud' should live as long as 'The Odyssey.'" Still another critic, Ralph Straus, said, "The novels of this brilliantly original writer have a kind of white-hot splendour that rouses all of one's admiration."

One of Shiel's friends was John Gawsworth, a poet who was once considered the probable successor to John Masefield as poet laureate of England. But Gawsworth's renown as a rhymer of verse may have been secondary to his prowess as a hoister of flagons. His drinking bouts at the Alma Pub were legendary. Shiel appointed Gawsworth as court poet and next in the line of succession to the crown of Redonda. Each man made a small slit on the inside of his wrist; the two men tied their wrists together; and the supposedly royal blood of Shiel mingled with that of Gawsworth.

Shiel saw being king of Redonda as something of a lark, and there is no evidence he ever took his title seriously. Once he achieved renown as a novelist he liked the idea of creating an aristocracy of intellect by conferring titles of Redondan nobility on his literary friends.

Meanwhile, back on Redonda, the guano mining operation was producing a thousand metric tons each year. In 1872 the island, which had been a dependency of Montserrat, was annexed by Antigua. Then phosphate was discovered beneath the bird guano. By 1895, more than 130 people from Montserrat worked on the island. Shiell the elder did not approve of bird manure and phosphate being taken from his son's kingdom and he waged a bitter if unsuccessful protest. His only solace was that the British did not dispute the sovereignty of his son.

In 1914, when the guano mining operation ended, about a thousand tons of phosphate were stockpiled near the pier on Redonda. The phosphate and the pier slipped into the sea and rendered the island virtually inaccessible. Afterwards, boats had to anchor off the southwest corner and the crew had to go ashore in small boats.

Shiell the elder attempted for years to have his son officially recognized by the British govenment as a legitimate ruler within the Commonwealth. He showered Whitehall and the Colonial Office with letters. In 1938 a Civil List pension was awarded to M. P. Shiel—Felipe I, to use his Redondan title. However, the pension had nothing to do with service to the empire; it was for his literary output.

Shiel died in obscurity in 1947. After he was cremated, Gawsworth, as his successor, was given custody of the remains. One story has it that Gawsworth hastened from the cremation to the Alma for a sustaining draft, passing the package of ashes to the busy barkeep for safekeeping. The barkeep hastily placed the package on a shelf. Gawsworth looked up from his drink and was astonished to see a fine stream of ashes falling from the package onto an open sandwich behind the bar. The barkeep finished preparing the sandwich and slid it down the bar to James Agate, a prominent London drama critic. The critic noticed Gawsworth's hypnotic stare but ignored it; he knew Gawsworth's penchant for ale. Gawsworth watched Agate eat the sandwich. He picked up his package and, as he departed, solemnly said to the critic, "You've just eaten part of M. P. Shiel."

"You're drunk," said the disgusted critic.

With great gusto, Gawsworth assumed the title—he called himself King Juan I—and was crowned in a Soho pub. By now, better known as a bibliophile than as a poet, he had a knack for convincing some of the most famous literary names of the day to become Redondan royalty. This, in turn, gave him access to their literary archives. Because Gawsworth spent so much time appraising manuscripts and books, he often referred to himself as a "literary dung beetle."

But Gawsworth was spending as much time in the Alma Pub as he was examining manuscripts. And he began the slide into what one of the first members of Redondan royalty called the "Almadonda phase." Gawsworth apparently came to believe that his mission no longer was to be a poet or an expert on literary archives, but rather the man who could create a literary aristocracy and, in the process, earn free drinks for the remainder of his life.

Some of London's literati, especially the Fitzrovians—those who hung out in the bars of Soho, Chelsea, and Fitzrovia—laughed at Gawsworth and called him "King of the Seagulls." He continued to pass out titles to anyone who would buy him a pint. The more he drank, the more generous he became with titles. More than three dozen writers, British and American, distinguished and otherwise, along with an occasional publisher, were ennobled.

Only a few months after Shiel died, Gawsworth issued State Paper 1. It was handwritten upon eighteenth-century handmade paper and conferred titles upon Arthur Machen, Ellery Queen, Arthur Ransome, Dylan Thomas, Eden Philpotts, and Frank Swinnerton. Royal appointments, with succession granted to male heirs, also were granted. Philip Lindsay became the duke of Guano; Lawrence Durrell, the duke of Cervantes Pequena; and Henry Miller, the duke of Thuana.

In 1949 Gawsworth issued Duchies of the Realm to Alfred A. Knopf and Dorothy L. Sayers. Royal appointments were given to J. B. Priestley and Rebecca West. Another long list of honors came in 1951. In 1960, Royston Ellis, who had been a beatnik poet in London a decade earlier, was made duke of Gypino de Redonda. Two years later his title was changed to duke of Tintinnabulation, perhaps because he had moved to Dominica and wrote paperback fiction under various pseudonyms while managing a five-piece touring band. Not unnaturally, a feeling grew among the "ancient" literary aristocracy of Redonda, the "Shielians," as those loyal to King Felipe I referred to themselves, that Gawsworth was somewhat less than discriminating in passing out titles.

But it was all good fun that brought a measure of excitement to the bars of the Fitzrovians, especially to the Alma. Then Gawsworth went too far. Americans were paying astronomical prices for any sort of royal memorabilia, and Gawsworth took advantage of this to sell off many of the royal accoutrements, including his crown. The sword of state, which once had belonged to General Cipriano Castro, a Venezualan general, also was sold, as was the manuscript of the Redonda national anthem, written by Leigh Henry, the Grand Duke Basalto de Redonda. The title of the anthem is "O God Who Gave Our Island Soil in Trust for Evermore"—a title almost as big as the island.

At the same time Gawsworth began selling the royal doodads he handed out honors even more promiscuously, and the followers of M. P. Shiel became increasingly dismayed. Fabian of the Yard (Robert Fagan, a highly publicized London detective) became duke of Verdugo and was appointed commissioner of police for Redonda. The vicar of Soho was appointed to the "arch-episcopal see" of an island whose only inhabitants were rats, crabs, seabirds, the burrowing owl (*Speotyto cunicularia*) that had become extinct on Antigua because of the mongooses, and the large dung beetles that had an extraordinary fondness for the nitrogenous excrement of seabirds.

(It would not be known until years later, but in 1960 Gawsworth was party to an accident that, when discovered, sat the Shielians' teeth on edge. The remainder of Shiel's remains had been put into a tea caddy and placed on his mantel. Gawsworth was involved in another of his frequent moves and the inevitable happened—one of his friends brewed up the contents of the caddy.)

In 1966 Gawsworth placed an ad in *The Times* of London offering an "irrevocable covenant" to the legendary throne of Redonda for £1,000. Replies poured in. Even the crown prince of Sweden, apparently bored with being a mere prince, sent a deposit of £50. Gawsworth cashed the check at the Alma and a grand night was had by all.

Gawsworth's offer to sell the crown of Redonda was the final straw for the Shielians. The peers of the realm decided they had had enough. The older officials of the court of King Felipe I, a group called the Privy Council of Five, called a meeting in the Fitzroy Tavern and were successful in stopping the sale of the title.

Nevertheless, Gawsworth apparently took money from those who responded to his advertisement and he apparently conveyed the title to each of them, because for years afterwards various "kings" surfaced. Perhaps the best known of the pretenders was Cedric Boston, a Montserratian living in London and a man whose aristocracy was almost entirely gay. In the early 1990s, Boston's realm took a serious blow when his grand chamberlain, the Reverend Paul De Fortis, a priest in the Church of England, wrapped himself in chains, and, in an esoteric homosexual bondage rite, accidentally killed himself. The accident received wide play in British tabloids.

But well before that, the Shielians had confronted Gawsworth and announced that the realm of Redonda had become tainted with his my-kingdom-for-a-bottle antics. The Colonial Office was formally asked to make some sort of statement regarding the legitmacy of the crown of Redonda. But even the Colonial Office saw no harm with this fictional kingship and said, in effect, that while the government was not sure if Gawsworth had the right to call himself king, if it made him happy, why not?

But the Shielians did not give up. They sought to issue a decree that would deroyalize all Gawsworth appointees made after 1951, stating that the kingdom of Redonda could not exist once it was separated from the literary works of M. P. Shiel.

The furor discredited Gawsworth. The man who once had won England's Benson Prize for poetry and who, at an early age, was given the special privileges that go with being made a Freeman of the City of London, spent his last years as a dish-washer, sleeping in doorways and cardboard boxes. He died in 1970 and was cremated, his ashes scattered across the crocus lawn of a London crematorium.

Gawsworth's title was passed to British novelist and publisher Jon Wynne-Tyson, the literary executor for both Shiel and Gawsworth, which made him, by precedent, the royal successor—King Juan II. Wynne-Tyson was the polar opposite of Gawsworth, a workaholic of a writer, editor, and publisher who is devoted to environmental matters. Wynne-Tyson told a British newspaper writer that he was a "reluctant monarch" and that Gawsworth had debased the kingship by handing out honors to so many drinking buddies. He said he wanted to restore the original concept whereby a Redondan dukedom is an honor that the recipient enjoys primarily because it is bestowed by fellow writers, with all parties recognizing that the title is amusing and harmless.

Wynne-Tyson and I corresponded several times, and in one of his letters he said, "The only point I see in the Redonda legend is if the island can be seen as a symbol of the places we should be leaving to the birds. The literary associations help to make it a fun thing, but only so long as no one begins to take it too seriously, or too lightly and too boozily. All a question of balance."

The first years of Wynne-Tyson's reign as King Juan II were as calm as the reign of Gawsworth was tempestuous. But in 1978 a wealthy American industrialist, A. Reynolds Morse, aka the Grand Duke Nera Roca, launched the First Shielian Discovery Expedition. He wanted to visit Redonda and the neighboring islands and gather information on M. P. Shiel. Because Redonda was part of the Associated State of Antigua, Morse went through Antigua. Apparently he was not well received there, for he wrote that Antigua, "with its additional hassle with customs, immigration and mini-airplanes, has certainly held the good and evil of tourism at bay." Morse sailed around Redonda but did not land. He decided that if the realm of Redonda is to live, it must be through its nonresident aristocracy.

Nonetheless, his interest caused the Birds to remember that Redonda was part of their country. In the aftermath, they sent caretakers to the island, opened a post office, and said the phosphate mining operation would be resumed.

By the next year Morse's discouragement in dealing with Antiguan officials had waned. Because Wynne-Tyson and several other prominent officials agreed to accompany him, he mounted the Second Shielian Discovery Expedition. In April 1979, the group left English Harbour aboard a chartered yacht. Desmond Nicholson, who then was vice-chairman of the historic sites commission on Antigua, was aboard, and it was on this trip he was elevated from Royal Archaeologist to the duke of Artifact. Also aboard was the duke of Androecia, Professor Richard Howard of Harvard; the duke of Strata, Jack Murphy, who was head of the geology department at the Denver Museum of Natural History; the duke of Cielo, A. A. "Bert" Wheeler, then the head of the National Trust on Montserrat; and the duke of Wadadli, the adviser to an Antiguan minister of government, who, while others in the expediton climbed the peak, stayed on board the yacht with his girlfriend.

Ever mindful of Antiguan sensitivities, King Juan II made it clear that his was an ecological mission rather than a political conquest. Nevertheless, the Birds viewed the trip with some apprehension. They did not understand that today monarchies are tolerated because they are a form of fantasy, and they regarded even the whimsical monarchy of Redonda as a threat. When Wynne-Tyson and his band of merry men anchored and climbed into small boats and made their way through the surf to the rocky beach, they were greeted by a postmaster, who offered them first covers for a new stamp issue. Two Rastafarians, whose sole job was to keep an eye on the expedition, stood nearby. They said they had been told to accompany the expedition throughout their stay on Redonda. "The government of Antigua has no sense of humor," sniffed A. Reynolds Morse.

After a perilous climb to the top of Redonda, King Juan II read a proclamation, most of which was lost in the roar of the powerful easterlies, and planted the new flag of Redonda, a tricolor fashioned from a pair of pajamas from Marks and Spencer.

Wynne-Tyson returned to England and wrote *So Say Banana Bird,* a powerful and multifaceted novel about a sailor who winds up on a Caribbean island that clearly is Antigua, and featuring another island that clearly is Redonda. In it, Wynne-Tyson lacerates the Birds and the Antiguan government.

Today the flag that King Juan II raised atop Redonda is kept in a small open box at the Museum of Antigua and Barbuda, along with a handful of artifacts gathered from both the 1979 Shielian Discovery Expedition and the 1992 expedition sponsored by the Museum of Antigua and Barbuda.

For the last decade, Redonda has been quiet. According to records at the museum, records whose accuracy is assured by the duke of Artifact, the yacht *Kilcullen* anchored off Redonda in 1980 and sent a landing party ashore to hoist the Irish tricolor alongside the flag of Redonda in a tribute to the Irish origins of M. P. Shiel. In 1984 Jon Wynne-Tyson's wife, Queen Jennifer I, became the first female monarch to land on Redonda. A few weeks later, J. Rainey, the owner of Tropical Studios on Antigua and the official court photographer, sailed to the island for a photographic documentation of Redonda's natural history. The duke of Artifact came along and replanted the Redondan flag atop the summmit.

Today the island's location makes it an easy landmark for aircraft. The surrounding waters have become a favored drop site for drug smugglers, especially those from Antigua, who come out in high-speed cigarette boats, pick up drug shipments, and then return to Antigua. The post office was blown away in a hurricane and the Birds never resumed the phosphate mining operation.

10

Behind God's Back

Barbuda is unique in the Caribbean. Even in a region noted for being quirky and out of step with the world, Barbuda stands out. One of the few things it shares with its sister island of Antigua, some twenty-nine miles to the south, is that people who have not been there mispronouce the name. The proper pronunciation is *Bar-BEW-da,* and the island often is confused with either Bermuda or Barbados.

Barbuda, unlike many Caribbean islands, is not volcanic and mountainous; it is a flat coral island with a karstic plateau called the Highlands that rises to about two hundred feet on its eastern side. Droughts are even more common here than on Antigua, and the land is a barely fertile scrub wilderness dominated by thornbush and cactus, and roamed by donkeys, feral cattle, and deer. A chart of Barbudan waters cautions mariners to exercise "extreme caution" because of inadequately surveyed reefs and uncharted coral heads. The waters on the Atlantic side of the island are filled with shipwrecks. Barbuda has no harbor, although there is a small dock called The River on its southwestern edge. There has never been anything on this poor and inconsequential island to justify regular ship traffic. A lagoon on the west side offers protected waters, but the approach is through a reef, over coral heads, and into a shallow, twisting, and ever-changing channel that intimidates almost everyone except Barbudans and the foolhardy. Barbuda is one of the least-populated islands in the Caribbean, and the island lacks safe water, has few proper toilets and no permanent doctors or dentists.

But the island does have what many consider the loveliest beaches in the Caribbean: small, isolated, cliff-wrapped and shell-strewn pink beaches that even today are rarely marred by footprints.

Until independence, the largest commerical source of income on the island was the Coco Point Lodge, a faded but expensive caravansary favored by wealthy Republicans and presided over by William Cody Kelly, an imperious lawyer from the great city of Cincinnati. The Coco Point Lodge is one of the few hotels in Antigua and Barbuda to have a "proprietary club license," which allows Kelly to refuse entry to anyone he chooses. Issuance of this license always has been opposed by the trade unions because it is seen as a way for white-owned hotels to exclude local black people. It also is seen as one of the most egregious examples of how, for the right amount of money, outsiders can gain favors whose effect is to discriminate against Antiguans and Barbudans. Kelly has taken full advantage of his license. He does not allow nonguests inside the door, even to have a drink or a meal. Since the club is on a remote point on the south end of Barbuda, the only people this affects are Barbudans.

About eighty Barbudans work at Coco Point, and roughly the same number work as fishermen. About one hundred people are employed by the government and most of the remaining income is derived from pensions or from remittances of family members living abroad. More than three times as many Barbudans live in New York as on the island. And large expatriate communities are found in England and Canada.

The history of Barbuda and the story of its calamitous marriage to Antigua began in 1685, when Charles II leased the island to Christopher Codrington, the Englishman who, in 1674, had established Betty's Hope on Antigua. Codrington used Barbuda as a stock farm and provisioning center, and for the next two centuries, while England, Spain, France, and Holland were developing and trading and fighting over various colonial outposts in the Caribbean, Barbuda was ignored. Remote and isolated, it knew nothing but peaceful days and placid ways. It would remain that way until the Birds began to plunder it in the 1980s.

Everything that is important and significant about Barbuda

stems from the Codrington lease. It was the lease that caused Barbuda to be a dependency for more than three centuries. And the island never had plantations where slaves worked in the canefields. Officially, Barbudans were slaves, but they were a different sort of slave from those found on other Caribbean islands. They were not field hands. They were woodworkers, boat builders, weavers, sailmakers, fishermen, lobster divers, leatherworkers, and charcoal-makers, and they enjoyed what for slaves was a rare privilege: having only one or two supervisors. In additon, Barbudans could use lands outside the village as swidden garden plots in burned-off clearings and as communal open range for animals to graze. Perhaps on no other Caribbean island did slaves have the independence and freedom that they enjoyed on Barbuda.

The remoteness of the island, the barren soil and xerophytic vegetation, the frequent droughts, the dangerous reefs—all the things that for so long prevented the settlement of Barbuda—made it an exceptional place in the plantation system of the West Indies. And from the beginning, Barbudans were known for their cantankerous and independent spirit. They never tried to mold the island into something it was not: they simply accepted the land and lived with it. Not until independence from Great Britain in 1981 did ecological and sociological deterioration began.

Associated statehood, in the eyes of Barbudans, codified their subordinate status to Antigua and to a people who raided their fish pots and patronized them as the bumpkins of the Caribbean. Associated statehood also meant that new types of entrepreneurs, with disruptive ideas about development, were beginning to look upon their island. Hotel developers saw mile after mile of beaches devoid of hotels. They regarded the droughts, which for so long had prevented successful commercial farming, as heaven-sent for tourists who wanted no rain during their visits. And they saw the flat terrain, with its meager scrub bushes, as needing only minimal work to become golf courses.

Until associated statehood, it had been little more than an annoyance for Barbudans that their island was linked to Antigua. But now the very essence of Barbudan life—land control—was threatened. Thus was born the feeling that if Barbuda could not remain a ward of the Crown, it should be separated from Antigua and make its way in the world alone—that it would be better off as an independent mini-state than as a dependency of Antigua.

Only two years after associated statehood, the Bird government granted a Canadian group exclusive development rights on Barbuda. The Canadians wanted to build a marina and hotels and to take Barbuda into the twentieth century by providing electricity, a telephone system, paved roads, and piped water. Everything would be financed by selling Barbudan land to foreigners. Barbudan opposition to the project was ignored by the Bird government. But the Crown intervened and said that no development of Barbuda could be considered unless it first was approved by the Barbudans.

The Barbudans knew their victory was temporary, that the Canadian project would be the first of many efforts by Antigua to develop the island. So the Barbudans sent Britain a petition for separation from Antigua. It was rejected.

Soon afterwards the Bird govenment offered to grant land titles to Barbudans who built new homes outside Codrington, the only village of the island. Living outside the village had been prohibited by law since the days of the Codrington lease. The system of communal land was such a part of the Barbudan tradition that the people immediately rejected what they recognized as a ploy by the Birds.

In 1976 V. C. Bird attempted to mollify the Barbudans by establishing the Barbuda Council, the island's first self-governing body. An election was held and all seats were won by candidates backed by the Birds. Opposition candidates then turned their efforts to working on another petition of separation to the Crown. The heart of the petition was the numerous citations regarding efforts by the Birds to sell Barbudan beaches to outsiders. It was submitted to Great Britain in 1978 and it exemplified the candor that marks political discourse in Antigua. It said that independence for Antigua would give it "sovereign rights over the lands and beaches of the Island [of Barbuda] and in the name of 'Development' make land deals with enterprising foreigners and use the money obtained to swell their bank balances in overseas secret accounts, reduce or pay off the huge debts that Antigua has incurred over the years, as well as assist in the numerous ambitious programs they have for the development of Antigua."

Toward the end of 1980, when V. C. Bird led a delegation to Lancaster House in London, where the conference on independence had been convened, the issue of independence was clouded by Barbuda's public threat to secede from the new nation. One Barbudan told the conference that Barbudans were prepared to undertake full independence on their own. Another Barbudan went on BBC and said his fellow islanders would prefer mass suicide on the beaches to independence in conjuction with Antigua.

While Antiguans excitedly talked of independence, Barbudans morosely talked of a shotgun wedding. Independence would remove Barbuda from the protective umbrella of the British Crown and make it subordinate to the Bird government.

But V. C. Bird and Lester had done their homework. They pointed to the Barbuda Council, which the Bird government had created, as an example of their good intentions toward Barbuda, and, as was to be expected, objections from Barbudans were ignored. When the British Parliament passed the Termination of Association Act, Barbuda, in the words of anthropologist Riva Berleant-Schiller, was "condemned to independence."

Barbuda was in the hands of the Birds. In a few months the worst fears of the Barbudans would be realized.

11

Sandmen, Bad Men, and Llamas

Independence faltered early in Antigua. The Great Dream turned into a hideous nightmare as independence became the avenue by which Bird and his sons could pillage and plunder without fear of reprisal. Nowhere was the rapacious fervor of the Birds more quickly evidenced than on Barbuda.

The stories from Barbuda are many, but the story of Winston Derrick stands out. Derrick is a big gregarious man with a permanent smile on his round, bearded face. He is a white Antiguan who, in 1984, signed a fifty-year lease for fifteen acres of land on the south end of Barbuda, which included the long-empty Dulcina Hotel. A year or so later Lester Bird, whom Derrick had known since the two were small boys, asked Derrick to relinquish the lease. "We want the land," Lester said, using the imperial *we*. Derrick refused. He had a valid lease and he had plans to develop the property. Lester publicly accused Derrick of smuggling drugs. The astounded Derrick marched into Lester's office in a state of high dudgeon. "Why are you telling people I smuggled drugs?" he demanded. "You know it is not true."

Lester shrugged. "We want the place," he said.

Derrick went home and thought about his dilemma. If Lester wanted the property badly enough to level such accusations, Derrick's life would be miserable. There was no guessing what Lester's next move might be. And no matter how hard Derrick resisted, Lester probably would wind up with the property.

So Derrick came up with what he considered a fair deal, and he wrote Lester a letter saying he would relinquish the lease for EC$500,000 and forty-five acres of land suitable for tree crops. While he was waiting for a response, a Canadian consortium offered to buy out his Barbuda lease for EC$750,000. But Derrick is an honorable man and a deal with Lester was on the table. So he turned the Canadians down. Then a group of British investors wanted to buy out the lease, and again Derrick said Lester had the first option. A few days later the British investors said they had been told that even though the property was leased to Derrick that they should deal with the appropriate minister of government—Lester Bird. The next thing Derrick knew, a note arrived on official government stationery saying the government of Antigua had rescinded his lease and that the property was being leased to the British. The note was signed by Lester.

While Derrick was still reeling from Lester's note, the British investors said they wanted to appraise the Dulcina Hotel and its contents. Derrick figured no harm could come from a simple appraisal. The British took over the hotel and began gutting it. Derrick told them to get off his property and he notified them he was going to court. He hired a caretaker to protect his hotel. Within days he received another note from Lester ordering him to give the British "full and quiet enjoyment of the demised property."

Because Derrick had known Lester for so long and because the two men had been close friends, he picked up the telephone and called Lester.

"Come see me," Lester said.

When Derrick showed up at the appointed time, Lester was out of the country. The next day police appeared at Derrick's house and told him if he trespassed on the Barbuda property he would be arrested. His caretaker at the Dulcina Hotel was evicted.

Derrick filed an injunction against the British asking that they remove themselves from his property. It took a judge only a few minutes to look at Derrick's lease and grant the injunction. Derrick then filed suit against the attorney general of Antigua and the British investors. When Lester entered his deal with the British, he was so confident that he had agreed to indemnify them if they incurred any expenses in connection with the lease. Derrick won his suit and received a judgment for EC$160,000.

The judge would not consider punitive damages, saying these would have to be paid by the Antiguan government.

Lester gave the British investors a lease for twenty-five other acres of beachfront property. And there, on one of the loveliest spots in the Caribbean, they built a dozen plywood shacks. About a year later officers from Scotland Yard showed up with extradition papers for the English developers, who were accused of numerous misdeeds back home. Derrick asked the court to sell their twenty-five acres to pay his damages. And Lester, who realized his attempt to seize the Barbuda property had failed, agreed that the Antiguan government would pay Derrick some EC$100,000. But agreeing to pay and paying are worlds apart for the Bird government.

"The Antiguan government is spending taxpayers' money to take land away from me," Derrick said. He had spent EC$60,000 to defend a lease that in most countries would never have been contested, and he didn't know how much longer he would continue the battle to regain his property. "If I push it too far, they will say this whole problem is because I am white. They would make it a racial thing." He shrugged. "An endless series of hobgoblins are loose on Barbuda."

Few tiny island-nations ever have gone through such a wild roller coaster ride as did Antigua in the decade of the 1980s. The Bird government went on a borrowing, spending, and building spree that may be unequaled in the Caribbean. It was as if Antigua, which had been at the tail end of those British colonies becoming independent in the 1960s and 1970s, not only had to catch up with them overnight, but had to surpass them in everything, especially in building the infrastructure necessary for tourism. Concomitant with the euphoric borrowing, spending, and building rampage was a series of events that demonstrated how Space Research, Robert Vesco, and New Aragon had been little more than warm-ups for the big-time world of international scandal. During the 1980s Antigua became synonymous with avarice and the V. C. Bird government became synonymous with knavery. And during the 1980s the relationship between Antigua and Barbuda became even more tempestuous. The two islands were fighting before the independence celebration was over. And while the disintegration of

Antigua took place in the public eye, that of Barbuda, as always, happened in relative obscurity. And if Antigua had been systematically exploited by British colonialism, it was nothing compared with how Barbuda was exploited by Antigua.

The plundering of Barbuda began less than a year after independence. The first step was a law sponsored by Lester Bird that declared the central government had the discretion to decide whether Barbudans could own land on Barbuda. It was a law most Machiavellian. Barbudan solidarity, for the first time in centuries, began to fragment. One group of islanders said the bill was the first step toward "eventual privatization of the land which has been held in common since Emancipation and to date has not been sold or purchased by anybody" and that it "erodes the traditional, customary, and constitutional authority handed down to the Council." These traditionalists feared that Barbuda's economic needs would make it vulnerable to exploitation from all quarters.

But other Barbudans praised the Antiguan government for the new law and said the island should be opened to private investment. They claimed that those opposed to the measure were hiding behind the guise of their love for Barbuda, undermining development by playing to a fear that outsiders would take over the island.

Concerns expressed by Barbudans at the 1980 London conference had been extraordinarily prescient. Much of what the Barbudans anticipated, including what Riva Berleant-Schiller called "corrupt or questionable investors, exploitation of Barbudan resources for Antiguan ends, disregard for the Council, and diversion of revenues to Antigua," was about to come true.

The first of those "corrupt or questionable investors" was Robert Vesco. Hot on his heels was Ed Joiner, an Atlanta developer with grandiose plans of putting hotels and golf courses atop the Highlands, building a railroad, and starting a bank. Joiner's seed money came from people in Atlanta whom he had convinced to invest in a phony energy company. He left Atlanta with the Internal Revenue Service in hot pursuit. On Barbuda, he became involved in local politics—which was deeply resented on Antigua. But his downfall came when he threatened Lester. Within days, Joiner was deported. He later served time in the

Atlanta federal penitentiary for his investment scam with the energy company.

As for "exploitation of Barbudan resources" and the "diversion of revenues to Antigua," nothing is more illustrative than the sand mining that occurred. As usual, a Bird was involved.

Barbudan sand became a vital ingredient in the building boom that swept the Caribbean in the 1980s. For more than fifteen years, three bargeloads of sand have left Barbuda every day for Antigua and for places as far away as the Virgin Islands. The resulting hole is seven meters deep and about one-quarter square mile in extent. The sand is dug from the narrow peninsula of Palmetto Point on the extreme southwestern corner of the island. The ocean is to the south and west while the lagoon is to the north. In a hurricane, the peninsula could be washed away.

A company controlled by Lester Bird mined the sand and paid the Antiguan government about seventy-nine cents per cubic yard. The sand then was sold on Antigua for $5.55 per cubic yard. The Barbuda Council filed suit against the sand mining company, demanding that all money that had come out of the operation be given to the council and that the council then take it over.

Hilbourne Frank, a Barbudan who taught school in England for many years before coming home and entering politics, spent a lot of time figuring out what would happen if the Barbuda Council were to take over the sand mining business. One month's profits would equal two thirds of Barbuda's annual budget. The level of services on the island could be increased tenfold and Barbuda would have money left over to invest. After five years, interest alone on the investments would cover the cost of administering Barbuda's government.

But Barbuda never had a chance to prove Frank's math. The attorney general of Antigua, who is appointed by Prime Minister Bird, joined the suit on behalf of Lester's sand company. The case was lost even before it came to court.

In 1983 the Bird government created the Barbuda Industrial Development Agency and gave it powers superseding those of the Barbuda Council. A close friend and aide-de-camp of Lester Bird was appointed chairman of the agency. Barbudans appointed to the agency were those who favored development and cooperation with the Bird government. So while the Birds can point to the Barbuda Council as proof of the island's autonomy, in truth the council is virtually impotent on the most important issues facing the island.

An example was a project approved by the Antiguan government over the bitter opposition of the Barbudans—a plan to use the island as a dumping ground for sludge consisting of compressed and treated human effluent from the United States. Barbudans fought back as they always do—emotionally. They put out a flyer that said "Washington Shits on Barbuda" and another that said Barbudans did not want their island to become a depository for "Rich People's Poo-Poo."

The opposition from Barbuda was so virulent that the Antiguan government, fearing the consequences, canceled the project.

Then Antigua approved a project whereby toxic wastes would be dumped on Barbuda. Again the Barbudans objected so vehemently that Lester Bird, the only minister whose portfolios gave him authority to deal with an outside company wanting to dump toxic waste, realized he would be publicly exposed. This project also was canceled.

As what may be the only two examples of battles won by Barbuda in the war with Antigua, these skirmishes proved to be valuable learning experiences for Lester. Throughout the 1980s incursions continued against Barbudan autonomy. Almost on a weekly basis foreigners would step off chartered airplanes and be escorted about the island by Antiguan officials. "It is all very hush-hush," Hilbourne Frank said. "We don't know who those people are."

But Frank, who became the leader of the Barbudan Separation Movement, continued to fight. He raised the money to hire John MacDonald, one of Britain's best-known constitutional lawyers, and filed suit seeking to establish that the longstanding practice of swidden farming and stock-grazing on open range gave Barbudans the rights in common to land ownership. The suit was to resolve once and for all the murky question of land ownership on Barbuda. The government of Antigua said the central government controlled all former Crown lands within the nation. And, as no one on Barbuda owned land, everything on the island was considered Crown land. When the case was heard in early 1988, Antigua carried the day.

A few months later Mel Fisher, the American treasure hunter who discovered the seventeenth-century Spanish galleon *Atocha* in the Florida Keys, announced he had an option for a ninety-nine-year lease on 654 acres of Barbudan land. His plans for the island were even more ambitious than those of Ed Joiner. Fisher was the front man for what was essentially a real estate project managed by a Florida developer. His leased land included the triangular acreage that wraps around a frigate-bird sanctuary on the northwest corner of the island. A marina was planned for the lagoon just south of the bird sanctuary, and an airport was to be built a few hundred yards south of the marina. Plans for Barbuda included a "rejuvenation and recuperation" program in a luxury hotel that would also contain a cosmetology center, a hyperbaric-treatment center, a biomedical clinic, and a longevity center. There were to be a four-hundred-unit condominium-hotel, a golf course, and a "preservation laboratory," in which Fisher was to display "anticipated treasures from shipwrecks of Spanish galleons in the area." According to Fisher, the complex also would include an underwater lounge, restaurant and observatory, along with six underwater suites, a search-and-salvage center, and an offshore bank. The prospectus said yachtsmen would have safe dockage at the secluded marina and that visitors could dive on the dozens of shipwrecks littering offshore reefs.

Had the Barbudans been apprised of Fisher's plans, their eyebrows would have raised, and not only from surprise at the scope and magnitude of the project. Did Fisher plan to blast a passage through the coral-studded canal going into the lagoon? Even if he did, how could yachts come through the offshore reefs when a heavy ground swell made the entrance to the lagoon virtually impassable for three or four months each year? As for tempting guests with the thought of diving on bullion-filled wrecks, didn't Fisher know the Barbudans' history of salvage? Anything of value had been taken off those wrecked vessels within hours of the time they struck the reefs.

It was through a story I wrote in *The New Yorker* that the Barbuda Council learned of Fisher's plans. Barbudans would never have agreed to building a marina and airport only a few hundred yards from the fragile mangrove swamps where frigate birds nest. And they did not understand how Antigua could grant salvage rights to anyone, since those ancient rights belonged to Barbudans.

Mel Fisher's project died a few months later, probably because publicity scared away potential investors.

But not all new projects were to fail. The imperious William Cody Kelly, who has been known to speak of Barbuda as "my island" and who jealously fends off any potential competition, was indirectly responsible for the biggest development on Barbuda. I had several telephone conversations with Kelly. Most of the chats were one-sided; he rattled on about all his important friends while I listened. But he had little to say about the new hotel down the beach from the Coco Point Lodge. This resort, the most expensive in the Caribbean, was built solely out of pique. One night the wealthy Italian industrialist Aldo Pinto and his wife, Mariuccia Mandelli, a designer who markets clothes under the Krizia label, were guests at Coco Point. They and a group of friends were having a party and wanted Italian food. They were happy, perhaps even boisterous. The manager at Coco Point was used to the sedate ways and mild manners of Republicans. After he refused to cook Italian food he tossed out Pinto's party.

Pinto and Mandelli decided to build the most fabulous resort in the Caribbean on Kelly's doorstep.

I talked to Pinto shortly after he announced the project. In addition to various remarks about Kelly, he said all of his dealings had been with Antiguan officials, that the Barbudans were not a part of his negotiations.

Pinto invested more than $10 million developing two hundred acres of land. The K-Club has a mile of perhaps the grandest pink beach in the Caribbean. To obtain enough flat land for a golf course Pinto had to drain both a salt pond and a considerable amount of mangrove swamps. There was no opposition, for the Antiguan government considers salt ponds, marshes, and mangrove swamps to serve no purpose except for developers who can utilize them in a constructive fashion. Pinto not only had the only golf course on Barbuda, but his resort has undreamed-of amenities for which guests pay $1,000 a day.

Nevertheless, the first few years of the K-Club have been rocky. Mariuccia Mandelli's attitude as a fashion designer carried over into her management philosophy at the K-Club: she changed managers the way she changed hemlines. The new resort was slammed by various publications, including a particularly biting review in *New York* magazine, and its future remains unclear.

Unlike the K-Club, the future of Barbuda seems certain. The uniqueness of the island is being destroyed at an ever-increasing rate. It is only a matter of time before a big hotel or a large condominium development is announced.

The Barbuda Council has continued its battle with the government of Antigua. A group of Italian investors, impressed with what Aldo Pinto had done, announced the construction of a new hotel on Palmetto Point. The Barbuda Council granted permission to fence the property. But the fence enclosed more than twice as much land as the council thought the Italians had leased. When the council asked the Italians to take down the fence and confine it to the original acreage, the Italians refused. The Barbuda Council ordered a backhoe operator to rip out the fence. Then the Italians angrily announced that they had leased from Antigua all the land that had been fenced. They had not responded to the Barbuda Council's earlier request because they knew the power lay in Antigua and they did not want to bother with the Barbudans. The Italians took the Barbuda Council into court, won, and the Barbuda Council had to replace the fence.

But the event of the 1980s that perhaps best symbolized the unending defiance of the Barbudans, and the incident that symbolized the tragedy that is Barbuda, revolved around the bizarre and unlikely episode of the llamas.

In April 1989 a chartered Boeing 707 arrived in Antigua from Chile with 268 llamas aboard, and the llamas were taken by barge to Barbuda, where a group of American investors had made arrangements with the Bird government to build a quarantine station. The investors, taking advantage of the faddish nature of llamas, fueled in large part by rock star Michael Jackson, would use Barbuda as a way station before importing llamas and other exotic animals such as lions, tigers, and elephants into the United States.

Barbudans did not pay too much attention when the fences

and buildings went up at the quarantine station. But when it become known that the llamas were en route, a Barbudan lawyer notified the importers that this project had not been approved by the Barbuda Council and that the animals would not be allowed on the island. Even so, the American importer ignored the Barbudans.

Like a giant wave, rumors preceded the llama-filled barges. Every Barbudan heard that flesh-eating wild animals and AIDS-infested monkeys were being imported as part of a plot by the Antiguan government to decimate the Barbudan population. In a classic example of bad timing, the barges arrived in Barbuda on election day for a parliamentary seat and for seats on the Barbuda Council. The only issue was whether a candidate was pro-Bird or anti-Bird, and, by extension, whether Barbuda would allow the Bird government to take over Barbuda.

It was a measure of how the election would turn out that the barges were met by a group of Barbudans who could only be described as a mob. Hundreds of Barbudans, many carrying pitchforks, machetes, and anything else that could be used as an instrument of mayhem, were at the dock on the south side of the island. They refused to let the barges off-load and they refused to allow water to be taken to the llamas. The llamas were creatures of the high Andes and were eminently unsuited to the heat of the Caribbean. Within hours, about two dozen had died.

On Antigua and Barbuda, arson has long been an accepted method of political expression. Before the night was over, Barbudans rioted and burned the trucks and station wagons belonging to the quarantine station and set fire to the new barracks. Even the Birds know there are times when it is best to walk away; they ordered police to leave the scene.

The next day the barge turned around and made the all-day trip to a small island off the Atlantic coast of Antigua where there is little shade and no water. By the end of April, the llama count had dwindled to 179, even though the American importers had paid an Antiguan to carry food and water to the llamas every week. The Antiguan subcontracted the chore to someone who did not take the job seriously, and by mid-1992, only about 40 of the llamas remained. But by then they had been adopted by various civic groups on Antigua and food and water were regularly supplied. Their numbers appeared to have stabilized.

Burning the quarantine station and turning back the barge are remembered as historic events on Barbuda—great victories over Antigua and over foreign businessmen. Hilbourne Frank, because of his outspoken opposition to the Birds and his unending efforts to bring about Barbudan autonomy, won election to Barbuda's sole parliamentary seat that day. His battles against Antigua and his fight for Barbudan autonomy have not ceased.

Frank is a tall and lean man with a canescent halo of hair around a face that ranges between kind and avuncular. His soft eyes give no hint of the determination that has enabled him to ignore overwhelming odds and fight Antigua for so long. When he talks of Barbuda, his voice is filled with the sort of sadness one hears when someone speaks of a terminally ill relative.

"When we look back, we realize that our association with Antigua has not been a fruitful arrangement," he said. "All of our imports have to come through Antigua. We have suffered a lot because of the lack of communication with the outside world. You have hardly heard of us. Antiguans feel that we are just a village in the countryside and not a people or a nation as we have been throughout our history. A lot of the social services which a country should have, we never had. The majority of Barbudans are still angry and frustrated about the coercion, the destiny that was forced upon us in association with Antigua. If the Antiguans are going to take away our birthright, our land, it is the same thing the slave masters did. If we have no say in what should happen to our lands, we are little short of slaves. Antigua is not interested in our welfare. They only want to grab our land. Our expatriates know that no matter how long they are away, when they return they are entitled to some piece of Barbuda. We have the name of being a sister island of Antigua. But that is only in name. In reality, we are worse than a subjugated dependency."

In September 1991, Frank wrote the secretary general of the Commonwealth of Nations in London, and stated that a "constitutional crisis" existed between Antigua and Barbuda. He said

Barbuda "is still suffering from economic rape and political incest at the hands of Antigua." And he again asked that Great Britain either accept Barbuda back into the fold as a dependency or that Barbuda be allowed to go its own way as a separate nation.

There was no response.

Book Two

EACH ENDEAVORING, ALL ACHIEVING

12

War and Friendship

To comprehend the long and close relationship between America and Antigua, to know why the State Department continues to prop up a government it describes as "the most corrupt in the Caribbean," one first must understand events leading up to the 1983 Grenada invasion. It is in the years between 1979 and 1983 that one discovers how Vere Cornwall Bird became a creature of America's Caribbean policy and how Antigua became an American puppet state.

Grenada is 350 miles south of Antigua, where it dangles like a geographic afterthought at the end of the Windward Islands. The island is closer to Venezuela than to many of its Caribbean neighbors. One third of the world's nutmeg is grown here, giving Grenada the sobriquet "the Spice Island." The island is so small and so remote that it is almost impossible to imagine anything happening there that could have much of an impact anywhere else in the world, especially in America. But when Maurice Bishop and a group of left-wing revolutionaries overthrew the government of Grenada in 1979, the ripples forever changed the Caribbean and caused near-panic in the U.S. government. Perhaps the most significant and lasting effect was in Antigua.

It may be difficult to recall today, in the years after the collapse of the Soviet Union, how strong was the specter of communism in 1979. The Domino Theory had been discredited in Southeast Asia, but it still had ecclesiastical weight in the State Department, especially when the Caribbean, the very back door of America, was involved. If Grenada, only a hundred miles or so southwest of the American embassy on Barbados, could make such a dangerous turn to the left, it could happen anywhere in the Caribbean. And the phrase "We lost Grenada," became, like "Remember the Alamo," a rallying cry in the determined effort to see that such a thing never happened again.

The U.S. ambassador on Barbados made no secret of his distaste for Bishop, a London-educated lawyer. This coolness, combined with Bishop's leftist leanings, pushed Bishop even closer to Cuba, the Soviet Union, and Libya. The U.S. government was upset when it learned that arms from Cuba had arrived on Grenada, and it was deeply disturbed when informed that Grenada had established diplomatic ties with Cuba. At the time, America would hold its nose and deal with the Soviet Union or China, but Castro's brand of communism was anathema—a U.S. embargo has denied Cuba tourists, trade, or investment since the early 1960s. And when Bishop allied himself with Castro, he had, in the eyes of Washington, taken steps that could lead to a disruption of America's hegemony in the Caribbean. In fact, Ronald Reagan saw Grenada as a pivotal point in the ideological battle between democracy and communism, and, in speaking of Grenada, said America's national security was at stake.

In the years following World War II, after two centuries of British domination, the Caribbean—with the exception of Castro's Cuba—belonged to America. Then Maurice Bishop took over Grenada. Ronald Reagan's bellicosity in referring to the Soviet Union as the "Evil Empire" compounded the simmering Grenada situation. In order to embarrass the United States, the Soviets paid court to Bishop. This, in turn, caused even more alarm in Washington.

From the time he seized power, Bishop had been obsessed with the idea he might be overthrown. His fears were realized on October 19, 1983, when he and his closest associates were murdered by a fanatical faction within the New Jewel Movement, followers of a Leninist doctrine. This was too much for Washington, and Reagan ordered the U.S. military to invade Grenada.

For the first time in history a U.S. president had committed an act of war in the Commonwealth Caribbean. The invasion had enormous and lasting significance throughout the region, not only ending the left-wing regime in Grenada but demonstrating U.S. military strength and frightening any group in the Caribbean or Central America that might have entertained thoughts of challenging U.S. hegemony.

Between Bishop's ascension in 1979 and the U.S. invasion of Grenada in 1983, the U.S. government's attitude toward the Caribbean underwent drastic and significant change, and Antigua was a key player in the change.

After Bishop seized power, the State Department sent troubleshooter Philip Habib to the Caribbean to determine why democracy "lost" Grenada to a left-leaning government and how the United States could prevent another such incident. The U.S. embassy in Barbados then was responsible for ten nations in the eastern Caribbean. Habib said the embassy was spread too thin, that one embassy could not keep an eye on so many countries. He recommended that an embassy be opened in Grenada and that a new U.S. consulate be established somewhere to the north. The consulate would be responsible for Antigua and Barbuda, St. Kitts and Nevis, Montserrat, Anguilla, and the British Virgin Islands.

Antigua was the natural choice. In addition to the U.S. Air Force tracking installation and the navy base already on the island, Antigua's airport had the longest runway in the area. The island was a stop for cruise ships. But most important of all, Premier V. C. Bird was a close friend of the United States. It did not matter to the United States that Bird's government already was showing signs of avarice; the State Department considers corruption to be a given in most Caribbean and Central American governments. The United States needed a stalwart pro-American country as a base from which to show the flag and defend the region. Antigua was about to become an American satellite, a bastion of democracy whose role would be as an anchor against what Washington saw as the insidious, pervasive, and dangerous spread of communism.

In late 1979 Paul Byrnes established a consulate general in St. Johns, which officially opened on Monday, April 12, 1980. It is indicative of the State Department's attitude toward the Caribbean that no one at the State Department knew anything about Antigua and that most of Byrnes's background information came from travel brochures.

Not long after the consulate general opened, the State Department decided to erect a Voice of America transmitter on the island to convince people of the region that democracy had many advantages over the leftist theories espoused by Maurice Bishop. Byrnes sent the Bird government a detailed plan and pointed out that the BBC had a relay station on the island and America should pay no more than the BBC was paying.

From there, exactly what happened depends on who is telling the story. The Antiguan version is that Lester Bird, who was being groomed to become Antigua's foreign minister after independence, vehemently opposed the VOA transmitter on the grounds that the VOA often was a cover for the Central Intelligency Agency and that the transmitter would be used to dispense American propaganda. He was intransigent.

This version of the story has it that several months later, when Lester was off the island, the State Department went directly to V. C. Bird and asked for an immediate agreement on the transmitter as an interim arrangement. If a better location on another island was found, the antenna might be moved. The State Department couched the request in such a way that the prime minister considered the overture a special request from fellow septuagenarian Ronald Reagan. Bird saw this as a way to increase the ties between the two countries. He not only signed on the dotted line, but he allowed America to pay the same lease price for the antenna site that the BBC paid, despite the fact that the BBC had the leverage of dealing with a colony when that deal was struck. America got the VOA transmitter lease for several hundred dollars a month.

Lester was furious, both at what he saw as duplicity by the State Department and at what he called a "peppercorn lease"—one virtually given away. He had been outmaneuvered and he did not like it.

A longtime State Department employee says of the lease, "We got it for a song," but denies there was a deliberate effort to go around Lester. He says the State Department did not know Lester was off the island when V. C. Bird was approached.

Tim Hector weighed in with editorials against the "CIA-sponsored radio station" and predicted the transmitter would broadcast programs designed to destabilize and subvert neighboring islands.

Almost overnight the transmitter rose from a site on the north side of the island near the navy base. Soon it was sending a message of democracy to part of the eastern Caribbean. The transmitter was not nearly as powerful as had been hoped—it barely reached Grenada. And rather than being a quick fix, it was to stay for more than a decade.

When Antigua became independent on November 1, 1981, the U.S. consulate general was upgraded to a full embassy and the title of the senior State Department official became chargé d'affaires. The embassy was a matter of great prestige on Antigua, where officials thought they now had a hotline to Washington.

And when dozens and then hundreds of pregnant Antiguan women flew to the American Virgin Islands so they could deliver their children on United States soil and thereby have them born as United States citizens, it was the U.S. embassy on Antigua that provided the documentation. Within a few years the official number of Americans on Antigua was to number in the thousands. *The F-77 Report*, a State Department document regarding the evacuation of American citizens in the event of an emergency, today considers some four thousand Americans to be on Antigua. But that number is extremely misleading. Only several hundred Americans, mainly retired people, live there. Almost all of the others are what the State Department calls "nontraditional Americans"—children of Antiguans who, when in advanced pregnancy, visited American soil for the sole purpose of having their children born U.S. citizens.

When America invaded Grenada, a squad of ten soldiers from the Antigua and Barbuda Defense Force were part of the token Caribbean involvement. Lester Bird, who opposed Antiguan participation, was overruled by his father. The prime minister had decided that he and Ronald Reagan were close friends.

The invasion was a watershed in U.S.-Caribbean relations. Never again would the small islands of the region look on America in the same fashion. They were independent nations, but after October 1983, they knew that America was the colossus to the north, the behemoth that, like a sleeping elephant, should not be disturbed or angered.

Lester Bird did not accept this prevailing wisdom. As much as if not more than any other ranking Caribbean official, he confronts and challenges America. Space Research and Robert Vesco were precursors of what would become his diplomatic style. With one hand he would slap at the State Department while, at the same time, he would hold out his other hand and demand money, services, and concessions.

Antigua had been independent eighteen months when, in April 1983, Lester Bird canceled a treaty with the United States as a necessary first step in making sweeping changes in the tax, banking, insurance, shipping, and trust laws of his country. Lester was about to set up Antigua as an offshore financial center.

By January 1984, U.S. Special Forces had finished training the first cadre of Caribbean police in anti-insurgency techniques. The United States wanted to train police on every island in the eastern Caribbean to recognize, combat, and overcome any efforts by left-leaning politicians to take over a government. Lester complained that the United States was "militarizing" the Caribbean.

Three months after the Grenada invasion, on January 13, 1984, a State Department paper was issued as a rationale for the close relationship between Antigua and America. The document said Antigua is "strategically placed in the Leeward Islands, thus a potentially dangerous hazard would be posed for the region if it falls to a hostile power." Despite the pervasive corruption of the Bird government, this would continue as State Department policy even after the Soviet Union and communism collapsed in the early 1990s. That the only issue was V. C. Bird and his government's friendliness to America became evident during the mid-1980s, when the United States learned that ministers of the Bird government were buying government-owned land—valuable beachfront property as well as the former sugar plantations V. C. Bird had bought from the British—at ridiculously low prices, or, in some instances, no prices at all. Although probity and rectitude would obviously not be the attributes either of the new nation of Antigua or of its top officials, the State Department said nothing.

V. C. Bird knew that his country hosted two of the most important U.S. military bases in the Caribbean, both of which had a critical national defense role and were symbols of America's hegemony.

The U.S. Air Force operated the Antigua Air Station, a tracking facility that monitors satellite launches out of Cape Canaveral by means of an impressive array of antennas scattered at remote sites around Antigua. But a more significant function of the base then was secretly to monitor Soviet satellites and to eavesdrop on radio conversations between Cuba and Russia as well as on the radio traffic of all Soviet aircraft and naval vessels in the Caribbean.

As for the Navy base, it is tucked away over the crest of a hill on the northeast corner of the island. No signs anywhere on Antigua announce its presence or point to its location. But for years this installation, through a vast network of undersea detection equipment known as the Sound and Surveillance System, or SOSUS, tracked the movement of the Soviet Union's nuclear submarines as they entered the Caribbean en route to Cuba or toward American shores.

After Grenada, when America began to pour money and new construction into Antigua, these two bases assumed even greater significance.

13

Peace and Friendship

One of the most curious aspects of America's relationship with Antigua is the lack of institutional memory by the United States. Chargés d'affaires rotate through Antigua every few years. The U.S. embassy is so small—the smallest in the world—that there is almost no room for records. Paperwork is kept a few months, then transferred either to the embassy in Barbados or to State Department archives in Washington. The most tumultuous events are quickly forgotten.

Robert DuBose was the chargé d'affaires during the mid-1980s. Lanky, languid, and full of himself, DuBose had not exchanged more than three sentences with me before letting me know he was a Harvard man. He waited expansively for me to offer my credentials. But I was so astonished at the idea of a middle-aged man identifying himself in this fashion that I did not respond.

Over a two-week period, I talked with DuBose several times at the embassy and I spent a long Sunday afternoon with him at his mountaintop home north of St. John's. I was amazed to find that he knew nothing of Space Research, Robert Vesco, or the Sovereign Order of New Aragon.

Not only does every chargé d'affaires begin his tour of duty unencumbered by history, so do the country officers responsible for Antigua at the State Department. Caribbean Affairs is something of a stepchild in the Latin American Bureau. At the end of its small suite of offices is a young country officer responsible for nine countries in the eastern Caribbean.

The same lack of institutional awareness is found at the two military bases. I have interviewed several commanding officers of the Antigua Air Station and found that while they are crisp and clear about their job and their mission, their knowledge of U.S. involvement on the island is vague. It is the same at the U.S. Naval Support Facility. The commanding officers of both facilities are briefed prior to their assignments, but they have little in-depth knowledge of military events that happened on Antigua prior to their arrival.

For the U.S. government, every day is a new day on Antigua.

Antiguan land leased by the United States during World War II was returned to Great Britain in 1950. Although the U.S. military retained landing rights at the airport, the privilege rarely was exercised. In 1956 the United States obtained from Great Britain a "right of entry" to establish the Air Force tracking station. Though it was not mentioned in the lease, the U.S. Navy facility opened in the same year was part of a top secret system for monitoring Soviet submarines in the Caribbean. The number of U.S. military aircraft increased significantly at what then was called Coolidge Field, the air base built in 1941 and named in honor of Captain Hamilton Coolidge, an American pilot killed in World War I. The field, now called V. C. Bird International Airport, may be the only airport in the world named for a living head of government.

In the early 1960s, not long after V. C. Bird became chief minister, the United States needed additional land for the Air Force tracking station. John F. Kennedy wanted the United States to catch up with the Soviet space program, but there was not enough money for all that had to be done. V. C. Bird contributed free land and a large building. Although the reason for the gift is not clear, one could speculate that Antigua was turning its back on the British colonial past and wanting to ingratiate itself with a new ally. America was the most prestigious ally of all. Whatever the reason, V. C. Bird knew the significance of his gift and he was to remind numerous chargés d'affaires of his role in assisting America's entry into the space race.

Through a series of leases, the United States has since maintained a continual presence on Antigua. But what once was free from the British has, because of Lester Bird, become increasingly expensive. Lester realized even before his country became independent how badly the United States needed the two bases and that they would pay for the privilege.

The United States was to find that paying higher and higher rents, onto which were tacked exorbitant "maintenance fees," meant little. The Birds were to begin a series of efforts, some of them successful, to encroach on, and to take back, the land they had leased. This was seen by some as an extension of a common syndrome during slavery and colonialism, the sly passive aggression toward economically powerful leaders. Others saw it as avarice and venality.

Whatever it is, the Bird government began a systematic campaign of appropriating U.S.-leased lands. Navy property was leased to a fish-freezing facility and to a furniture manufacturer. A series of Antigua squatters moved onto Navy property and began building homes. When the Navy forced the illegal tenants to evacuate, the Bird government threatened to sue the U.S. government. Then the Air Force found that raw untreated sewage from a nearby village was collecting in a large pool on Air Force property. The Bird government repeatedly ignored Air Force requests to divert the sewage. Not until the Air Force served notice it was about to seal the drainage pipe did the Antigua government send in a crew. Then a marina adjacent to the Air Force station fenced its property—and included several acres of Air Force land. The Air Force complained, but to no avail.

These efforts at encroachment continue. In 1992, the driver of a dump truck showed up at the naval facility saying he had authority to move fifteen loads of sand that had been piled on the beach where the Navy was building a new pier. The Navy commanding officer sent him packing.

On one of my visits to Antigua, I was in the embassy talking with Robert DuBose when he received an emergency phone call. Bulldozers were clearing land around the VOA transmitter and a large sign had been erected saying the site would be the location for the "Pink Lady Disco." For several days Prime Minister Bird ignored DuBose's complaints. When DuBose found that what he called "organized crime figures from the United States" were behind the Pink Lady Disco, he successfully threatened to send armed men from the Navy base to stop the bulldozing. "Antigua operates under the law of the bulldozer,"

DuBose grumbled to me. "Whoever has the largest bulldozer wins."

It is not known exactly when the United States began paying rent for Antiguan land or what the initial fees were. These records have long since been relegated to the archives, and neither the Air Force nor the Navy commanding officers can clarify the issue. But by the mid-1980s, the Air Force and the Navy each paid an annual lease of $750,000 to Antigua. In 1988, when the contract was up for renegotiation, they each found their rent had jumped to $1.25 million. The Air Force then leased 535 acres of land. Lester asked the State Department to return 63 acres that would be converted into an industrial free zone. He said a European consortium had agreed to finance the infrastructure for the free zone, and, when completed, the free zone would attract enough foreign investment to turn Antigua into the "Hong Kong of the Caribbean." Lester notified the State Department that the project was crucial to Antigua and he demanded urgent action. The State Department had major reservations about the free zone. The financing was dubious, and there was some concern that the remote acreage, which had a dock large enough for coastal freighters, might be used for narcotics trafficking. Nevertheless, the United States agreed to return the 63 acres to Antigua if Antigua would not ask for another increase in the lease payments until the contract expired in 1998. By late 1992, there was still no financing and no foreign investment in the free zone. And the Birds were pressing for another rent increase.

In addition to the annual rent, the contract calls for the Air Force to pay a "fair and reasonable" airport maintenance fee of $40,000 annually. This fee covers whatever damage might be done by the landing of some thirty military aircraft each month. About five of these flights are medical flights to Puerto Rico or flights carrying dependents. The other U.S. aircraft are C-130s, which are used to drop paratroopers into the ocean, and C-141s, which are used as "range aircraft" that twice each week come from Charleston to Patrick Air Force Base and then down the chain of islands in the Atlantic tracking range.

The arrangement between the United States and Antigua for use of the airport is described by the State Department as "one of [the most], if not the most, generous arrangements with a foreign government anywhere in the world." U.S. aircraft land at V. C. Bird International Airport at any hour and with no prior notice. They pay no landing fees and the crews do not go through customs or immigration.

In addition, no taxes or duties are imposed on the import or export of any equipment at the tracking station or on the personal effects, including automobiles, of U.S. personnel. The list of concessions, which include fiscal exemptions, extraordinarily lenient rules regarding civil claims against military personnel, and the exemption of U.S. vessels from all toll charges, goes on for several pages in the lease agreement.

An equally important part of the arrangement, and one that is not generally known on drought-stricken Antigua, is that the parking aprons, taxiways, and runways of the airport constitute the largest single catchment system on the island. Built by the U.S. Army when the airfield was under construction, an underground system of pipes leads directly to the nearby U.S. Air Force station, where a 2.5-million-gallon container is kept full—enough to supply both the Air Force and Navy for several months. The Air Force also has a reserve storage tank holding 1.6 million gallons. Meanwhile, Antigua imports water at a cost of about $20,000 per bargeload.

Today the Antigua Air Station occupies a relatively small portion of the 472 acres under lease. The purpose of the base, according to an unclassified mission briefing, is the computerized collection of data from missiles launched at Cape Canaveral and from satellites. Its secondary mission is to conduct surveillance of space. The Antigua Air Station is part of the Eastern Test Range, which runs from Florida, through the Bahamas, U.S. Virgin Islands, then to Antigua and on to Ascension. The Antigua Air Station transmits commands to missiles and satellites, and it can, if necessary, relay destruction commands to a missile gone amuck.

Much of the computerized collection of satellite data comes from satellites belonging to nations other than America. The Antigua Air Station, from its main base near the airport and from eight outlying instrumentation sites around the island, uses telemetry and radar to probe the secrets of those satellites. And although neither the State Department nor the Air Force will confirm it, several of the antenna-strewn locations around Antigua almost certainly are part of the supersecret National Security Agency's SIGINT—signals intelligence—platforms that eavesdrop on everything from shortwave radios to car telephones.

The air station is unusual in that only two Air Force personnel are stationed there: the commanding officer, who is a major, and a clerk, an enlisted person. A civilian contractor from America operates the tracking station with eighty-one technical people. An additional eighty-one Antiguans constitute the skilled and unskilled labor force. The American employees spend an estimated $500,000 annually on Antigua. Salaries for local workers amounts to $563,000 annually. In addition, the Air Force buys more than $800,000 worth of fuel each year at the airport.

The U.S. Naval Support Facility is an innocuous title for an innocuous base. The Navy outpost, around the corner and over a small hill from the Air Force station, occupies 182.6 acres of land. The highly classified SOSUS for keeping track of Soviet submarines, the longtime raison d'être of the Navy facility, was replaced with new technology in the mid-1970s, when the base was scaled down to a caretaker status. It was about to be closed but Maurice Bishop came to power in Grenada and the United States decided every facility in the Caribbean was needed. In 1985 the base was redesignated as a "support facility," which means the base has no intrinsic value other than to support other, more important, military missions. The Navy acts as host to elite units from various branches of the U.S. military that come here to practice waterborne operations—parachuting rafts and personnel into the ocean so the troops can practice assault missions, often on the beaches of Barbuda. Most of the troops are Army Special Forces, but also represented are Navy SEAL, Marine force recon, and Air Force commandos. The base also stores weapons and ammunition. The U.S. units that come here for underwater training bring their own explosives.

The annual civilian payroll at the Navy facility is about $900,000. The Navy payroll is about $1.5 million.

The senior military people at both the Air Force station and the Naval Support Facility have been generous in giving out base passes to Antiguans, an odd and unusual practice if the bases are as important as the U.S. military says they are. After all, foreign nationals usually are not allowed such access to sensitive U.S. military bases. The passes, which for a long time had no picture or identifying number, only the bearer's name, allowed entry for hundreds of Antiguan civilians, who believed a great cachet was attached to visiting the Air Force's Satellite Club, eating at the restaurant, and drinking American beer—all at rock-bottom military prices.

At one period, more than one thousand such guest passes were issued. But when Operation Desert Shield began, the commanders of the two U.S. military facilities pulled all the passes and introduced a new and tightly controlled system of allocating numbered identification cards upon which was affixed a laminated photograph. While the system cut back substantially on the number of passes, it had no effect on the privileges. One practice on the Navy base, highly unusual and perhaps without precedent, allows Antiguan employees at the Navy Exchange to purchase duty-free goods. A former Air Force commander complained without avail both to the State Department and to the Department of Defense that the Navy was violating rules and regulations of the U.S. government.

The beginning of the 1990s was significant in another respect for the two bases. The U.S. military was making major cutbacks and the State Department was retrenching. Strong consideration was given to closing both bases. The Navy base was an easy call, for its function could be carried out in Puerto Rico or the Florida Keys. Its primary advantage was its being one of the few places left where the local government had no objection when U.S. troops systematically blew up the reefs, killed fish, and made barren large expanses of the sea bottom. Now the rationale for the base, to use the euphemistic military phrase, is "the freedom of action granted to U.S. troops."

The Air Force base presents a more complicated picture. At first glance the station seems a vital tracking station. Because clouds cause attenuation of electronic signals, Antigua's clear skies are important for around-the-world satellite tracking. But the Antigua Air Station could be replaced by ships; and although it is not widely known, the Air Force already has one such tracking ship in its inventory.

In 1990 it was decided that both bases could be shut down without downgrading either the Air Force satellite-monitoring program or the Navy training program. Nevertheless, the bases remain open. The prime minister wanted them to stay. And the deciding rationale was that they provided a stabilizing influence for a government friendly to the United States. Removing the bases, according to the U.S. logic, could cause the Bird government to be replaced by a government that might not be so friendly.

After it was decided to keep the bases open, both facilities received additional funding. Considering the small size of the bases, the money was substantial. The Air Force got $10 million to renovate and expand existing technical equipment and to build new barracks, office spaces, and a fire station. Another $10 million will build a new Consolidated Instrumentation Facility (CIF), which will automate radar and telemetry facilities. The Navy received $10 million, some of which went to finance increased security measures, such as a ten-foot-high fence around the base. Construction began on a $5.5 million boathouse that was custom-made for training Special Forces troops but which also could be used to launch clandestine operations. A deeper channel was dynamited and dredged and a pier was built so naval vessels could tie up at the Navy base rather than in St. John's harbor. The Navy did not have to prepare an environmental impact statement, and local environmental groups complained that the dynamiting and dredging caused extensive damage to a large reef.

Antigua, both the government and the community, has always offered much to the American serviceman. The favorite attraction is the three brothels in St. John's, among the largest in the Caribbean. Many of the young women who work in the brothels are the golden-haired and tawny-skinned women of the Dominican Republic. After the Navy vessel *Belknap* visited St. John's, crew members came down with a particularly virulent strain of antibiotic-resistant venereal disease. U.S. military officials asked local medical authorities to examine the prostitutes and, if they were found to be carrying a sexually transmitted disease, have them treated. The Antiguan government refused. The United States placed the brothels off-limits, which made them even more attractive to sailors.

About eight U.S. Navy vessels make port calls in St. John's each year. The vessels usually stay three or four days and, according to Navy statistics, each sailor spends about $100 a day.

America's military presence is also seen in the U.S. Army Special Forces instructors who train the Antiguan police and Defense Force. The U.S. Coast Guard contingent on Antigua has the dual function of advising the Antiguan Coast Guard and conducting surveillance for narcotics smugglers. On Antigua, as in many Caribbean islands, the local coast guard comes under the supervision of the police. According to American intelligence reports, the *Liberta*, the single boat in the Antiguan Coast Guard, has been seen picking up narcotics shipments that were air-dropped into Antiguan waters—shipments that were never reported as seized.

The friendly and often sensitive relations between the Bird government and the U.S. military dictate that the two American commanders be under the supervision of the chargé d'affaires at the U.S. embassy. The commanders tend to look on the chargé as something of a baby-sitter, and tend to believe they can perform their military jobs as well as deal with the Birds. Part of their confidence comes from the fact they are commanding officers in a "new" military environment where officers are expected to have some diplomatic skills. But part of their confidence springs from economic muscle. After all, the two bases are second only to tourism in the amount of money they pour into the local economy, and now, because the tourism industry is down and the bases are engaged in construction projects totaling about $30 million, the U.S. military is an even greater financial power.

In addition to the U.S. military presence on Antigua, America is heavily represented through a contingent of more than two dozen Peace Corps workers and through the Agency for International Development. It is difficult to isolate the precise amount of money AID has spent in Antigua, for many of the programs are spread out among islands of the eastern Caribbean. But examination of AID and State Department projects shows what appears to be a disproportionate amount for Antigua—about $75 million in the five years surrounding independence and perhaps another $35 million during the next decade. The money was spent on projects ranging from an $18,000 "chemical lime analysis" up to $9.7 million to expand the water supply system.

Since the late 1970s, the United States has spent almost $200 million to prop up the Bird government.

14

God's Link Between Heaven and Earth

In the corruption of Antigua, two case studies stand out. One involves Vere junior, the other, Lester. The incidents reveal how each man thinks, his boldness, and the scope of his imagination. Although the incidents are well-known across the island, in Antigua the payoff is not in public awareness of multimillion-dollar scandals; the payoff is that nothing is ever done to the guilty or to show that justice has been served.

The first of the two scandals concerns Vere junior. In late summer of 1985, Prime Minister V. C. Bird, Minister of Aviation and Public Utilities Vere Bird, Jr., and Minister of Economic Development Lester Bird stood side by side in the hot humid weather and proudly watched as the local Anglican bishop prayed over the newly resurfaced runway at V. C. Bird International Airport. The three Birds were the tallest people present, and because they also were the three most powerful men in Antigua, a certain aura radiated from them. A large crowd listened attentively as the bishop blessed the runway as "God's link between heaven and earth," rejoicing that their new nation could overcome numerous obstacles to complete such a large undertaking as resurfacing a nine-thousand-foot runway. Antigua was in control of its destiny. The tourism industry was safe. And, as Antiguans had come to expect, a man named Bird was responsible. What Antiguans did not then know was that the runway was more cursed than blessed, and that it would soon be at the center of an $11 million international fiasco.

In the tourism-dependent Caribbean, whoever has the biggest airport wins. An airport with a runway long enough to accommodate long-range passenger jets is a fundamental prerequisite for any island wanting to compete in the tourism industry. The most desirable tourists—those who stay five days or more and bring money for hotels, meals, rental cars, restaurants, bars, and gaming tables—come by air. Cruise ship visitors, by contrast, stay on the island perhaps a half day. And as a general rule, most of their vacation money has been spent on the cruise and they have little to spend during a brief island stopover.

The United States gave Antigua a jump start in the airport business. When the American military pulled out of Antigua in the late 1940s, it left behind Coolidge Field on the north coast, a first-rate airport. Antigua's fledgling commercial air operations then consisted of an occasional flight by British West Indies Airlines, an operation so idiosyncratic that even today its initials are said to mean "But Will It Arrive" or "But Walk If Available." The few commercial flights used the three-thousand-foot runway at Fort James on the western side of Antigua. In 1951 those flights moved to Coolidge Field, which then became a joint-use operation; that is, one used both by Caribbean airlines and by the U.S. military. In 1960 the Canadian government erected a terminal building. During 1971–72 the Canadians extended the main runway to nine-thousand feet—long enough to accommodate fully loaded passenger jets from London and make Antigua's airport comparable to those on Martinique and Guadeloupe. In fact, once the recession of the early 1970s was over, the airport became a hub for the northern part of the English Caribbean. From the British Virgin Islands south to St. Lucia, Antigua was a major player in the airport game. In the late 1970s, after V. C. Bird returned to office as premier, the Canadian International Development Agency agreed to build a new $10 million terminal. The United States contribution was to build the parking lots.

After Antigua became independent, the increased traffic from heavy wide-bodied jets began to cause serious runway deterioration. Cracks in the overlay allowed water to penetrate to the lower strata and weaken the subgrade. About halfway down the runway was a major depression. Loose stones worked through the binder material onto the runway surface, where they constituted a serious operational hazard. Hot weather melted the runway surface and the wheels of wide-bodied jets pushed the loose surface into washboard-like ridges. The overlay was rolling and cracking. By the end of 1983 the airport was in serious trouble.

Estimates to fill in and repair the depressed area and to resurface the runway ranged from $740,000 to $1.8 million. The United Kingdom, the United States, Canada, the Caribbean Development Bank, and the oil-rich country of Trinidad and Tobago all were approached for loans to finance the project, and all said no.

By early 1985, Vere Bird, Jr., was coming under extreme pressure from the airlines. The airport was unsafe for passenger operations and unless the runway was resurfaced by the beginning of the next tourist season in November—when the airlines added extra flights—the airlines would cease operations in Antigua.

Vere junior was already working on one airport project, a secret arrangement that would not be revealed for several years. He had formed Antigua and Barbuda Airways International, Ltd.—ABA, as the company was known—but it had no airplanes, no pilots, no flight attendants, and no ticket counter. It was a phantom company designed for a single purpose: to set up a monopoly arrangement with British Airways. Under terms of the agreement between ABA and British Airways, the airline was guaranteed three flights per week on the London–Antigua route. In return, 1 percent of net revenues on the route would be paid to ABA. The airline also agreed to give fifty first-class tickets each year to ABA, and another fifty seats for promotional purposes. The agreement said that if the Antigua government allowed any other carrier, except for ad hoc charter flights, to operate the London–Antigua route, the agreement would be null and void.

The 1 percent commission—about $280,000 annually—was deposited in ABA's bank account. The Antiguan signatory to the agreement was Cordell Weston, permanent secretary in the Ministry of Aviation and the top assistant to Vere junior. When Tim Hector asked Weston how a company with no offices, telephone, or staff, spent its money, Weston said all the information was with the auditors. Asked when the auditors would release the information, he said, "Well, auditors, boy I tell you, they do twenty jobs at the same time. Who knows?"

But all of this would not be known for another year or so. In the interim, everyone's attention was focused on the resurfacing project. Vere junior galvanized public attention when he announced to the Cabinet that, even though numerous sources had turned down loan requests, he had arranged for Maryna, Ltd., a French consulting group, to recruit an engineering firm that would resurface the runway. The financing would come from France. Almost as an afterthought he added that the original resurfacing project had been expanded to include a new runway lighting system, and that the cost had risen from around $1 million to about $10 million.

Vere junior, on behalf of the government of Antigua and Barbuda, signed the airport contract on July 2, 1985. The contract included a clause saying the government would pay Maryna, Ltd., fees of $1.3 million. The contract also said the Antiguan government would supply free of charge the concrete and gravel needed to rebuild the runway substructure.

The first glitch came when the Antiguan government refused to supply the concrete and building materials. An additional $1.1 million was added to the contract so the French engineers could buy the gravel. The supplier was a company controlled by Lester Bird, the same company involved in sand mining on Barbuda.

The airport project took fifty-three working days. The airlines agreed to continue operations and went ahead with plans for increased flights during the 1985–86 tourism season. After the airport project was completed, a ceremony was held and the Anglican bishop blessed the runway.

But within a few short months the quality of the $11.1 million job was in doubt. One night the prime minister was returning from a trip to America, and as his aircraft was about to land, the airport lights went off. His aircraft aborted the landing and then circled while technicians worked frantically. The prime minister said someone deliberately had turned off the runway lights and that a plot was afoot to kill him.

Then the French newspaper *Le Figaro* began running a series of articles about the French construction company that had resurfaced the runway. The newspaper said the company had declared bankruptcy and was in liquidation while negotiating with Vere junior on the airport project. Tim Hector called on his sources and began expanding the story. He wanted to know how a project originally estimated to cost about $1 million grew to cost $11.1 million. Where did the extra money go? Hector revealed that Maryna, Ltd., was not a French consulting firm at all, but an Antiguan company owned by Vere junior. The story exploded into what would afterwards be known as "the airport scandal."

The Birds of Antigua may have had their differences in the past, but those differences were always in private. In public, the Birds flocked together. They were a united family. But the runway issue shattered that unanimity and began the disintegration of this extraordinary family. Antiguans were astonished when Lester publicly hinted that his brother was profiteering on the runway project. This was like watching a particularly bold shark take the first bite out of a fish that everyone had thought was too big and strong to come under attack. Other ministers, who, under normal circumstances, never would have attacked Vere junior, moved in for the kill. They stood up in Cabinet and talked of "the airport scandal" and called on the prime minister to take action. But the prime minister chased them all away from what they thought was a vulnerable target by angrily defending his firstborn son. He said that he did not expect his ministers to die broke, that Vere junior had done nothing that each of the other ministers had not done at some time or another, and that they were complaining simply because they had not received a piece of the action. The prime minister bitterly opposed suggestions by Tim Hector and others that he convene an administrative inquiry into the airport project.

To Lester the scandal was of such proportions and the blame for the malfeasance was so obvious that they provided an opportunity to advance his own plans to become prime minister, and, at the same time, destroy his primary opposition. He announced that if anyone brought the Antiguan government into disrepute, as Vere junior had done, then the unwritten rules of a Westminster parliamentary democracy demanded that the person resign.

The prime minister said Lester's comment was "imperialist propaganda designed for the colonies."

The outcry against Vere junior grew to such proportions that even the prime minister could not control it. He agreed to an inquiry and to making the results of the inquiry public. On January 13, 1987, Sir Archibald Nedd, a prominent British-trained West Indian jurist, was appointed to investigate the airport project. His mandate was to examine the runway rehabilitation, the circumstances surrounding the $11.1 million loan, and how the money had been spent. Finally, he was to determine if there was any wrongdoing or dereliction of duty by anyone involved.

The prime minister had not been able to stop the investigation, but he was able to limit severely Nedd's investigative power. He denied Nedd the power of subpoena and would not grant him authority to take sworn testimony. But Nedd knew how to improvise and adapt. He called on the International Civil Aviation Organization, and, through the U.S. embassy, the Federal Aviation Administration, to investigate and analyze the work done at the airport. The prime minister squelched the results of both investigations. And when Nedd's report was submitted, a report on which the government had spent more than $100,000, that, too was squelched. To this day, the report has not been made public except for a single clause stating that in the absence of evidence that might have been withheld, there was no indication of criminal wrongdoing.

The preface of Nedd's full report sets the tone by reminding readers of the difficulties under which he conducted the investigation; particularly the problems encountered when witnesses were able to give unsworn testimony and therefore were "free from the hindrance of remembering the sanctity of the oath taken." Nedd wrote that, when Vere junior told the Cabinet that he had recruited a firm of French consultants, there was, in fact, no such French firm. Maryna, Ltd., was an Antiguan company represented by the law firm of Bird and Bird; moreover, Vere junior was Maryna's principal shareholder, director, and chairman. When Vere junior wrote to the chairman of Maryna, Ltd., seeking help in recruiting an engineer for the airport, he was writing to himself. While the airport contract was clear and unambiguous about the nature of the work to be done, there was no independent evidence to prove the work had been carried out properly. And when Nedd asked to bring in an independent engineering firm, the prime minister refused the request.

Although the contract called for a minimum three-inch overlay, the FAA analysis found that many cross sections were only two inches thick and some were as little as one and a half inches thick. And because the runway had numerous slumps and low spots, the FAA said the optimum solution would have been to remove the concrete slabs that formed the runway foundation and rebuild from the ground up—a job that would have required closing the runway for at least a month. Instead, the engineers drilled holes through the slabs and pumped in grout to fill the voids—a measure which was at best a short-term solution.

Much of the report, especially when one considers the restraints under which Nedd had to work and his understated style of writing, are of an incredibly damning nature. It points out that the government of Antigua and Barbuda never investigated a company that it was paying more than $11 million but simply took Vere junior at his word when he said the firm had experience throughout the world. When Nedd asked for proof of the French company's expertise, he was given two company brochures.

The contract between the government of Antigua and Barbuda and Maryna, Ltd., gave the company full responsibility for making sure the resurfacing was inspected and certified to be in accord with international airport standards. Maryna, Ltd., also issued frequent payment certificates to the French engineers.

Nedd's strongest criticism was that Vere junior, acting as minister of aviation, chairman and director of Maryna, Ltd., and as Maryna's legal representative, had "conducted himself in a manner unbecoming a minister of government." Nedd did not believe he had been told the truth by many government officials whom he interviewed, and he had been forced to make finding of fact based on the testimony of unsworn witnesses, "some of whom could hardly be described as being completely disinterested or having no ax to grind." The refusal of the Bird government to place at his disposal a competent engineer made him doubt the sincerity of the government in asking for the investigation. According to the report, the "best evidence of bad workmanship" on the airport project was that, a few months after completion, the airport lighting system was so defective that night landings were prohibited until the system could be repaired.

Tim Hector, as usual, had the last word. He revealed that Cabinet minutes had been altered to show the Cabinet had approved spending $11.1 million at the airport when, in fact, it was an independent decision by Vere junior. Hector, who enjoys hanging derisive nicknames on the Birds, began referring to the minister of aviation as "Vere 'Runway' Bird."

The name would stick for a few years. And then Vere junior would become involved in a larger scandal that would give Hector the occasion to pin an even more serious nickname on the prime minister's oldest son.

15

Taller Than a Palm Tree

Americans like to quantify their knaves. And once Americans venture beyond the beaches of Antigua and discover the antics of the Birds, they always ask which of the sons has been involved in the greater skulduggery. "Which one is the biggest crook?" is how the question usually is framed.

The answer is difficult. Vere junior and Lester are not, as it might at first glance appear, Tweedledum and Tweedledee. The two brothers are polar opposites in their approach, their methodology, and their associates. The conventional wisdom is that Vere junior is a bumbler, that his schemes are as egregious as they are clumsy, and that his overweening greed causes him to gravitate toward like-minded men. This same wisdom says that Lester soars with the eagles, that his associates are some of the slickest and most sophisticated investors to be found, and that whatever he may have done, he has never been caught, for he is too smooth and too smart to make mistakes.

But conventional wisdom can be wrong. Lester has made mistakes. And one of the biggest was the Royal Antiguan Hotel.

If, while in Antigua, you are interested in streetwalkers, drugs, or guns, or if you want to find a person to torch someone's house or beat up an enemy, you will be directed to Christian Street in Grays Farm, a street referred to locally as "Forty-second Street." Antiguans like to know where they fit into the larger scheme of things, and they are proud that Christian Street offers all the temptation, venality, and violence of New York.

It is no surprise that such a street is found in Grays Farm. This ghetto on the southwest corner of St. John's near the market and the bus station and the harbor is the most heinous slum in all of Antigua, a mephitic nightmare of spavined shacks and open sewers and desolation and disease. Grays Farm is a hellhole.

For as long as anyone can remember, the road from St. John's to Deep Bay was through the middle of Grays Farm. But in the late 1980s a new road was built. Wide and scenic, running along the southern edge of the harbor where the eye was irresistibly drawn to the green waters of the basin or to the open prospect of the Caribbean, it circled the edge of Grays Farm and was the only road on Antigua comparable to one in America: wide and smooth and even with a white stripe down the middle. Once the road passed Grays Farm it curved back to the south and dumped into the old road that led from St. John's to Deep Bay. A right turn at the intersection took tourists past Bruce's, one of the largest and most infamous brothels on Antigua, then across the salt marshes that have been filled in with dredge material from the harbor. Another right turn and tourists were on a poinciana-lined road that curved over a hill and around a corner to Deep Bay.

Lester built the new two-and-a-half-mile road from St. John's to Deep Bay as a grand avenue to his signature project as minister of tourism and minister of economic development: a hotel that would be the most prestigious government tourism development in all of Antigua and a monument to his vision of what Antigua could become.

In the beginning the hotel was called the Royal Antiguan. Then the management was taken over by Ramada and the name was changed to the Ramada Renaissance. Most Antiguans refer to the project by its location: Deep Bay. This hotel, like the airport scandal of Vere junior, has become symbolic of the Bird's excesses with public funds. And it represents Lester's most visible failure as a public official.

Since the early days of tourism on Antigua there has been an unwritten law that no hotel could be taller than a palm tree in the belief that no hotel or condo should overpower or dominate the natural beauty of the beaches. This has been interpreted to mean two stories tall. For more than a quarter of a century the palm tree restriction was observed—that is, until the inception of the Deep Bay project.

The hotel was nine stories tall, far taller than any known palm tree. It was built on one of the earliest known Amerindian sites on Antigua. Destroying a prehistoric site to erect the most modern hotel on the island is even more ironic than Christian Street being called Forty-second Street.

I visited Deep Bay during the early days of construction and saw that the northeast face of a hill had been scraped away to provide room for the structure. Guests in rear rooms would look out upon a denuded hillside almost close enough to touch. In front of the hotel, an isthmus that blocked a salt marsh from the sea was cut open. Another marsh was drained and thousands of fish were killed.

Engineering and feasibility studies usually cost about 2 percent of the project's projected value, but at Deep Bay the costs were $9 million, or almost 20 percent of the total.

While the hotel was ostensibly a project of the Antiguan government, overall supervision came through the Deep Bay Development Company, a quasi-governmental group chaired by Lester Bird. Cecil Wade, a prominent businessman and chairman of the loan committee at the Bank of Antigua, was appointed deputy chairman of the Deep Bay Development Company. Makeda Mikael, Lester's top assistant, ran the company on a day-to-day basis.

Lester Bird, in his ministerial capacity and as chairman of the Deep Bay Development Company, borrowed $43 million in deutsche marks to finance what was to be a 320-room hotel with two 9-story wings. The money was to be repaid in U.S. dollars. The Italian government guaranteed the loan. The board of the Deep Bay Development Company was not fully aware of the quid pro quo nature of the deal Lester had struck with the Italians until a meeting was held at which board members were discussing possible design changes at the hotel. Some members wanted a two-story hotel. Because the beach was a half mile away, others wanted to move the hotel closer to the water. While these and other possible changes were being discussed, it was announced that an Italian ship carrying precut steel frames and all the construction materials needed for the hotel had arrived at the dock. Realizing that the board of which he was deputy chairman had no real function, that Lester Bird had already made the significant decisions about the hotel, and that Lester was a one-man show who would make all the major decisions in the future, Cecil Wade resigned.

It is axiomatic in Caribbean countries that local people always get a slice of major construction projects. The contractor must hire local laborers and buy construction materials and furnishings from local vendors. But because the Italians guaranteed the construction loan, they were allowed to bring in everything they needed, from building materials to live animals for food. More than 95 percent of the laborers were from Italy. And not only the construction materials but the furnishings and fixtures were from Italy. The hotel plumbing system was Italian. Italians built the swimming pool and lined it with Italian tile. One of Antigua's best-known manufacturing facilities is the Sealy Mattress Company, but it was Italian mattresses that went on Italian beds in the hotel.

This is significant because the government of Prime Minister Bird grew out of the trade union movement and Lester Bird was chairman of the Antigua Labour Party. While most unions try to take care of their own, Lester abandoned the very group that was the base of his political power.

In March 1990, as the Royal Antiguan was about to come under a management contract with Ramada, Tim Hector once again caused consternation and embarrassment to the Birds by publishing documents from Ramada executives showing that it was not the government of Antigua, but rather Lester Bird, who owned the hotel. Lester contended his name was listed as owner because, as head of the Deep Bay Development Company, he was holding the hotel in trust for the government. Tim Hector then revealed that the trust document had been signed only by Prime Minister Bird and not by the standard signatories for such legal papers, the governor-general or the attorney general. Hector also wondered why, if the hotel were owned by the government, no audit of hotel finances had ever been presented to Parliament or the Cabinet, as was required by law for all government agencies.

But Lester had more to worry about than Tim Hector. He had promoted the hotel with full-page ads in major American magazines and people were staying away in droves. I stayed at the hotel for a week not long after it opened. Since then I have visited the hotel on every trip to Antigua. The roof leaks, windows do not fit their frames, room air conditioners leak water onto a spotted carpet, light fixtures in the rooms and along the halls have fallen and not been repaired, and windows have been broken and not replaced.

When the hotel's Italian plumbing system failed, local workers could not repair it—instead they replaced it. When the blue tiles in the swimming pool and the fountains fell off, local workers could not repair them and the pool and fountains were drained and left empty for several years. Because Antigua had never had a building taller than a palm tree, there was no equipment to wash windows or do external repairs and maintenance. Today the windows are covered with grime and the exterior is streaked and sadly in need of paint. One can only speculate about the dimensions of the disaster should the hotel ever catch fire.

I talked with numerous airline crews who stay at the Ramada and found that the mere mention of the hotel caused them to grimace in distaste. These crews travel widely, but they agreed that nowhere do they stay in a hotel with such abysmal conditions as the Ramada Renaissance in Antigua. They complained of roaches, mice, sagging beds, and service that ranged between nonexistent and insolent. They also told me that they had had numerous conversations with Ramada executives and that the executives were extremely embarrassed about the hotel and wanted to get out of the management contract. When I called Ramada's headquarters, the executives would not discuss the Antigua hotel.

Today, three of the hotel's four restaurants have closed. In my numerous visits there for breakfast, lunch, and dinner, I have never seen more than a half-dozen people in the dining room. In October 1991, a few days before Antigua's tenth anniversary of independence and a time when one would think the hotel would be filled with dignitaries and teeming with guests, I was having lunch when a tourist walked in, looked around in bewilderment, and asked a waitress, "Am I the only guest in the hotel? There must be people somewhere." I had arrived early for lunch that day and when I left at two P.M.

guests had occupied only four tables in the enormous outdoor dining room. Even then there had been an interminably long wait for the menu, for food, and for the check. It was ten minutes after I paid my tab before the waitress returned with change. As I left I noticed the cavernous lobby was empty except for bored employees and the woman who operates Peter Pan, Lester's travel agency.

In front of the hotel I chatted with a cab driver who told me how he came there at four-thirty A.M. each day so he could be first in line for airline crews traveling to the airport for early flights. He said bitterly that many days the airline crews were the only fares to be had.

But the greatest problem for the Antiguan government is that fluctuations in the money market caused the cost of the hotel to rise from $43 million to about $90 million. The value of the hotel, even by the most charitable appraisal, is no more than $40 million. In 1989 Donald Trump offered to take it over but Lester turned him down.

(While Trump was negotiating with Lester, Ivana was aboard the *Trump Princess* anchored off Mill Reef on the southeast corner of the island. Ivana, accompanied by a half-dozen or so of what one Mill Reef employee described as "ladies in waiting," came ashore for a picnic. When told by Mill Reef employees that she was on private property, Ivana angrily replied, "The prime minister told me I could swim on any beach in Antigua." That is correct, she was told, as long as she stayed below the high tide line. Above the high tide line is private property. Ivana insisted on staying and the Mill Reef people acquiesced. They knew that Ivana was off a boat and that she would be there only a day or so. Donald Trump himself was so taken with the guarded enclave of Mill Reef that he applied for membership. The Donald's flamboyance and vigorous self-promotion are the antithesis of the quiet millionaires at Mill Reef, and the application was quickly denied.)

A for sale sign still hangs on the hotel at Deep Bay. Lester was quoted in 1988 as saying he had an offer of $85 million but would not consider anything under $100 million for what he called "one of the finest structures in the whole eastern Caribbean." By late 1992 the hotel continued to be an enormous financial drain on the government. Part of the drain, albeit a very small part, came from Ivor Bird, the younger brother of Vere junior and Lester and the man who runs the family-owned radio station. He is a regular patron in the hotel restaurant and bar, where he always signs a tab. When, eventually, hotel management asked him to pay and he refused, Makeda Mikael, Lester's top aide, told him to pay up or be barred from the premises. Ivor went to the prime minister and complained that Mikael had insulted a Bird. The prime minister told Lester to restrain Mikael. Ivor's hotel bills were ignored.

To celebrate New Year's Eve in 1990, Prime Minister Bird decided he would have dinner at the Ramada Renaissance. The public works department hastily resurfaced the two-and-a-half-mile road and repainted the white stripe down the middle; and the prime minister enjoyed a smooth and pleasant ride to the hotel, where by all reports, he and Cutie had a pleasant dinner and a happy new year.

But today the road that Lester built is filled with enormous potholes. The edges are falling away in great scalloped pieces. If a driver's attention wanders from the view of the harbor as he drives from Deep Bay toward St. John's, he might look off to the right, toward the backside of Grays Farm, where open drains and sewers excrete long languid fingers of glistening fluids that ooze across an open landfill and collect into a wide pool.

16

Good Intentions

In few places is the axiom "The road to hell is paved with good intentions" more clearly manifest than it is in the tangled financial affairs of Antigua. Two more of Lester's projects were a harbor-dredging operation that cost $20 million and the waterfront shopping center of Heritage Quay that cost about $15 million. Vere junior, not to be outdone by his younger brother, obligated Antigua for a $43 million desalinization–power plant whose cost rose to about $70 million (no feasibility study was done to determine if the desal plant was the best way to solve the island's chronic water shortage), a $10 million telephone system, and the $11.1 million airport resurfacing project.

All these undertakings have two things in common: First, most of them are failures. The Ramada Renaissance, by any criterion, is a flop. Heritage Quay, known as "Lester's Folly," is a slick and polished complex where most of the duty-free stores are owned by government officials. Too few tourists shop there and the enterprise lost money from the beginning. The harbor-dredging project became an embarrassment when it was announced that Lester turned down a bid from a Venezuelan company that was about half the price of the winning American company. In fact, much of the increased rent from the American military bases was earmarked to pay the American dredging company, with which Lester has close ties.

As for the government-financed projects of Vere junior, the "airport scandal" remains the best-known. The desal plant was to be on-line early in 1987 and, according to Vere junior, would solve all of Antigua's fresh-water problems. After running two years behind schedule, the plant opened. But the pipes to carry fresh water to remote parts of the island were inadequate and the desal plant was pumping thousands of gallons of fresh water each day back into the sea. Sometimes the power plant works and sometimes it doesn't.

The second thing the projects of Lester and Vere junior have in common is that they do not generate enough revenue to service the loans it took to build them and are creating an enormous drain on Antigua's near-bankrupt government. All of this was predicted by both the World Bank and the International Monetary Fund. The IMF knows that a developing country needs to borrow money. But the borrowing should be a transition step, not a necessity in order to keep a country afloat. And the borrowed money should go toward projects that have a high rate of payoff. A country's economic strength and financial performance is best revealed in how quickly the country moves away from dependence on external aid. Antigua, by the mid-1980s, had become a chronic borrower; it could not exist without rescheduling existing loans and finding new ones. The Birds wanted not only to rehabilitate and expand the infrastructure of Antigua, but to do it overnight. They ignored both the World Bank and the IMF. Today Antigua has the highest per capita debt in the Caribbean and one of the highest in the world—about $400 million for a nation of 63,200 people. Largely because of the Birds, Antigua has become a nation held in captivity by foreign banks and unwilling and unable to pay its debts.

The man at the center of these complicated international dealings was Minister of Finance John St. Luce. St. Luce is much respected for his financial wizardry, and he is given credit for keeping Antigua afloat through the one-after-the-other financial storms of the 1980s. A succession of chargés d'affaires at the U.S. embassy has privately confided to me that St. Luce would be the ideal choice to succeed V. C. Bird as prime minister. In the eyes of Americans, St. Luce enjoys what is almost a unique reputation for an Antiguan official: he is perceived as being an honest man. The same State Department officials who privately supported St. Luce for prime minister also agreed that he had no chance of reaching that peak. He was seen as lacking the moxie or the political street-fighting ability to win a battle with his close friend Lester Bird.

In 1989 I talked with St. Luce about the possibility of his becoming prime minister. There was none of the quiet dignity or decorum about his office that one would expect in a ministry of finance. Instead I quickly realized why St. Luce has the reputation of hiring more constituents and more "ghost workers" than any other minister. While this might seem to belie his reputation as an honest man, it must be placed in the context of small-island politics, where government is a major employer and where, in order to stay in office, a minister must hire numerous constituents. Throughout the office, desks were manned by as many as three people, each of whom had the job of answering a single telephone that sat in the middle of the desk. When the telephone rang, there was no frantic grabbing for the receiver. Each of the three simply waited for one of the others to answer the phone.

St. Luce reminds one of a mongoose, slim with bright eyes, quick movements, and a wary manner. And like the mongooses on Antigua, he had no natural predators. He was so good at his job that no one wanted to challenge him for such an onerous and almost impossibly complex task.

I found him to be a man caught between ambition and caution. On the one hand he described himself as a "healer" who had helped rebuild the ALP, a man who, if he became prime minister, "would send a top-level team to the U.S., Canada, and Britain to seek technical assistance and to reschedule our debts." But the closest he would come to criticizing the Birds was when he said, "Having three members of the family in government—well, you can speculate on the problems that creates." When I asked him why he did not attack the prime minister or Lester, he grinned and shrugged. "V. C. Bird still has the charisma to tell Antiguans to anoint his son as prime minister," he said. "He could do that and they would listen."

As I was leaving, he said, "You might be interested to know a new expression that has arisen here on Antigua."

"What is that?" I asked.

" 'We want to see the back of the Birds,' " he replied. St. Luce wanted to make sure I understood he was not the originator of this phrase. His eyes widened and he held up an admonishing finger. "That is a well-known expression here," he said. "Very common."

This extreme caution was even more manifest when I visited St. Luce again in the summer of 1991 after he had become the minister of information. He gave me a stack of documents whose dates covered the last five years of his tenure as minister of finance, and he asked if I would cut off the letterhead, which showed the documents were copies of the official minutes of Cabinet meetings. The reason he gave me the documents was clear. Each began with a quote from St. Luce in which he cautioned the Cabinet of approaching financial disaster: "The Honourable Minister of Finance, once again, briefed members of Cabinet on the difficult financial situation of the Government of Antigua and Barbuda," and "The Honourable Minister of Finance brought Cabinet up to date on the prevailing difficult financial situation of the Government," and "The Honourable Minister of Finance provided Cabinet with the usual report on the adverse financial situation."

The Cabinet ignored St. Luce and made a valiant effort to equal the spending spree begun by Vere junior and Lester. One way the government found a little extra money was to stop making payments to social security and medical benefits programs soon after independence. By 1985 the government contributions to those programs had fallen behind $1.3 million and $1 million, respectively. Today the programs exist in name only.

In September 1986, the Cabinet, in negotiations with trade unions, gave government workers a 25 percent raise that cost government more than EC$600,000 each month, or upward of $7 million annually. The raise was backdated to the first of the year. When government pensioners complained, the Cabinet rushed to give them the same backdated raise. Individual ministers obligated the government for debts that Cabinet minutes referred to as "far exceeding the provisions of the budget."

By 1987 the government of Antigua was in arrears not only on the rocketing foreign debt but in paying salaries. St. Luce suggested to ministers that when they traveled overseas they should be paid on a per diem basis rather than the present system of simply saying, "I need thirty thousand dollars" or "I need eighty thousand dollars" and then not having to fill out

Prime Minister Vere Cornwall Bird, Antigua's greatest hero and one of the grand old men of the Caribbean. In recent years the prime minister has presided over what the U.S. State Department calls "the most corrupt government in the Caribbean."

Vere Cornwall Bird, Jr., the oldest son of the prime minister, refers to himself as "Fungi Man" because he is so unassuming and down to earth. Vere junior was at the center of an $11 million airport scandal and was allegedly involved with gun runners for a Colombian drug cartel. Today he is the second most powerful man on Antigua.

As a young man, Lester Bird was known as "Giant Malt" because he was the biggest, smoothest, and most urbane of his contemporaries. Lester Bird had the opportunity to become the hope of Antigua and a spokesman for the Caribbean. But he traded his birthright for a bowl of porridge.

Behind this intimidating sign lies an unnecessary and virtually useless United States Naval Support Facility. Although the facility's training function could easily be performed elsewhere, the U.S. government recently spent about $10 million for expansion.

TROPICAL STUDIOS/J. RAINEY

From Clouds Restaurant, the diner looks down on Dickinson Bay and Runaway Bay, the most popular beaches on Antigua. Behind the beaches, in the left of the picture, is McKinnon Swamp. Untreated sewage from numerous hotels is discharged into the swamp, where it overflows onto the beaches.

TROPICAL STUDIOS/J. RAINEY

One of the most historic sites on Antigua is this tamarind tree near Bethesda. It was here that Vere Cornwall Bird confronted Alexander Moody-Stuart and said cane-field workers would strike until British sugar barons raised their pay. "We will eat cockles and the widdy widdy bush," Bird said. "We will drink pond water."

TROPICAL STUDIOS/J. RAINEY

British publisher and author Jon Wynne-Tyson, who also is King Juan II, stands atop Redonda's 971-foot peak and proclaims to an attentive Rastafarian.

TROPICAL STUDIOS/J. RAINEY

Antigua Air Station, part of the Eastern Test Range, uses sophisticated radar and telemetry equipment to collect data from satellites and to conduct surveillance of space. In 1990 the base was almost closed. Then the U.S. government spent $20 million to expand the facility.

TROPICAL STUDIOS/J. RAINEY

V. C. Bird International Airport, perhaps the only airport in the world named for a living chief of state

TROPICAL STUDIOS/J. RAINEY

Rossano Brazzi was a 1950s movie star, a friend of Ronald Reagan, and the front man for a shadowy group of down-at-the-heels European royalty; that is, until he was charged with gun-running.

AP/WIDE WORLD PHOTOS

Gerald Bull, shown in 1965. Bull tested artillery pieces on Antigua that evolved into the Supergun of Saddam Hussein. Bull was assassinated in 1990.

AP/WIDE WORLD PHOTOS

Robert Vesco defrauded investors of more than $224 million and faced criminal charges in connection with an illegal $200,000 donation to the 1972 reelection campaign of Richard Nixon. He fled to the Bahamas and, in 1980, to Antigua, where he was protected by the Bird government. Today he lives in Cuba.

AP/WIDE WORLD PHOTOS

The Flashes, once the largest salt marsh on Antigua and a habitat for thousands of wild ducks, today is the largest solid-waste dump on the island, an expanse of burning garbage.

TROPICAL STUDIOS/J. RAINEY

The smallest U.S. embassy in the world is presided over by a former football star who has twice been investigated by the State Department.

TROPICAL STUDIOS/J. RAINEY

From atop Shirley Heights, the visitor has a view of English Harbour, Nelson's Dockyard, and Falmouth. Each Sunday afternoon, one of the best parties in the Caribbean takes place atop Shirley Heights.

TROPICAL STUDIOS/J. RAINEY

The Ramada Renaissance Hotel at Deep Bay. The nine-story structure is the first and only hotel to violate Antigua's unwritten law that no hotel should be taller than a palm tree. The decrepit hotel is badly in need of maintenance, three of its four restaurants are closed, and most of its rooms remain empty.

TROPICAL STUDIOS/J. RAINEY

expense reports or return any unused money. (Even though government officials received large travel advances, it is common for those officials to stay with friends or relatives when they travel, and thus to have few expenses for lodging or meals.)

Antigua's external debt, including arrears, rose from $59 million in 1984 to $181 million in 1986, to $245 million in 1987. The $245 million was 95 percent of Antigua's gross domestic product (GDP). In 1991 the debt, according to the Antiguan government, was less than $300 million and, for the first time in years, was being serviced. However, a 1991 conference of Caribbean economists said Antigua's debt, including arrears, had reached $400 million.

In March 1990, shortly before St. Luce resigned as minister of finance, he delivered his final budget speech. He was looking ahead to a race for leadership of the ALP, which is seen as a stepping-stone toward becoming prime minister, and there were some who expected him to cut loose with a stem-winder of a polemic. But St. Luce did not want to antagonize V. C. Bird. So his speech was a panegyric in which he promoted the demonstrably fallacious economic policy of V. C. Bird. "The Government quite often acted as a catalyst with its bold, risk-taking and imaginative programmes in most sectors of our economic structure. This was a necessary step because as we should all know by now, in small less-developed countries such as ours, there is insufficient capital formation to provide the economic base for the required take-off." Furthermore, the prime minister had provided leadership that has "won world-wide acclaim" and led the ALP to victory in the campaigns of 1976, 1980, 1984, and 1989. We applaud our Prime Minister and Father of our Nation for the high caliber of his statesmanship during his long period of national service." St. Luce ended the speech with: "We, the Members of this Honourable House, salute our great national hero and leader—Doctor, the Right Honourable Vere Cornwall Bird."

Using the title "Doctor" was a particularly obsequious note, and a gesture as empty as the speech was specious. V. C. Bird came back from America in the mid-1980s saying the University of South Carolina had awarded him an honorary doctorate. He used the title often and he had it imprinted on many official government documents.

Wondering why an American university would award a doctorate to V. C. Bird, I called the public affairs office at the University of South Carolina. The spokesperson remembered no such award. She spent several hours checking with various sources at the university and then called back. The university never awarded an honorary doctorate to V. C. Bird.

17

Heart of the Caribbean

Antigua's Department of Tourism is in a faded and sun-blasted two-story building near the waterfront in St. John's. The high ridge up beyond the edge of town, where the prime minister's office and the U.S. embassy sit, blocks the prevailing easterlies, and along the waterfront there is not the faintest trace of a breeze. The open front door of the tourism office faces a narrow street, and the buildings across the way seem oppressively close. After the pedestrian has crabbed along the narrow sidewalk in an effort to avoid both the cars that speed by an arm's length away and the cloacal ooze in the gutters, the darkened interior of the Tourism Department is a welcome relief.

A vivacious young receptionist with a crisp and professional demeanor sat at a desk on the left, anxious to be of help. But because help in the Tourism Department often is a long time coming, visitors hunted for chairs and sat against the wall, pulling in their feet each time an employee walked past and wondering why the building was not air-conditioned, and why—even with an appointment—the wait was always interminable when one was to meet with a government official.

"In the Antiguan government it's sort of like mañana," one American told me. "But without that sense of urgency."

Yvonne Maginley is director general of tourism for Antigua, and either because she has been in the job for a long time or because it is her nature, she is an imperious woman who talks to few people other than her boss, the minister of tourism, and to her employees. As I waited, passersby wandered in from the street to use the receptionist's telephone or the bathroom or simply to talk. Employees from other parts of the warren-like building popped in and out of the reception area—a hall that runs the length of the building with little offices off to one side—and they bustled about, stared at the visitors, then disappeared in the rear of the building. Phones rang constantly. And from out on the street came the faint refrain of Antigua's unofficial anthem, a transmogrified version of "Island in the Sun," whose chorus says, "I had a little girl in St. John's town." It is impossible to escape this song on Antigua.

After I had waited for more than an hour, Yvonne Maginley sent word that she had no time but that I could talk with Irma Tomlinson, a mid-level tourism official in an upstairs office. Mrs. Tomlinson, a large woman with a pleasant face and generous smile, sat behind a desk that was angled into a corner of her small office. A single file cabinet against one wall created a narrow aisle through which Mrs. Tomlinson entered and exited the sanctity of the space behind her desk. In front of the desk were two straight-backed chairs. On the wall to the left was a small sign that said, "Cows may come and cows may go, but the bull in this place goes on forever."

A plate heaped with Saltines sat before Mrs. Tomlinson, and every few minutes she reached for a cracker, popped it into her mouth, and chewed away. We had barely begun talking when her telephone rang. The phone conversation lasted about ten minutes but did not slow up Mrs. Tomlinson in her eating of the crackers. Other employees frequently entered the office, looked at Mrs. Tomlinson, then walked away. While she was talking, Mrs. Tomlinson opened a desk drawer, pulled out a box of ballpoint pens, each of which was inscribed

ANTIGUA AND BARBUDA
HEART OF THE CARIBBEAN

She pushed the box across her desk, motioned for me to take one, and continued her telephone conversation. She did not notice that I tried three pens before I found one that operated properly.

After a while she hung up the telephone and picked up on our conversation in mid-sentence. A moment later an employee walked in and interrupted. Mrs. Tomlinson and the employee engaged in a spirited exchange for about five minutes and then the employee left as suddenly as he had entered. Mrs. Tomlinson munched her crackers and explained how Antigua is different from other islands in the Caribbean.

"We are unique," she said in what obviously was a well-rehearsed spiel. "We have an almost perfect climate. We have a very low humidity, far lower than that of the other islands. The trade winds blow almost constantly. People are very friendly. We are not overly commercialized. The greatest distance on the island is about fifteen miles. We have a strong British influence here. We have an anchorage for yachts. There are a lot of old buildings that have been restored. And we have not yet lost our ambience."

Buried within Mrs. Tomlinson's soliloquy was the distilled essence of problems faced throughout the Caribbean. It was no accident that she began by saying, "We are unique." The curse of the Caribbean is its homogeneity. Sure, some islands are of volcanic origin and some are not, some are English and some are French or Dutch or Spanish, some have better restaurants or accommodations than do others, but to many tourists the region is a confusing clump of islands that all offer more or less the same combination of sand and sea and sky. Every island wants to be unique, not out of a sense of national identity but because of an urgent need for each island to find something—anything—that separates it from others in the Caribbean, something that will fix its identity in the minds of tourists.

Mrs. Tomlinson's comment about low humidity shows how far tourism officials will reach in their search for the distinction. The wind that blows across Antigua comes off the sea with a fetch of several thousand miles; and as soon as a visitor steps from the air-conditioned coolness of his aircraft, he knows the humidity is cloying, stultifying, and enervating. In fact, according to an AID-funded environmental profile of the islands, Antigua's relative humidity is significantly higher, not lower, than that of the other islands.

And a myth has grown up about just how friendly the people of Antigua might be. Several years ago the Tourism Department printed thousands of bumper stickers saying ANTIGUA NICE to combat a growing feeling among tourists that Antiguans are not friendly. As with other islands, there is an inverse relationship between the friendliness of locals and the length of time an island has been independent and a player in the tourism game. Antigua has been independent long enough for tourists to have experiences that are distinctly unfriendly. It starts at the airport, where visitors are met by Customs and Immigration officials who seem unable to smile and who give new dimensions to the word *surly*. Purse snatching has become common in St. John's, particularly during carnival, and a conversation with almost any unaccompanied female tourist reveals numerous horror stories, particularly from the northwest side of the island, where some hotels caution females about walking the beaches at night. The experience of Jamaica, Trinidad, the Bahamas, and Barbados shows it is an easy and natural step from purse snatching to robbery, from hassling female tourists to rape. Antigua has crossed the line. And if trends from throughout the Caribbean are any indication, the situation will get worse.

One thing that can be said with certainty about Antigua can be said about most Caribbean islands: it is small, very small. The overriding and unshakable truth, but one that the government has had great difficulty understanding, is that it is an island with no natural resources other than those that appeal to tourists.

For Antigua, tourism is everything. About 70 percent of Antigua's GDP is based on tourism. The economic soundness of government and the financial well-being of hotels, restaurants, bars, and cab drivers depend on visitors. When Antigua traded in a single-sector dependency on sugar for a single-sector dependency on tourism, the country based its future on one of the most lucrative but also one of the most ephemeral and whimsical industries in the world. Perhaps more than any other industry, tourism is subject to every changing outside breeze. If the price of gasoline goes up in America, Antigua's tourism industry goes down. If America, and to a lesser degree the United Kingdom and Canada, sneeze, Antigua catches a cold. If a hurricane even skirts Antigua, as Hugo did in 1989, tourism plummets. When America focused on Operation Desert Storm, the 1990–91 tourism season was devastated. And when America experienced a recession during the 1991–92 and 1992–93 tourism seasons, Antigua felt even greater pangs.

In addition to being susceptible to outside forces that can neither be anticipated nor influenced, tourism is an industry that presupposes an infrastructure both expansive and expensive—modern roads, safe water, dependable electricity, direct-dial telephones to America and Europe, and trained service personnel. A case can be made that in each of these areas, Antigua is, at best, marginal.

Nick Fuller is a West Point graduate who served as a vice-consul on Antigua during World War II. He liked Antigua so much that he took an early retirement in 1949 and returned to the island where, on the site of what had been a beach club for U.S. Army officers, he opened a bar and called it the Bucket of Blood. Navy Seabees were working on the island, and they liked to hang out in a bar owned by an American. Occasionally a Seabee would stand up and say he could whip any man in the house, and because Fuller was a West Point graduate he usually felt constrained to defend the honor of the Army. "I took an old infantryman's delight in tossing a squid out of my place," he said. But by then Fuller was pushing forty and he knew the day was not far off when a young Seabee would wipe up the floor with him, so in 1951 he opened a hotel on the foundation of the old Army NCO club and called it the Lord Nelson Club. That was when Pan American flew the majestic DC-6, better known as the Pan Am Clipper, from New York to Antigua with a brief stopover in San Juan. The flight took nine hours, cost $194.60, and brought Fuller many guests. Today the Lord Nelson Club is one of the oldest continuously operated hotels on Antigua.

Fuller can still be found at the hotel. A daughter is the manager. Someday, one of his grandchildren will take over. A family-owned and family-operated hotel is almost without precedent on Antigua and, for that matter, throughout the Caribbean, where absentee ownership and transient management have been the great curse of the hotel industry.

Fuller remembers how tourism on Antigua expanded in the late 1950s and early 1960s, when more than thirty of the island's forty-six hotels were built. In 1959 Cuba was closed to Americans and tourism in the eastern Caribbean experienced massive overnight growth. Fuller saw the changes brought to Antigua.

"I remember when the few cab drivers were honest," he says. "Now you get in a cab and tell them you want to come to the Lord Nelson and they say 'Ten dollars' and they don't tell you that is in local currency, not U.S. dollars. So a tourist pays them U.S. dollars—three times the going rate. They're a bunch of barracudas today."

The number of annual visitors who arrive in Antigua by aircraft and who stay more than five days (spending about $160 daily) reached a high in the late 1980s of slightly under 200,000. Approximately the same number of people arrive by cruise ship for half-day stopovers. From the beginning, the largest single group of Antigua's tourists have been Americans—about 47 percent of all visitors. Most of them come from New York, New Jersey, Pennsylvania, and Massachusetts—eastern seaboard states with bitter winters; places where city-hassled and cold-flogged people can easily jump aboard a jet for the four-hour flight to Antigua.

After America, and probably because of former colonial ties, the second largest number of tourists come from the United Kingdom (13 percent), followed by Canada (8 percent), whose government has been so financially generous to Antigua that the Canadian flag flies at the airport. The European market is now at 13 percent and growing while the U.S. market is weakening.

Caribbean tourism has still another burden, a dirty little secret that almost never is discussed with outsiders, and a secret that, over the long run of years, may be the greatest burden facing the industry. This is the attitude problem on the part of many people who work in the airports, hotels, restaurants, and bars.

Tourism is a service industry. Reduced to the simplest terms, tourism is poor blacks waiting on well-off whites. Waiting on whites can be difficult in Third World countries, where people are beginning to feel their black identity. In some of these island nations tourism is seen as an extension of slavery. Jamaica Kincaid scorns the hotel training school in Antigua because it "teaches Antiguans how to be good servants, how to be a good nobody, which is what a servant is." In the Dominican Republic, catering to tourists is called *putería*—whoring.

Antiguans are dismayed with the economic disparity between local people and their visitors from abroad. Most hotels are owned by foreigners and the revenue is spent outside the country. Many Antiguans live at a survival level, while nearby a hotel puts up tourists who spend over $200 a day. The hotels are often further isolated from local people by being surrounded by fences and patrolled at night by security guards. All beaches on Antigua are public, yet it is not uncommon for hotels to erect high fences on their property line, fences that extend into the sea and block local people from the beach.

A special wrinkle to the resentment against tourism is found on Antigua, where emancipation is talked about as if it happened only a few days ago. Jamaica Kincaid says the word is used as if referring to a contemporary occurrence. And she says that Antiguans "cannot see the relationship between their obsession with slavery and emancipation and the fact they are governed by corrupt men, or that these corrupt men have given their country away to corrupt foreigners."

In the ten years that I have been visiting Antigua, I have seen a significant change for the worse in the attitude of hotel workers. I have seen the same syndrome in the Bahamas and in Jamaica, but it does not exist in the Turks and Caicos Islands, which remains both a crown colony and a bit player in the tourism industry. Nor does it exist on Barbuda, which is insignificant in the tourism industry.

If one can generalize, the islands of the Caribbean are places where pink tourists drink white piña coladas and complain about local black people. Tourists belly up to the bar, stare into the circular troughs of their drinks, and denigrate black employees as if those people were devoid of hearing and feeling. On Antigua I once stayed in a small hotel where most of the guests were English. When the English come to a former colony, they hear echoes of empire; they talk of "coming out here" as if they were trekking somewhere east of Suez; and they have that peculiar English manner of treating hotel employees as if they were pieces of furniture.

Little wonder at the open resentment displayed toward tourists by many hotel workers. Once I was sitting at the beach bar of the hotel favored by English tourists when a guest ordered a nonalcoholic drink made from a banana, crushed ice, milk and sugar water—it is called a Rasta Banana and tastes much better than it sounds. The waiter continued his conversation with a girlfriend for a few minutes then used half of the banana to make the drink. When the guest complained that the entire banana should go into the drink, the waiter complied, but he added so much extra ice and milk and sugar water that the drink was thin and watery. He filled the guest's cup, accepted his money, then turned and poured the remainder of the drink for his girlfriend. She tendered no money. At the same hotel I saw another bartender walking along the narrow cement path through the brambles toward the beach bar when he met a guest going in the opposite direction. The bartender put his head down and continued on the path, forcing the barefoot tourist into the brambles.

Antiguans, like the people of other tourist islands in the Caribbean, are caught in the great dilemma of trying to mix nationalism with tourism. They have not reconciled to the fact that they are financially dependent on an industry that demands they be servants.

I never thought much about what it is like to live in a tourism-dependent country until one day when I was having lunch at the Calypso Restaurant in St. John's. Diners at the Calypso sit outside under awnings. I watched tourists walk up and down the street. Many of the men wore wildly colored Bermuda shorts, T-shirts, and tennis shoes. The women wore too much makeup and too few clothes. Then a group of white businessmen wearing suits walked in. A local woman sitting at the next table nodded approvingly and said, "Some of the white people seem to be dressing a bit better."

Antigua is one of the most expensive destinations in the Caribbean. Mrs. Tomlinson and other Antiguan tourism officials take great pride in this and boast about Antigua being "upmarket." But when tourists pay several hundred dollars a day for a room and exorbitant prices for meals and drinks, they expect a commensurate level of service, the same service they are used to in other parts of the world. And they do not always get that service in Antigua. If a tourist walks into a dining room and his waitress is having a snack, chances are she will not interrupt her meal to wait on the guest. When she does come to the table, it is accompanied with much sighing and reluctance.

A front-desk receptionist who is on a break is not disturbed by a ringing telephone. In fact, ringing telephones rarely cause concern in Antiguan hotels. I have seen American businessmen grow almost apoplectic when a hotel telephone operator refused to put through an overseas call, or, when the person being called doesn't answer in one or two rings, the call is terminated. (Government ministers do not have such problems. They have direct-dial telephones in their offices and cars and they use them often to call friends and family abroad. The government pays the bill.)

Antigua is host to a large Rastafarian community, and many of the Rastas are quite aggressive in peddling trinkets on the beach, particularly to unaccompanied young women. Many guests and many hotel officials have complained and have reminded the government of an ordinance prohibiting unlicensed beach sales. But nothing happens.

A discussion with Antiguans about the attitude of hotel employees often brings the response that Antiguans should not be judged by British or American standards, that they should be considered only by Antiguan standards, by the standards of a relatively new country with severe financial restraints. This argument is specious in the extreme, for many tourists have traveled widely and know it is possible to have a high level of service in a relatively undeveloped country.

If a white tourist meets an Antiguan and the two go to lunch or dinner, it is almost unheard of for the Antiguan to pick up the check. There is a pervasive attitude on Antigua that if a person is white, he must be wealthy. Coupled with this is a feeling that Antiguans deserve whatever they can get from whites, sort of a reparation for the historical evils of all other whites. And if a white tourist wants to economize on his Antigua trip, he is looked upon with derision as part of the "blue jeans crowd."

Antigua is only beginning to have an inkling that there are universal standards in the tourism industry, and that Antigua is not meeting those standards. The industry is beginning to falter. The Tourism Department says the tourist season on Antigua is now year-round, but about half of the island's hotels are open only from November until April. While the larger hotels have high occupancy rates, the smaller hotels barely manage to keep their doors open.

Without tourism, most Caribbean islands would wither in the

sun. Antiguan officials are being forced to rethink their ideas about tourism and even to talk publicly of fundamental changes in philosophy: things such as establishing a work ethic and realizing that tourism is a fantasy business wherein the tourist is buying a dream, and for the length of the dream—the time the tourist is on the island—everything must be perfect.

This idea, which seems so basic, is causing enormous consternation on Antigua. The tourism industry is in a state of flux. The only constant is the number of small shiny black birds found at every outdoor restaurant. These little birds hop about the tables in a cocky stiff-legged fashion while their glistening eyes remain fixed on whatever food is available. Tourists at first are pleasantly astonished. Often they encourage the birds by moving a toast crumb or a piece of bread across the table. As the birds become more aggressive and begin stealing food off the plates, the tourists become less amused. The tourists usually end up flailing away with arms or napkins in futile efforts to shoo the birds away. Finally, they give up and pay their bills and leave everything for the birds.

18

Antigua Is Too Beautiful

> Antigua is too beautiful. Sometimes the beauty of it seems unreal. Sometimes the beauty of it seems as if it were stage sets for a play, for no real sunset could look like that; no real sea water could strike that many shades of blue at once; no real sky could be that shade of blue—another shade of blue, completely different from the shades of blue seen in the sea—and no real cloud could be that white and float just that way in that blue sky; no real day could be that sort of sunny and bright. . .
>
> —Jamaica Kincaid, *"A Small Place"*

The northwest shoulder of Antigua has the most concentrated collection of hotels and restaurants to be found anywhere on the island, and its mile-long, scimitar-shaped beaches of Dickenson Bay and Runaway Bay are the most popular in Antigua. Some of the island's best-known resorts and restaurants front on Dickenson Bay and Runaway Bay: Halcyon Cove Hotel, a favorite for American businessmen; the lofty and chic Clouds Restaurant; Sandals, the exclusive couples-only retreat out of Jamaica; Antigua Village, Buccaneer Cove, Siboney Beach Club, Marina Bay Condominiums, Spinnakers Restaurant, Coconut Grove Beach Restaurant, French Quarter Restaurant, Sunset Cove Condominiums, Runaway Beach Club, and the Crazy Crab Restaurant. These hotels and restaurants are particularly popular with Canadians, and there are times during the tourist season when the beach is filled with the exultant laughter of those who, only hours earlier, were wrestling with the woes of a Canadian winter.

Many Antiguans look upon these cavorting tourists with secret amusement. Few Antiguans will swim off these two beaches. They say the torpid waters are murky and cloudy and that swimming here will cause their skin to itch and break out in a rash. They say the beach sometimes feels as if it has been covered with a clear oil and that the offshore waters are slick to the body. They say the sea has a peculiar odor and that occasionally the air is filled with the odor of sewage and something that smells like rotting fish.

The reason for all this is best seen from the open dining area at Clouds Restaurant. For the diner at Clouds, the eye cannot help but be pulled to the sea and the sweeping panoramic view of the sort that draws people to the Caribbean. Here one sees what Jamaica Kincaid sees—the unreal beauty of Antigua in sunsets that beggar description and a sky and a sea of shades of blue that are found no place else on earth. It is a view that causes a tourist to realize in a single moment that the expense of the trip is worthwhile.

But then, if one looks away from the sea and gazes inland, a large body of water is seen nestled behind the beach, behind the point that juts into the sea and delineates Runaway Bay from Dickenson Bay. Once the body of water was known as McKinnon Salt Pond, and it was the largest wildlife habitat on the northwest coast. Part of the pond was filled by the company that built the Marina Bay Condominiums. Today the abundant mangrove thickets around the pond are dying; and McKinnon Salt Pond now is known as McKinnon Swamp, separated from the sea only by the road that runs behind the beach. The overflow from the swamp goes under the road and then spills across the beach and into the sea, where wind and tide disperse it in Runaway Bay and Dickenson Bay.

McKinnon Swamp would have no overflow were it not for the hotels and restaurants along the beaches. Because Antigua has no central sewage system, each hotel is supposed to have a sewage treatment facility. But when those treatment plants break down, as they often do, the sewage is pumped into McKinnon Swamp. Halcyon Cove is a good example. Until 1991 Halcyon Cove was owned by the Antiguan government. It was sold to generate much-needed cash. The sewage treatment plant had been broken for about three years before the sale. During that time the waste from tourists in 127 rooms and 16 suites, along with the waste from the hotel's restaurants, was drained into McKinnon Swamp. Other hotels along Dickenson Bay and Runaway Bay did the same thing.

Halcyon Cove did not pump all of its sewage into McKinnon Swamp. Several large pipes run from the hotel across the beach and into the sea. After seeing fecal matter floating a few yards offshore, I asked a hotel employee what was pumped through the pipes. He stammered, rolled his eyes skyward, and said, "Dishwater."

Edward Henry is the curator at the Museum of Antigua and Barbuda and a man as much concerned with preserving the island's environment as he is with preserving the island's history. He was permanent secretary in the Ministry of Education until he retired in 1983; and since then he not only was instrumental in establishing the museum, but he was a founder of Concerned Citizens for the Environment, Antigua's first environmental group. Edward Henry has pictures of what happened when hotels dumped their waste into McKinnon Swamp.

Like many Antiguans, he noticed the odor from McKinnon Swamp and he saw the change in the nearby beaches. But it was not until the fish kills that he realized what had happened. By the end of the 1980s, the carrying capacity of the swamp was exceeded and the mangroves around the edges of the great lake began to die. In July 1989, high summer temperatures caused the sewage from hotels to transform McKinnon Swamp into a giant bowl of nutrient soup that virtually depleted the oxygen in the water and asphyxiated hundreds of thousands of fish. The surface was littered with their carcasses, and when the wind rose and blew the carcasses to the leeward edge of the swamp they piled up and rotted and filled the air with their stench and the water with their deteriorating bodies. Edward Henry has the pictures.

The Antiguan government did not repair the sewage treatment plant at Halcyon Cove and it did not insist that other hotels repair their plants. Instead, the government adopted a measure used by polluters in many countries, one based on the adage that "the solution to pollution is dilution"—seawater was pumped into the swamp to flush the sewage and the rotting fish across the beach and into the waters of Dickenson Bay and Runaway Bay.

Since the summer of 1989 there have been additional fish kills in 1990, 1991, and 1992. Each was photographed. But Edward Henry says fish kills in McKinnon Swamp are like shipwrecks off Barbuda: there are many more that are undocumented.

Today McKinnon Swamp continues to overflow across two of the most popular beaches on Antigua, dispersing its offal among the tourists, who are so happy to be in the sun they do not notice what else they are in. Seawater continues to be pumped into McKinnon Swamp from one side while sewage continues to be pumped in from the other.

This is only one example of the overwhelming environmental crisis facing the island. Antigua's beaches are being destroyed. Solid wastes are piling up. Raw sewage and domestic wastes are unchecked. Agrochemicals, hazardous wastes, and toxic wastes are not controlled. Not only is the foundation of tourism threatened, but public health is endangered, too.

Consider the beaches of Antigua. Antigua boasts it has 365 beaches, one for each day of the year. Those beaches and the clear offshore waters are the main reason tourists come to the island. Yet on many beaches, sand is taken away for construction projects at a rate faster than the natural accretion process can replace it. Laws forbidding the taking of sand are not enforced, and the beaches of Antigua and Barbuda are disappearing.

Barbuda is the most dramatic example. The largest export sand-mining operation in the eastern Caribbean takes more than one thousand cubic yards of sand from Barbuda each month. On Antigua, one of the first sights for a cruise ship visitor entering the harbor at St. John's is on the port side, where the remains of Fort James, an English redoubt of the seventeenth century, are located. A great necklace of white beach once stretched below the fort and graced the entrance to the harbor. But the sand was taken away for construction. Then the dredging of the harbor for a deep-water pier and a turning basin so changed the ecology that retaining walls had to be installed to halt erosion. Now Fort James, one of the most historic parts of Antigua, is threatened. All around Antigua, any day of the week, large trucks filled with sand can be seen coming off the beaches.

Consider the salt marshes. In the late 1980s, when St. John's harbor was dredged, silt was pumped through large pipes to the south side of the harbor and then across the open fields east of the Ramada Renaissance Hotel into "the Flashes"—the largest expanse of salt marsh on Antigua, an area perhaps a mile wide and almost three miles long. For years the Flashes was a favorite habitat of wild ducks, but today it is the largest solid-waste disposal area on Antigua. What once was a highly productive food factory for wildlife is a great lifeless expanse, a pan-like surface whose edges are piled high with refuse and whose interior is dammed in several places by silt. Tons of solid waste lining the borders burn twenty-four hours a day. A great pall of greasy and foul-smelling smoke suppurates from the area. Here is dumped industrial waste, toxic waste, old cars, and—perhaps the greatest insult of all—the garbage and debris from the cruise ships. Edward Henry says that officials representing the cruise ship lines told Antiguan officials their ships would stop in St. John's only if, during the stop, they could dump garbage.

As Edward Henry and I one day stood amid smoking tons of solid waste, he grew pensive. "An oil spill the magnitude of the *Exxon Valdez* could ruin fishing and tourism throughout much of the eastern Caribbean," he said. "It would cause the economic collapse of dozens of islands. But Antiguans think of the environment as a place to dispose of garbage. Garbage is strewn and littered about this island." In his research, Edward Henry discovered that each year this small island is littered with six million plastic and tin food containers, twelve million glass bottles, one quarter million quarts of lubricating oil, half a million pounds of agricultural chemicals, four million pounds of paper products, forty-two thousand tires, and fourteen hundred scrapped cars. "How can tourism thrive in an atmosphere of uncontrolled littering that is visibly displeasing to tourists?" he asked.

Consider the land of Antigua. During the years of King Sugar, the vegetation and the landscape of Antigua were altered more significantly and more dramatically than on almost any other Caribbean island. Uncontrolled livestock grazing severely damaged vegetation that provides cover for the land. When roads were graded and building sites were cleared, there were no contouring or drainage ditches—simple but effective means of erosion control. And now when the rains come to Antigua, the water washes the soil into the sea. With no permanent natural lakes or perennial rivers, Antigua has a greater and more urgent need for a national water policy than does any other Caribbean country.

Consider the marine and coastal habitats. A direct link exists between the health of the mangrove swamps, coral reefs and seagrass meadows and the production of fisheries. Almost all fish harvested for human consumption live part or all of their life cycle near coral reefs. About 85 percent of the problems affecting marine and coastal habitats originate from events on land. For instance, more mangrove swamps were drained or killed in the 1980s than in all of Antigua's previous history. Edward Henry estimates that as much as 50 percent of Antigua's offshore reefs have been destroyed by either sewage or construction. A tourist who breaks a piece of coral from a reef can be fined up to $5,000 and be sentenced to a year in jail. But there is no punishment for those building marinas or hotels or condominiums.

One of the more curious facts about Antigua is that so many marinas around the island have been dredged. Antigua has been famous for centuries as an island whose scalloped coast provided some of the best natural anchorages in the Caribbean. During the hurricane season, dozens of Antigua's natural harbors are used as safe and secure bolt holes by yachtsmen. Yet the construction of marinas goes on. Jolly Beach is a good example. At the Jolly Beach Hotel, the largest hotel complex on the island, offshore reefs were destroyed by dredging for a marina. Now the marine growth on the reefs is gone and the reefs are dead. The Swiss businessman who owns Jolly Beach has turned this remote and rural part of Antigua into a moonscape. The land where cows once grazed was bulldozed. The mangrove thickets where local people once gathered shrimp were cleared. Off Jolly Beach, the sea bottom has turned into a desert. When a delegation of local people went to see Prime Minister Bird about the enormity of the destruction, he offered no help.

Consider the sewage of Antigua. One of the most difficult adjustments for tourists who leave their air-conditioned hotels is learning to cope with the odor of fecal matter. If there is one pervasive odor on Antigua, it is the stench of human excrement. Antiguans appear not to notice, but sometimes the problem reaches such proportions that even they complain. One example was when the septic tank at the prison, which is located at the top of the hill above St. John's, overflowed and crepitous ordure filled the gutters. Perhaps the complaints came because the effluent of criminals is more malodorous than the effluent of the affluent.

The most startling and the most dangerous example of raw sewage is found below Holberton Hospital, which sits near the prime minister's office on the eastern edge of the ridge above St. John's. The hospital has a sewage treatment plant, but like the treatment facilities in many hotels, it has not worked in years. An open ditch leads from the hospital down the hill and carries not only sewage but hospital wastes: surgical waste, biopsy material, delivery room waste, syringes used in treating an increasing number of AIDS patients, and all the other jetsam of a busy hospital. The refuse goes under the road and through a field where, even in the worst of droughts, the weeds are tall and green. The weeds are filled with rats and roaches and should be cut down, but the man who owns the land is a good trade union man and a strong supporter of the Bird government and it is feared that asking him to cut the weeds might offend him. After going through the weeds, the refuse continues down the ditch to the Fiennes Institute, the place where Antigua's old and poor are housed. From there the by-now fetid material oozes down the hill through St. Johnson Village, which is part of Lester Bird's constituency, and on down a ditch from which goats, cows, and chickens drink, and where children play.

The sugar industry, upon which Antigua depended for so long, and the tourism industry are alike in many respects. Both are susceptible to outside influences. Both are labor-intensive. Both provide work that often is at the lowest end of the wage scale. The profits of both are repatriated to the homeland of the owners. Both have a dramatic impact on natural resources. Antigua's environmental crisis is exacerbated by its overstressed economy, and its options in attacking environmental problems that have arisen from development are limited.

When a study called the *Environmental Agenda for the 1990s* was about to be published in 1991, those involved in the research went to Lester Bird, then minister of economic development, and gave him an overview of their bleak conclusions. He ordered that the information not be concentrated in the summary, as is customary; but, following the same pollution-control philosophy manifested at McKinnon Swamp, it should be diluted by being spread throughout the lengthy study.

Antigua's environmental problems can no longer be ignored or overlooked, nor can the pace of development be sustained. The island ecosystem is too small, too fragile, and too complex. Resorts planned for Barbuda would alter a major part of that island's wetlands. At full occupancy, the resorts would increase the number of people on the island by 40 percent. It is impossible to imagine a proportionate commercial level of change in America or Canada or the United Kingdom within a comparable time frame.

The great irony in all this is that today the people of the West Indies are becoming more and more aware of their heritage. On Antigua this means that a people who for generations celebrated British holidays, sang British songs, and learned history through a filter of British teachers is realizing its own contributions. The Museum of Antigua and Barbuda is a leader in the West Indies in identifying and preserving that heritage: the cricket bat of Viv Richards, the Antiguan batsman who set world records; the history of the trade union movement; and the history of the Caribs and Arawaks who lived on Antigua. Now the museum is working to preserve archaeological relics and structures of historical and architectural significance, and—perhaps most important of all—to save the fragile environmental heritage from the mixed blessings of development and tourism.

Edward Henry is trying to show Antiguans that when they break coral and sell it to tourists, they are selling their island; that when they steal sand from the beaches, they are stealing their patrimony; and that when garbage and sewage and solid wastes are strewn about the island, they are destroying their nation. He becomes melancholy when he considers the size of the task. "This nation of Antigua and Barbuda is a disaster-prone place that is almost entirely dependent upon foreign revenues," he says. "And I have been disheartened by the inability, the lethargy, of many Antiguans to do something about our environmental problems. Nothing happens. They sit there with their hands in their laps."

19

V. C. Bird Is in Charge and Let No Damn Dog Bark

For Tim Hector, the 1980s were a glorious romp. A tragicomedy was being played out and he had an exclusive on the story. The Birds were larger-than-life characters against the backdrop of a new nation where, it often seemed, half the rogues and brigands and wheeler-dealers of the world had gathered, and money was being spent madly on bizarre projects, and knavery gathered momentum by the hour.

More often than not, Hector was part of the stories he covered. Because of his take-no-prisoners style of writing, he came under frequent attack from the Birds. In 1984 Lester made a speech saying Hector was in Guyana, where he "planned to overthrow governments in their various territories." As it turned out, Hector was in Antigua. He wrote a story saying "Lester Bird now stands publicly exposed as a public liar." The Bird government became so paranoid about Hector that, in 1985, a Canadian diplomat was detained at the airport and questioned by police about his connection with the newspaperman. The Birds continued to accuse Hector of being everything from a Communist to a trained terrorist to a puppet of Castro. (For the record, Hector says he is a leftist, and that people on Antigua are not sophisticated enough to know the difference between a leftist and a Communist.) Even if all the charges leveled against Hector were true, the more important point would be that, because of his newspaper, he has been the loudest and most enduring voice of opposition against the Birds. Even though Antigua has a television station, a cable television operation, two radio stations, and around a half-dozen newspapers—the number varies according to political events—Tim Hector was virtually alone in his hard-nosed and aggressive reporting during the 1980s. *Outlet* was the only thing approaching a system of checks and balances in Antigua.

Lester for years was chairman of the ruling ALP. Fifteen of Parliament's seventeen seats are occupied by members of the ALP; and most of those fifteen, at one time or another, have been Cabinet members. In reality Antigua has a government by Cabinet rather than a government by Parliament. ABS Radio and ABS Television are owned by the government and controlled by the prime minister. Frequently the prime minister goes on television or radio to remind Antiguans how "cattle, horse, and donkey mess" covered the land and how he delivered them from drinking pond water and eating widdy widdy bushes. This hardy perennial of a speech has become known to younger Antiguans as the "pond water speech."

The government radio and TV stations are essentially promotional vehicles for the Bird government, and rarely are they available to anyone with dissenting views or for any news that might embarrass the Birds. If Antiguans had to depend on government radio and television for their news, they would not have been aware of much of what happened on the island during the 1980s.

The slogan of ABS Radio, delivered in stentorian tones, is, "Give us sixty minutes and we will give you the world." An example of how the Birds use ABS is seen in a 1991 incident, when Lester found himself in political trouble. As a diversionary tactic he called for the formation of a "multisectorial group to address the needs of the nation." Even though the message was meaningless—there was no group formed, and even if one had been formed, it would have had no power—this was the lead story on ABS for three days. It consisted of mentioning Lester's name frequently and listing the various organizations that would make up the "multisectorial group."

Then there is ZDK, a radio station owned by the Bird family and managed by Ivor. As with ABS Radio and ABS Television, newscasts are mostly sports news and good news about the prime minister. Because of the British heritage, the *Z* is pronounced *zed,* and the slogan is "Bad zed."

Vere junior controls Antigua's only cable television system.

The system is profitable both because it is a monopoly and because Vere junior pirates his material from a satellite. When executives at Viacom, the American company that owns the satellite, complained, one of Bird's ministers of government replied that Antiguans have a right to take whatever comes from the sky. "All we did was turn a dish to the heavens," he said.

The number of newspapers in Antigua varies because one of the first things a political opposition group does is crank up a newspaper. The more or less regular newspapers are predictable in their coverage. *The Nation* is a government-owned print version of ABS Radio and ABS Television. To read *The Nation* is to know that V. C. Bird is the only person who can lead Antigua, that each tourism season is greater than the preceding season, and that Antigua enjoys a prosperity unequaled in the Caribbean. *The Worker's Voice,* published by the Antigua Trades and Labour Union, is loyal to the Bird government. Vere junior has a newspaper called *The Sentinel,* and Lester sometimes publishes *On Line* and *The Herald.*

Thus the prime minister controls not only the most powerful trade union, the ruling political party, and the government, but he has a virtual media monopoly unique in the Caribbean and increasingly rare anywhere in the world. The influence of the prime minister on what Antiguans see and hear through local media is almost impossible to overstate. It has led to the Antiguan expression "V. C. Bird is in charge and let no damn dog bark."

Outlet is the only Antiguan newspaper of note that can be classed as independent. Since Hector leads the Antigua Caribbean Liberation Movement and often is an ACLM candidate for office, it is impossible to distinguish between Hector the politician and Hector the publisher; and it is difficult to know if Hector's opposition to the prime minister grows from his frustration as a politician or his indignation as a newspaperman. As do other politicians with their newspapers, he frequently uses his paper to promote himself and his party. But he alone has been unswerving in his criticism of the prime minister and relentless in his pursuit of investigative stories.

Outlet has double the circulation of any other newspaper on Antigua—about six thousand copies locally, with another couple of thousand mailed to subscribers in England and America.

Every Friday, people wait in line to buy it. If people voted for Hector with the same enthusiasm they read his newspaper, he would have been prime minister many years ago. No other paper on Antigua generates the conversation, the anger, the derision, and the respect of *Outlet*. Every minister of government, though he may publicly demean and criticize Hector, reads it avidly. Those ministers are frightened of Hector, and most of them leak stories to him not so much from a conviction that the public has a right to know, as from fear that Hector might turn on them. Even the prime minister has sometimes ordered his staff people to pass information to Hector.

Hector's brand of journalism is rough-and-tumble, freewheeling, and very personal. He can sling ridicule like a cheap nightclub comedian and he can thunder with all the outraged indignation of an Old Testament prophet. His impassioned feelings cause his front-page stories sometimes to appear more editorial than news. It is the sort of journalism that hammers and intimidates, that bites and stings; but there is woven throughout his work a shining thread of high-minded idealism. He believes the Birds are an embarrassment to black people everywhere and that Antigua both deserves better and can do better.

Hector's headlines and his photo captions are as bawdy as they are original. When Minister Robin Yearwood was caught issuing promissory notes for which the government of Antigua was responsible, Hector's headline thundered, "YEARWOOD LANDS ANTIGUA IN DEEP DOO-DOO." And when a minister campaigning for reelection said in a speech that if he were returned to office, "Every day will be a pussy salad," he was reelected—presumably because of his promise—and now, if his picture is published in *Outlet* the caption sometimes identifies him as "Pussy Salad."

In the 1980s, Hector not only wrote the first draft of Antiguan history, in most instances he wrote the only draft. During that decade, the Bird government passed out diplomatic passports with great abandon. Antiguan officials liked what they envisioned as the perks of high office—one of which was a large entourage of diplomatic-passport-carrying sycophants. When Lester came to the United States accompanied by a female friend said to be his "communications adviser," Hector wrote that one "disgruntled paramour" objected that "another of lesser rank" was taken to the United Nations with "full diplomatic rank."

He wrote about a boatload of beef that had been denied entry in America because it was contaminated with radioactive metal particles. It ended up in Antigua, where it was seized on the pretext it would be destroyed. Instead, a customs official and a prominent veterinarian sold the meat to local restaurants to be fed to tourists. Hector says meat America deems unfit for human consumption often winds up on Antiguan hotel tables.

When Princess Margaret visited in the mid-1980s, her advance men looked at the Independence Arch over Independence Avenue and said it was too shaky for the princess to pass under. They asked that the arch be taken down. Afterwards, Hector reminded his readers of how much money had gone into constructing and remodeling the arch, and he made it something of a metaphor for the Bird government.

For Lester, the 1980s were a time when his ambition grew at an exponential rate. Once he called the governor-general and asked what would happen if Parliament issued a vote of no confidence in the prime minister. Could he, as deputy prime minister, take over? The governor-general promptly notified the prime minister who, in turn, immediately solidified his position with his Cabinet. Tim Hector made all of this public. A chastened Lester said his call had been nothing more than an inquiry on a point of law. But then he proposed that Antigua become a republic and his father be elevated to the position of president while he became prime minister.

In 1987 Ivor announced he had leased twenty-six acres of beach property around Fort James, perhaps the most historic spot on Antigua, to a New York businessman named Tony Vimcuillo. A casino and hotel would be erected. Hector identified Vimcuillo as a member of New York's Gambino crime family and claimed that, if the prime minister approved the plan, Ivor would receive fees and equity of about $6.7 million. When Robert DuBose, the Harvard man serving as chargé d'affaires, heard of the deal, he cabled the State Department: "Another Bird has flown into the cookie jar." Hector wrote that Ivor held no government position and had no authority to lease government land. His stories referred to "Ivor 'Fort James' Bird," and

Antiguans became so aroused that the prime minister canceled the deal. Ivor was miffed enough to announce he would run for office against a minister who criticized him. But the big Birds—the prime minister, Vere junior and Lester—congregated and, after deciding there were enough of them in government, shooed Ivor back to the radio station.

Hector's Old Testament wrath was invoked after the home of the Reverend Neville Brodie, the senior Antiguan cleric on the island, was firebombed before dawn in March 1990. One Molotov cocktail came through the front door and another through the back. Brodie and his family barely escaped. Brodie had organized a demonstration to protest the open and flagrant fashion in which the three brothels on Antigua operated.

(The history of Antiguan brothels is worthy of note. When Bird was out of office from 1971 to 1976, a single brothel opened. Bird invoked his Salvation Army background and raised such a public outcry that it was closed. After Bird returned to office, three brothels opened. They grew until in 1992 *The New York Times* wrote that four thousand Dominican prostitutes worked on Antigua. So many women from the Dominican Republic work as prostitutes that Bruce's, the largest brothel on the island, is referred to as "The Daughters of Santo Domingo," an appellation that particularly annoys the Catholic Church.)

The Bird government ignored the firebombing for several days, probably because a senator and ardent supporter of V. C. Bird was the chief suspect. The senator owns an air-conditioned van equipped with several beds, a rolling brothel that makes its rounds on the island and gives a new dimension to the concept of home delivery. According to Hector, the senator had told the prime minister how important prostitution was to the tourism industry and that the religious community should be stopped from interfering in secular matters. The prime minister rumbled about deporting two Jamaicans who are religious leaders in Antigua and he hinted that Brodie was trying to "destabilize" his government.

The State Department report on human rights took notice of the incident by saying, "Although the police questioned several suspects, the investigation was quietly dropped; there were credible reports that this was due to the possible involvement of a prominent Antiguan official. Neither the protest march nor the firebomb attack were mentioned on the radio and television although these issues dominated public discussion for several weeks."

Hector wrote a story maintaining that the U.S. Air Force installation was a major drug center and had been used for distributing cocaine throughout Antigua. He reported that the C-141 that comes down from Patrick Air Force Base twice each week had been used to carry drugs from America to Antigua. The story was denied by the U.S. embassy, but the next week the embassy issued a press release stating that fourteen Americans, including one Air Force person, had been returned to the United States because of suspected drug involvement. The fallout from the incident is still seen in the thorough baggage searches before Air Force aircraft leave Florida for Antigua.

Hector particularly enjoyed covering the airport scandal, because that was when Vere junior and Lester began fighting in public. At a Cabinet meeting during those fractious times, Vere junior turned to Lester and derisively announced: "You are nothing but a servant"—a comment that by nightfall had reverberated around Antigua and resurrected rumors that Lester was the result of a dalliance between his father and the family maid.

Caribbean newspapers usually present a solid front against the outside world, and they rarely attack the few remaining elderly politicians of the region, particularly those who came out of the labor movement. But an editorial in the *EC News,* a Caribbean newspaper, stated that Prime Minister Bird, in defending Vere junior against the findings in the Nedd report, had rejected the notion that conflict of interest by a minister undermines the integrity of government, and that "this must be more than frowned upon by all committed to honest, open government. We can understand the anxiety of Prime Minister Bird to defend his son; but we cannot ignore his unwarranted criticisms of the findings of Nedd, who expressed tremendous restraint in preparation of the report."

Caribbean Contact, a publication of the Caribbean Conference of Churches, published a story reporting that the Bird government "proved it has not exhausted the capacity to stagger public opinion."

The Barbados Advocate said the prime minister "must be living in fantasy" and that "a smell of manure is emanating from Antigua's politics." The editorial ended: "That smell has now become a stench and any West Indian politician who wants to be taken seriously as a leader of probity and decency will have to be careful to distance himself clearly and publicly from the Vere Birds of Antigua."

One of the most popular television shows in the Caribbean, a show whose audio is also used on radio stations, is a program called *Caribbean Crossfire.* When the program devoted a segment to Vere junior and the airport scandal, the program was suppressed by ABS Radio, ABS Television, and ZDK Radio.

The Globe and Mail of Canada wrote that Antigua under the Birds was "almost feudal" and that the island was becoming the "laughing stock of the Caribbean."

Vere junior did not like being the target of newspapers from other islands and from Canada. So he hired Angela Cole, a public relations expert from Barbados, to clean up his image and advise him on how to take the initiative against increasing criticism. She looked at his record, talked to various people, and suggested he resign from office. According to Hector, Vere junior threw the young woman to the floor, battering her, then had her deported.

Tim Hector's prominence grew so much that even the United States became jealous. It particularly annoyed the U.S. embassy that each year Hector arranged for as many as a dozen young Antiguans to go to college in Cuba. A State Department representative went to the home of a prominent Antiguan and said, "People here like Hector because of those scholarships. What can we do to make them like us?"

The Antiguan stood up, walked into his kitchen, and turned on the faucet. After rumbling a few minutes, the faucet reluctantly regurgitated a slug of mud. "Make water come out of our faucets all the time and Antiguans will love you," he said.

The American nodded. "What else can we do?"

"You can provide scholarships."

The American was surprised. "You mean if the U.S. offered scholarships, Hector would send those students to America rather than to Cuba?"

The Antiguan laughed. "Of course. It is the scholarships that are crucial; not where the students go to college."

A few weeks later the embassy had arranged for a dozen scholarships. But the embassy had to work through the Ministry of Education and the ministry did not like the arrangements—no money was to change hands—so the program died a quick death. (Almost a decade later it was resurrected.) About the same time, the State Department also announced it would finance a $10 million upgrading of Antigua's water supply and sewage system. A major part of the system would be at Grays Farm, where a large pipe would drain effluent into the harbor. But the pipe was so low that the sea backed into the pipe and spread the waste matter on the open flats below Grays Farm.

Tim Hector chronicled it all. For week after week and month after month he owned the beat. And he never let up. His voice often was shrill and self-serving, but it was heard.

At the end of the 1980s Hector the politician as opposed to Hector the newspaperman was approached by the United National Democratic party (UNDP), which wanted to join forces with Hector's ACLM to defeat Bird's ALP. The ACLM is a small but noisy party and has never received more than 3 or 4 percent of the vote. Nevertheless, before Hector would consider joining forces with the much larger UNDP, he demanded enough parliamentary seats to give him control of the government. Of course the UNDP refused, the merger never happened, and the ALP won. Hector's greatest attribute as a journalist—his inability to compromise—cost him political power.

But several months later came a journalistic victory of such magnitude that the travails of the past decade—the arrests, the fines, and the days in jail—seemed almost worthwhile. The Queen's Privy Council in London tossed out his conviction under the Bird-imposed Public Order Act on the grounds that the act was unconstitutional, "insidious and objectionable," and unfit for a democratic society. The British court also ruled that the government of Antigua must pay Hector's legal costs from the lengthy litigation—about EC$150,000. But by late 1992 Prime Minister Bird had yet to authorize the payment, and Hector doubts he ever will get his money.

20

High Rollers

Lester Bird likes to smile, wave a big arm, and remind visiting businessmen that the Caribbean once was a haven for buccaneers. From islands such as Antigua, pirates and freebooters would sally forth into the shipping lanes, cozen up to unwary vessels, then hoist the Jolly Roger and swiftly descend upon the vessels and plunder them.

Today the pirates of Antigua do not have to sally forth; they plunder their own lair. And they no longer hoist the Jolly Roger before falling upon their victims.

The Caribbean remains a crossroads of intrigue and mysterious happenings, and fortunes are lost as quickly as they are gained. The arc of islands plunging from Puerto Rico to South America—a combination of tiny nations, different nationalities, numerous harbors, and remote airports—is like a giant strip of flypaper that collects the vermin of the world. Everything from "security consultants" in fatigue pants and olive-drab T-shirts to real estate fraud men to con men to scammers of every persuasion come to the Caribbean.

But Antigua stands out as a haven for them. If Gerald Bull is tossed out of Barbados and no other island will accept him, he finds sanctuary in Antigua. If Robert Vesco is tossed out of the Bahamas, he finds sanctuary in Antigua. If Ed Joiner flees from the IRS in America, he is welcomed with open arms in Antigua. People behind the Sovereign Order of New Aragon search the Caribbean and decide the Bird government of Antigua offers them the best deal. Treasure hunter Mel Fisher decides Barbuda is the place where grandiose dreams can come to fruition. There are dozens of other examples.

The truly savvy businessmen who come to Antigua, the ones who have done their homework, dress for success by wearing ALP colors: red ties, red socks, or a red handkerchief in the breast pocket of the suit. The Birds like this sign of support. They not only welcome the high rollers and their ventures, they fight to get a piece of the action.

Two of the high rollers of the 1980s were worth special consideration. Lester was involved with one of the men and Vere junior with the other. It is significant that Bruce Rappaport, who worked with Lester, remains on Antigua to this day and is said to be planning the largest single development ever to take place there. It is also significant that Maurice Sarfati, who worked with Vere junior, is hiding somewhere in Europe.

Bruce Rappaport was born in Palestine and is a close friend of Israel's Shimon Peres. In the late 1950s he moved to Geneva, where he opened a ship's chandlery and then switched to ship management. A brash man with a penchant for big cigars and international deal-making, he made his fortune shipping petroleum in Indonesia. After the government of Indonesia accused him of profiteering and tried to cancel his shipping contract, he sued the government. During the litigation, it was revealed that he had loaned $2.5 million to the man in charge of Indonesia's state-owned oil company. The suit was settled when Indonesia agreed to pay Rappaport $150 million of its $1.5 billion contract obligation to him. The president of Indonesia later described Rappaport as an "enemy of the country."

Rappaport then became involved in shipping oil from Gabon and in distributing Thai oil. All the while he was searching Africa, the Philippines, and the Caribbean for a government that was properly receptive to his ideas. He settled on Antigua. In 1982 Lester Bird sold Bruce Rappaport a 75 percent interest in Antigua's government-owned refinery, even though the refinery was government property and legally could not be transferred to a private citizen without an act of Parliament. The sale was not announced on Antigua and did not become public knowledge until it was published by *The New York Times* in 1988. Lester did not reveal the terms of the sale. The *Times* reported that Lester gave Rappaport a virtual monopoly on fuel-oil sales on Antigua, a concession worth millions of dollars annually. Since then Rappaport has arbitrarily increased fuel prices as much as 30 percent. He said he would open the refinery and provide jobs for hundreds of Antiguans. But the refinery never opened and the jobs never materialized. An outraged Tim Hector reminded readers that when Rappaport did not deliver on his promise of jobs, it was trade union people—the source of Lester's political strength—who suffered.

Rappaport gained further attention in the mid-1980s when the Bechtel Group, Inc., a San Francisco engineering company, was asked by Iraq to build a pipeline that would carry oil to a Jordanian port on the Red Sea. Bechtel called in Rappaport as a partner. His job was to secure from Israel a promise not to attack the pipeline. For $150,000, Rappaport hired E. Robert Wallach, a San Francisco lawyer and close friend of then attorney general Edwin Meese, to approach Meese about arranging a meeting between Rappaport and Robert McFarlane, President Reagan's national security adviser. McFarlane endorsed the $1 billion pipeline. Wallach then sent a confidential memo to Meese saying that payments of around $65 million would be made to Israel, part of which would go to the Israeli Labor party. The memo led to the 1987 appointment of a special prosecutor to investigate Meese and Wallach. The pipeline fell through, Meese resigned, and Rappaport continued his global deals from Geneva.

Today Lester and Bruce Rappaport remain close friends. When Rappaport's yacht anchors in Antiguan waters, Lester is his most frequent guest, and he occasionally travels to Geneva to confer with Rappaport. It was he who convinced Rappaport to refinance several loans of the Antiguan government, loans that in all likelihood never will be paid. Rappaport built Antigua's new archives building and paid medical bills for the prime minister at the Mayo Clinic. Rappaport owns the Swiss American Bank in St. John's, where more than $7 million thought to belong to the Irish Republican Army mysteriously turned up in the mid-1980s. Antiguans say that one way of causing Lester to lose his temper is to call him "Rappaport's boy" and to accuse him of flying to Geneva to get his instructions.

That Rappaport is Jewish activates the virulent xenophobia of Antiguans and has put him in conflict with the Hadeed family of Antigua. The Hadeeds are a Lebanese family who have lived on Antigua for about forty years. Extraordinarily wealthy, they are active in numerous pro-Arab causes, and one of the Hadeeds has served as Antigua's ambassador to several Arab countries. The Hadeeds lend the Antiguan government large amounts of money, and stories abound of their enormous influence in political affairs. One of the most intriguing is how, during elections, ham radios crackle with Arabic instructions on moving and switching voting boxes before the ballots are counted.

In a 1992 campaign for leadership of the ALP, the Hadeeds spent over a half million dollars supporting John St. Luce, while Rappaport spent even more supporting Lester. The fact that the campaign resulted in a tie, with St. Luce and Lester receiving an equal number of votes, only intensified the competition between Rappaport and the Hadeeds.

Lester is too wily to place his political and financial fate entirely in the hands of one man, even one as wealthy as Rappaport. He is very close to the Hadeeds and often has wheeled and dealed with them.

While Lester was involved with a billionaire businessman who has interests around the world, Vere junior was involved with a melon farmer named Maurice Sarfati, who conned millions of dollars from the American and Antiguan governments.

Sarfati is an Israeli national who was born in Lebanon in 1941. He was an airline executive from 1965 until 1982, when his career path took a rather abrupt turn: he went into partnership with the government of Jamaica to establish drip irrigation farming methods. The details of what happened in Jamaica are not clear. Tim Hector wrote that Sarfati was kicked out of Jamaica in 1983 and fled to Antigua, where he fell in with Vere junior, who promised him fifty acres of government land to grow melons and gave him extraordinary concessions. Roydan Farm, as Sarfati called his operation, would be exempt from corporate income taxes, customs and import duties, property taxes, and the approval of various licenses. In addition, Sarfati was allowed to use extraordinarily scarce public water to irrigate his crops.

The Ministry of Agriculture expressed concern about these concessions, and the Cabinet, in February 1985, refused to approve Sarfati's project. On May 4, apparently without any further discussion, the Cabinet reversed itself and said it had "agreed to the feasibility study carried out by the Roydan company . . . as approved by the Minister of Agriculture." But there was no feasibility study, nor was the project reviewed by the Ministry of Economic Development, as required by law. On May 6, Vere junior told Sarfati's lawyer that the government had approved the concessions and that he, Vere junior, would have administrative responsibility for the project. It was never made clear how the minister of public utilities and communications could usurp the authority of the Ministry of Agriculture and assume operational control of a farming project.

In July 1985, after Roydan Farms had begun operations in the center of the island, Vere junior appointed Sarfati "Special Adviser on Aviation" and "Special Envoy" of the Antiguan government as well as the managing director of Antigua and Barbuda Airways International, the shell company Vere junior set up to handle kickbacks from British Airways.

Sarfati began repaying the favors—literally. Sarfati's secretary later testified that on numerous occasions she delivered $5,000 checks from Sarfati to Vere junior. On one occasion Sarfati sent Vere junior's wife a check for $20,000.

Roydan was allowed to lease another two hundred acres of government land. The Overseas Private Investment Corporation (OPIC), a semi-independent agency of the U.S. government, lent Sarfati $1.3 million. OPIC has a reputation in the U.S. government for questionable loans, and the Antigua deal quickly went to the top of that list. It is almost certain that the Antiguan government guaranteed the loan, a promise that means nothing. But this is conjecture, because OPIC, like other semi-independent agencies, rarely explains its actions.

When Antiguan officials realized how much money Sarfati was generating, they wanted a piece of the action. Because government officials could be bought cheaply back then, Sarfati managed to appease them. Under the tax-free imprimatur of Roydan Farms Sarfati brought in everything from kitchen appliances to a Jacuzzi and expensive bathroom fixtures and gave them away. To minimize complaints from local farmers about his melon farm, which, because of its extraordinary demand for water, could cause them grievous damage, he paid the influential manager of the Antigua Sugar Industry Corporation EC$500 a month to be on his board of directors.

Sarfati needed all the friends he could get. Not only was he using vast amounts of water for which he refused to pay—he said the meter readings were wrong—but he laid an illegal pipeline from a government reservoir and began siphoning off water for his farm. The government of Antigua paid for the pipe.

Minister of Agriculture Hilroy Humphreys signed a contract in 1987 guaranteeing Roydan a line of credit for up to EC$20 million. There was no third party to monitor any drawdown on the money: it was strictly between Sarfati and Humphreys. Neither the Cabinet nor the Ministry of Finance knew of the arrangement until after the papers had been signed. When the deal was discovered, Humphreys said his signature had been forged. But a handwriting expert testified that the signature was authentic. Investigators subsequently found Roydan records that showed thousands of dollars had been transferred from Roydan to Humphreys's personal bank account.

In June 1987 Humphreys signed four EC$250,000 promissory notes and issued them to Roydan, Ltd. A few days later he signed three zero coupon notes totaling EC$1.78 million, and he issued another promissory note for EC$750,000. Still another promissory note raised the total amount of Antiguan government notes and bonds paid to Roydan to EC$4 million.

While other ministers have the authority to obligate the Antiguan government for multimillion-dollar expenses, only the minister of finance can issue promissory notes. Banking officials in Antigua know this, yet Bruce Rappaport's Swiss American Bank accepted the notes. Later, when the Antiguan government hired a Washington law firm to investigate Sarfati and the melon farm, the manager of the Swiss American Bank refused to talk to the investigators. Because the investigators did not have the power of subpoena, the role of the Swiss American Bank was never fully explored.

Later it was revealed that Sarfati guaranteed an EC$26,000 loan for Vere junior at the bank, and that Swiss American officials allowed the account to become EC$92,000 overdrawn. Roydan's account was at Swiss American and the bank paid overdrafts on the account of more than EC$1 million.

By late 1987 it was obvious to all that Roydan was in serious financial trouble. Bills were not being paid and notes were not being met. Even so, in January 1988, Vere junior, on official government stationery, wrote a glowing reference for Sarfati. A few weeks later, Roydan went into receivership with debts of about EC$8 million. The amount of the financial obligations that Vere junior and Hilroy Humphreys incurred on the part of the government could not be determined, because Sarfati's accountants, Price Waterhouse, refused to turn over Roydan records to investigators. But a big part of the debt was the OPIC loan. It is not clear what Sarfati did with the money he conned from Antigua and America. No one knows if it disappeared because of mismanagement, was squandered on bribes, or simply was squirreled away.

Sarfati fled Antigua. But his business arrangements with Vere junior were far from over.

Antigua is an economic petri dish where questionable growths develop and strange organisms prosper. One of the most long-lived of the questionable locals is Jeff Hawley, a white Antiguan who has been the bagman and personal aide to both Lester and Vere junior. It was difficult for Hawley to replicate his glory days of being an intermediate between Lester and Robert Vesco, and for the next few years one regular assignment of his was dealing with the U.S. embassy whenever Vere junior wanted an American visa for a friend. Chargés d'affaires at the U.S. embassy dismissed Hawley as an inconsequential opportunist, but then came an incident that caused a reappraisal of his talents.

As consular officer at the U.S. embassy during the early 1980s, Bryant Salter became a close friend of Jeff Hawley as well as the Birds, particularly Lester.

Salter was equally lenient in granting American visas to Antiguans and Arabs. As a matter of practice, American consulates do not usually grant visas to residents of a third-party country. But in the early 1980s Antigua became a conduit for Arabs who wanted to come to America. The Hadeed family was active in this, and Jeff Hawley was an intermediate between the Hadeeds and the U.S. embassy.

Afterwards, Salter was transferred to South Africa and then to Mexico. In 1988 a State Department investigation recommended that he be prosecuted for illegal sales of U.S. visas to Arabs in Antigua. The State Department turned over the results of its investigation to the U.S. Attorney's office in Miami, but the press of narcotics trafficking and money-laundering cases meant the Salter case had a low priority. The statute of limitations expired and the case was dropped. All this occurred while Salter was assigned to a consular office in Mexico. He was investigated there for the same possible offense, but no wrongdoing was found.

Neither of these investigations dampened Salter's desire to return to Antigua. While in Mexico Salter threatened to quit if he were not reassigned to Antigua. The request confused his superiors. "Antigua is not exactly a career-enhancing move," one of them told me. But because Salter was one of the first highly visible blacks to be hired and put on a fast track at the State Department, he was returned to Antigua in 1991, this time as chargé d'affaires. He resumed his friendship with Jeff Hawley and with the Birds, and confided to prominent Antiguans that he plans to retire from the State Department and live in Antigua, becoming a broker for American businessmen, a middleman between the Birds and investors.

"We in the State Department often are accused of becoming too friendly, too close, to officials in a host country," one State Department official told me. "Sometimes the charge is true and sometimes it is not. But even here in the State Department, Bryant Salter is considered to be at the top of the list of employees who are too close to local officials."

Another questionable growth that has emerged in the Antiguan petri dish is Dick Bertone, an American lawyer who is a close friend of Lester. Bertone was behind the plan to create a national airline for Antigua. He invited about fifty young women from around the Caribbean to Antigua, where they would apply for jobs as flight attendants, and he convinced various hotels to provide free lodging and meals. Plans for the airline fell apart, the women went home, and the hotels were left in the lurch. Bertone, like all good businessmen, picked himself up after the failure, dusted himself off, and proceeded at full speed on another venture. He went to London and negotiated with various charter airlines about flying to Antigua. Such high-level and significant negotiations are usually conducted by a minister, but Bertone holds no brief from the government. Tim Hector says Bertone owns the offshore oil rights of Antigua and Barbuda, a concession that could have been granted only by Lester as the minister of economic development.

Many of the mystery men who come to Antigua want to remain hidden from public view. Their favorite hotel for more than a decade was the Castle Harbour. One of the few large hotels in downtown St. John's, it sat on a knoll a few hundred yards below the U.S. embassy and overlooked St. John's, with a breathtaking view of the harbor and the Caribbean. The exterior paint was peeling and streaked with mildew. Room fixtures did not work. The expansive courtyard around the swimming pool was cratered. Nothing ever seemed to be repaired and an odor of decay hung over everything. Sometime in the mid-1980s the name was changed to the Flamingo, but the room keys remained imprinted with "CASTLE HARBOUR."

Historically, hotels in St. John's do not do well. Tourists want to be on the beach. But throughout the 1980s the Castle Harbour/Flamingo stayed open with one of the lowest occupancy rates of any hotel in the Caribbean. I stayed there on two occasions and never saw more than a half-dozen guests. And they were the sort who stared at every person entering the dining room as if trying to determine exactly who the newcomer was and why he would want to stay there. The hotel's zombie-like staff had little to do but lean against the walls in boredom.

Casino licenses are extraordinarily difficult to come by on Antigua. They have gone only to Halcyon Cove, which until 1991 was owned by the government; to the Ramada Renaissance, which is owned either by Lester or the Antiguan government; to the St. James Club near English Harbour, a habitat primarily of wealthy Europeans; and, in a jarring deviation, the Castle Harbour/Flamingo hotel. On the half-dozen occasions I visited the casino it was virtually empty. Nevertheless, the hotel stayed open.

When Robert Vesco was considered too frugal by Antiguan officials, it was a manager of this hotel who advised Jeff Hawley to "get the smart boys in, take a knife and open up and put the liver on the plate." And when a group of Louisiana good old boys mounted a paramilitary effort to overthrow the government of Dominica, it was in this hotel that they planned the coup. The effort failed and became known as the "Bayou of Pigs."

In 1990 the State Department assigned Roger Gamble, a sharp-eyed, blunt-talking fiscal expert, as chargé d'affaires in Antigua. He and I were discussing the never-ending scandals that have cropped up on the island. At the time embassy officials were under no restrictions about talking with visiting writers, and Gamble was complaining that Antigua was the only nation in the eastern Caribbean that refused to share information on narcotics traffickers and money launderers with America. When I asked about the Castle Harbour/Flamingo, Gamble hinted that the hotel was something of a washing machine. "We have serious concerns that money may be laundered there," he said. "It's the only explanation. There are never any guests."

21

"Captain, the Ship Is Sinking"

—*calypso song*

Sometimes it seems that not only the roads lack signs on Antigua, but there are no markers or guides for everyday life either, and existence is frenetic, confusing, and frustrating. So it seemed during one of my visits.

I was sitting in Roger Gamble's office at the U.S. embassy when he called the prime minister to arrange an interview for me. It was the spring of 1990; the prime minister was a virtual recluse and was rumored to be in declining physical and mental health. It was said that he had become so dotty he would occasionally order his permanent secretary to "Get me Moody-Stuart on the telephone" and then, later on, ask if Moody-Stuart had returned his call. Stories about the prime minister's declining health had been circulating for almost a decade; and I dismissed these latest ones as wishful thinking from opposition politicians, especially since the prime minister had said he intended to complete his term of office, which did not end until early 1994.

As Gamble talked to the prime minister's permanent secretary, he winced and I asked him what was the matter. Gamble put his hand over the mouthpiece, turned to me and said, "I can hear the permanent secretary talking to him. He's saying, 'Turn around. It's the telephone on the right. The second one. That's it. Now pick it up.' He's in bad shape. When I see him, I try to limit the appointment to no more than ten minutes."

After the conversation, Gamble thanked the prime minister, then turned to me and said, "He will see you at ten o'clock tomorrow morning."

The prime minister's office is a two-story wooden building that was once the home of the former British colonial secretary. It sits near the crest of a hill not far from Parliament. The winding road leading up the hill is unpaved and ends at a tiny guard shack. The gate was unattended, and the guard was asleep, sprawled out in a rocking chair on the porch of the prime minister's office. At the sound of my footsteps he opened one eye and gave me a quick once-over. I could almost hear him thinking: "White guy in a suit. Okay." The eye closed. My shoulder bag was not searched, and as I wandered into the waiting room, it occurred to me that the prime minister of Antigua must be one of the most approachable heads of state anywhere in the world.

The floor of the office was scuffed and covered with heel marks. Small plants in orange pots were lined up atop a divider that separated back-to-back desks in the large waiting room. Green Naugahyde chairs were shoved against the wall for visitors. The windows were open to the east wind and birds were singing. The permanent secretary, an elderly man of great dignity, introduced himself and said the prime minister would see me in a few minutes.

As I waited, a black car traveling at higher-than-normal speed raced through the gate and around to the rear of the building, where it stopped in a cloud of dust. Lester Bird alighted from the passenger side, popped through the rear entrance of the building, and without a word to anyone in the office, turned to climb the stairs to his father's office. He saw me, paused, nodded tightly, then continued up the stairs. Fifteen minutes later he came down. He did not look at me as he left the building. I waited. About a half hour later the permanent secretary returned and in an embarrassed manner said the prime minister was tired and would not be able to talk with me. He discouraged me from trying to reschedule the appointment. "The prime minister is very busy," he said.

I had been outflanked by Lester and I did not know why. I wondered if I could reach the prime minister through Cutie Francis, the former beauty queen who had become one of the most powerful people in Antigua. It was said that she even turned aside the telephone calls of Lester and Vere junior when she did not want them to disturb the prime minister. Tim Hector, who called her "Queen Cutie," had written numerous stories of her influence in the daily affairs of government, how she handled the prime minister's personal investments, and of her own growing business empire. Jamaica Kincaid refers to her as "Evita."

I dropped in on Cutie at Gifts Galore, a boutique she owns in St. John's across the street from the red awnings of the Kentucky Fried Chicken outlet. The shop contains everything from G.I. Joe toys to soap to off-brand crystal, a hodgepodge inventory that lines the walls and is stacked high on shelves. Cutie, sitting on a stool behind the cash register and listening to a religious program on the radio, was singing along with a song whose title appeared to be "I'd Walk the Last Mile for You." In between verses, she drank a Coca-Cola and munched on cookies. She wore no shoes. An old woman, clad in a simple cotton dress, sat at her feet. When I introduced myself, Cutie seemed surprised and pleased that I knew of her and of her connection with the prime minister. She slipped on her shoes, put on a stunning pair of gold and diamond earrings, and slid a newspaper over the package of cookies. She is a plain, rather plump woman whose most noticeable feature is her expansive bosom. About her is an air of command. She was very direct in her gaze and in her speech. When I told her I would like to talk to the prime minister, she asked that I give her a list of questions for him to approve. I sat down and prepared a list. But the next day when I returned, she shook her head as I walked in the door. "He said we didn't want any publicity," she told me.

In the 1980s Antigua seemed lost in a sea of corruption with a moral compass that could not find true north. Occasionally an anchor would be tossed out in an effort to slow the inexorable drift. One such effort was in 1989, when a book celebrating the golden jubilee of the Antigua Trades and Labour Union was published. The book was dedicated to "Prime Minister the Rt. Hon. Dr. Vere Cornwall Bird." It is not clear exactly what the union had to celebrate, and the book had little connection with reality. The years since independence had been marked with tumult and dissension, with one scandal after another. The United States recently had demanded the recall of Antigua's ambassador to the United Nations because of his alleged involvement in selling passports. Using his United Nations title, the ambassador had borrowed a quarter of a million dollars from a New York bank and then had defaulted on the loan. He was in the process of being sued.

Eastern Airlines had canceled service to Antigua, and Pan American soon would do the same. This did not bode well for tourism. Actions of years past were threatening the financial stability of the country. For instance, the prime minister, upon his return to office in 1976, had fulfilled a campaign promise and abolished personal income tax. Now, many companies were declaring their business profits as personal income and were thus avoiding corporate taxes. In addition, the lack of a personal income tax meant Antiguans had to pay high tariffs, duties, and import fees on virtually everything brought into the country. The International Monetary Fund several times asked the prime minister to reinstate the personal income tax, but he refused to do so. Antigua was virtually bankrupt.

"We have a very high standard of living," one Antiguan told me. "But it is costing us a hell of a lot to live the way we do."

One of Antigua's moral anchors is Dr. Keithley Ivor MacDonald Heath. Perhaps as much as anyone else, Dr. Heath represents the plight of educated and idealistic Antiguans who want a government that will bring their country into the twentieth century. Dr. Heath's problem is that he is far too gentle to prevail in the no-holds-barred arena of Antiguan politics.

In 1960, with a medical degree from Queen's College in Belfast, Northern Ireland, and as a Fellow of Surgery at the Royal College of Surgeons in Edinburgh, Scotland, Dr. Heath returned to Antigua and began practicing medicine at Holberton Hospital. Within weeks he was in conflict with both the minister of health and the government.

"I wanted to upgrade the services provided at the hospital," Dr. Heath told me. We sat in the spacious living room of his home and he looked through the open windows, where a light breeze stirred the gauzy cotton curtains as he recounted what has happened to him and to the island over the years. "Basically I felt that anything we did in Antigua should be done as well as they do it anywhere else. The position of the government was that we had limited funds, that the hospital did not bring in revenue, and we should accept the fact that in Antigua services need not be that high. Basically, I was told that my standards were too high. Whenever a minister of government became ill, he caught a plane and went to the United States or to the United Kingdom. He would not go to Holberton Hospital. It was good enough for our people but not good enough for a minister."

Dr. Heath is six feet three inches tall and very slender. His light complexion is topped by white hair. His eyes are gentle and his voice is soft and cultivated. It is impossible to imagine him losing his temper or departing in any way from being courtly, refined, and civilized. One of the few signs of emotion manifested by Dr. Heath was when he told how, in 1986, the government brought in a state-of-the-art piece of X-ray equipment costing $500,000. "When it arrived, we realized there was no place at the hospital to put it," Dr. Heath said. And for two years the piece of equipment sat in an air-conditioned trailer before finally being installed in the hospital.

"I've become quite worried about the political situation here," Dr. Heath said. The discipline and organization of his mind was apparent in the manner with which he easily and smoothly segued from one topic to another.

"After the Bird government took over the lands of the sugar estates, the government owned the sugar business. But the government said it could not give the people the wages they once had; that even though the trade unions had supported the government all along, there would be no salary increases. So the Bird government lost in 1971 and people went with the PLM. The PLM closed down the sugar industry. The ALP returned to power in 1976 with a promise to bring back the sugar industry. That brought the sugar workers, the traditional strength of the party. Bird also told them there would be no income tax, so that touched the white-collar workers, professionals, and businessmen. The ALP galloped back into office. What worries me is that then the government borrowed $30 million from the Caribbean Development Bank to restart the sugar industry, but the industry was not restarted. The government wanted new hotels, but what concerns me are the tax-free holidays the government gives to those who build the hotels. People with capital build hotels, then send the money earned in Antigua back to their own countries. And the government sells large acreage, sometimes as much as twenty acres, for a hotel where two acres would suffice. We are attracting many unsavory people to this island."

Dr. Heath stared out the window. It was almost as if he were talking to himself. "What pushed me over the edge was the 1984 election. The ALP won all sixteen seats. Let me back up and say that when Labour won in 1976, the opposition actually got more votes than Labour. Labour won very small majorities in the constituencies, but the opposition polled big majorities in some areas. It sounds like a paradox, but it isn't. Who controls the government does not depend upon the total votes, but on who wins the most seats. In 1984, the opposition got one third of the votes cast and won no seats. I realized we had democratically elected a dictatorship."

It was then that Dr. Heath became a founder of the United National Democratic party (UNDP) and entered politics. And what he discovered about the government and the people of Antigua was disturbing. "You can go back two generations in any Antigua family and you are back in the canefields," he said. "In a very short time we moved from the canefields to a sophisticated consumer society. But what do we produce? We are almost totally dependent on tourism. Agriculture has been allowed to die. We do not even produce eggs and milk to feed our people. Everything is imported. There is talk of doubling the number of hotel rooms, but there is no talk of upgrading sanitation or sewage facilities or the health services. The rug can be pulled from under our feet so easily that it is frightening. One epidemic would do it. Look at Trinidad ten years or so ago and the polio scare. Trinidad almost closed down. They canceled carnival. Today people are scared of disease, and here you can get hepatitis or typhoid easily.

"In England, in Macmillan's time, was a phrase: 'We never had it so good.' I hear that same phrase here. In America you have a different society. People are attached to the land. But here farmers left the land because if they work as bartenders or maids they earn more money than on the land. But on the land, you are working for yourself. In the hotels, you are rapidly getting back to conditions that existed before, when expatriate planters controlled the economy and, therefore, the people. We are rapidly getting to where our economy is not controlled by the government, because the government has loans which it is no longer able to service.

"I sit down and I wonder what we as a people have accomplished since independence. We are building hotels, but very often with no Antiguan involved. Agriculture has declined. The educational system is faltering. Health services have not improved. Our beaches and the beauty of our island have become secondary to attracting dollars. Septic tanks cannot cope with the volume of sewage. There are instances of straight fecal matter coming out of pipes into the ocean. It could lead to an epidemic in this country. Typhoid, jaundice due to virus, infectious hepatitis—lack of sanitation is associated with many diseases. But under the colonial system, water was tested frequently. Sanitation inspectors went into our back yards.

"The Bird government has not kept pace with the needs of this society. We have completely failed to maintain and develop the infrastructure necessary to develop both our people and future generations. And at the same time, corruption in government has produced a situation in which the values of our people have been so eroded that many of them accept the present situation as the norm. We are like people in a supermarket who have collected as many items as we want, but eventually we must go to the counter and pay. We cannot do this.

"I was born in Antigua. My father had to leave school at the age of twelve. He worked hard all his life. He educated all his children. Today he still lives in the same house where I was born. He is ninety-two. And he is a contented man. He gave his children opportunities which he never had. My father made many sacrifices for me. I have a debt to future generations on this island. There is no personal animosity toward those in power; my animosity is against the corrupt practices which are destroying this island.

"Under the British civil service, everything was well organized. The infrastructure worked. You could report something broken and something would be done. That has gone by the board. If someone comes to work late and just passes the time, there is absolutely nothing you can do about it.

"In most former British colonies there are two strong political parties, either of which can form a government. The people look at those parties to decide what policy they want to follow. You find this in Britain with the Conservatives and Labour; in America with Democrats and Republicans. But in Antigua we have only one political party which is seen as being able to run the country. Mr. Bird has made it clear he is the only one who can control the nation. A lot of people accept this. He points at the opposition and says, 'Don't put those people in. Last time they were in, you know what happened.'

"There is no discipline or order in this society. Government has stopped publishing the auditor's report because there are so many instances of money not being accounted for. We have had no auditor's report since 1985.

"Everything here is patronage. Even at the hospital; from doctors to cooks. There are good doctors here who have been blocked from working in this system."

Dr. Heath wanted to change all of this, but he was tossed out as leader of the UNDP and replaced by Baldwin Spencer, a well-intentioned and sincere man whose ambition appears to exceed his abilities. Dr. Heath did not take the loss personally. He simply returned to practicing medicine.

A year later, when I talked with him again, he said he had no intention of reentering politics. I asked him about all that we had discussed earlier and wondered aloud why another government was not voted in.

Dr. Heath sadly shook his head, and said, "I don't know. But I hope you don't ask me what is the future of Antigua."

Book Three

"ANTIGUA ME COME FROM"

22

"As Governor-General, I Must Stay Above Politics"

In the spring of 1990 Vere junior was caught moonlighting as a gunrunner to a Colombian drug cartel. Within days, Lester was in open warfare with his brother and his father over the allegations. The country was virtually paralyzed as it awaited the outcome of the internecine battle, and the government was under attack from all quarters. The International Monetary Fund said the government's civil service rolls were so bloated they should be cut by 40 percent. The Chamber of Commerce announced that "Antigua has to get rid of the image of corruption which has been tagged on it since independence." Roger Gamble sent a cable to Washington describing the bleak financial conditions of the Bird government and predicting that Antigua "will make little progress in bringing its fiscal house to order." Another cable said Vere junior's ministry deserved its reputation "as the worst ministry/government agency in Antigua."

But many people tried to put on a brave front. They reminded me of someone selling deck chairs on the *Titanic* even as the ship was sinking. The best example was seen at the governor-general's reception celebrating the queen's birthday. With the possible exception of the opening of Parliament each spring, nothing in Antigua evokes the glory of empire as does the festive and tradition-bedecked celebration of the queen's birthday in June. It is held on the lawn at Government House, the large rambling residence of the governor-general that fronts on Independence Avenue.

When the afternoon of the party arrived, police officers in

crisp white jackets and razor-creased black trousers stopped traffic so men in suits and women in fancy dresses could enter the grounds.

Governor-General Sir Wilfred Ebenezer Jacobs, the longest-serving governor-general in the British Commonwealth, greeted the visitors. Sir Wilfred is a courtly man of otherworldly charm who is very much aware of his exalted position. He is reserved and aloof toward many Antiguans. That night he had on a dark pinstripe suit, a striped shirt, and a dark tie. Although he has been awarded numerous honors by the British government, he wore only the GCVO—the Grand Cross of the Victorian Order. Sir Wilfred's bonhomie, which for him was rather unusual, indicated he had begun the celebration early. He readily agreed when I asked if we could talk during the evening.

The queen's birthday is a holiday of such significance that even the prime minister, who had not been seen in public for months, was in attendance. His official black car purred through the front gate, visitors parting before it, and the then-seventy-nine-year-old patriarch of Antigua, accompanied by Cutie Francis, alighted. He was stooped, and, if his slow shuffling walk was any indication, his knees were causing him considerable pain. After a few steps, he sat in a reserved chair in the front row, looked across the lawn toward the flagpole, and waited for the ceremonies to begin.

Vere junior and Lester were conspicuous by their absence.

Because the queen's birthday is a national holiday, various parties were being held around St. John's, a curious phenomenon for a people whose loathing of the British can be very much in evidence. A half-dozen outdoor celebrations across Independence Avenue and the noise from a much-amplified reggae band a few doors down the street almost overpowered the weak and quavering notes of the Royal Police Force Band on the parade field at Government House.

The red and black flag of Antigua was lowered and the band beat retreat. As the band rendered a quavery version of "God Save the Queen," a line of riflemen fired three ragged volleys into the gathering darkness. The band marched across the parade field to the edge of the trees, took their seats, and played softly as the party began.

As dusk fell, and as the band music rose and fell like a radio trying to hold onto a distant signal, lights around the yard were turned on; and the guests rushed toward the numerous bars set up at the far end of the spacious yard. Bartenders were ready. Dozens of glasses half-filled with Cavalier rum had been marshaled atop white tablecloths and needed only a few ice cubes and a splash of Coca-Cola to become the local drink of choice. Many guests kept their eyes on the front gate as they watched and wondered if Vere junior or Lester would make an appearance. And if both arrived, what would happen?

Within moments the first power outage of the evening occurred. In the blackness, the faint, rising and falling notes of the band drifted across the field, and the soft clinking of ice was heard. A few moments later the lights returned and there was another rush toward the bars. As guests downed their drinks, they looked around and whispered that neither Vere junior nor Lester had appeared. It was as if the sons of the prime minister might have staged the power outage so they could arrive under the cover of darkness.

Another power outage. Then another. And after each outage, there was a lemming-like rush for the bars.

Cutie was mingling and chatting. She never looked toward the prime minister, who sat in the shadows at the edge of the parade field. His hat was pulled low around his ears and added to his dark and melancholy appearance. After about an hour he fidgeted and looked up. Two uniformed members of the Defense Force materialized at his side to help him stand. The stooped old man limped toward the car, Cutie grimacing as she kept pace. Then the driver opened the car door and Cutie climbed inside. Slowly, the prime minister followed. The car drove away, and through the back window I could see Cutie's erect silhouette as she stared straight ahead. The prime minister's head was hunched between his shoulders and almost hidden under his hat.

I was staring after the prime minister's car when Sir Wilfred broke away from a group of people, pulled me toward the chairs where the prime minister and the official party had been sitting, and said, "We must have our little chat."

Sir Wilfred sat down, smiled expansively, crossed his hands

over his stomach, and nodded. "I've thought about this, and if I speak with you, I must be honest," he began. "And what I have to say would be controversial."

He smiled benignly. He looked up as several people approached to bid him good night, waved, and then turned back to me. The guests continued toward the gate when they saw he was not going to stand up and chat.

Sir Wilfred got straight to the point. "You must understand, first of all, that V. C. Bird did not form the first trade union," he said. "He came in after the fact."

When I nodded, Sir Wilfred continued, "He tells people today that he formed the union. But he did not."

Sir Wilfred looked up, smiled, and again waved as more visitors departed. He leaned toward me, hands outstretched. "And V. C. Bird did not force the British sugar barons, the plantocracy, off this island. It was because of the shifting economies of sugar that they left. They were ready to leave. They wanted out of the business."

The governor-general leaned back, pursed his lips, and continued. "And V. C. Bird is credited with bringing Antiguans out of colonial oppression. But the mood of the Caribbean was such that this would have happened anyway. He just happened to be in office at the time." He threw his hand wide in an expansive gesture. "The main thing V. C. Bird did was to buy up the sugar plantations and give land to the peasants of Antigua."

"Peasants?"

The governor-general paused, then nodded as if embarrassed. Sir Wilfred often complains to the police when local people make too much noise on Independence Avenue. He is a man who, on the rare occasions when he ventures away from Government House, does so in an air-conditioned limousine whose windows are tinted so darkly it is impossible to see who is in the rear seat. And when he goes on vacation, it is usually to London where, as the governor-general of a Commonwealth country, he is afforded special honors and privileges. He is more British than West Indian, the ultimate representative of the British Crown and a man who cherishes the prerogatives of office.

"I must be careful speaking to you like this," continued Sir

Wilfred. "You see, I was attorney general during many of V. C. Bird's travails with the Crown, and we have a historical animosity." He smiled. "As governor-general, I must stay above politics."

By now it was growing late, and only a handful of guests remained. Several couples waited a few feet away, insistent on paying their respects. Sir Wilfred stood up, smiled, and held out his hand. The men clustered around him while the women chatted among themselves. "Did you see the prime minister?" one of the women asked. "He was sitting there in the front row." Another woman nodded and said, "I saw him. But I was standing next to Cutie and talking with her." The third woman leaned forward. "Did you see . . . ?" She did not finish the sentence. She did not have to. The first two women shook their heads. Vere junior and Lester, the two most talked about men on Antigua, had not shown up at the queen's birthday party.

23

Fungi Man

In the spring of 1990, Vere junior retreated to his home at Friars Hill, a cowed and confused man. What had started out as a plan to make a few bucks on a shipment of guns had ended up an international scandal. A few months earlier he had been a leading contender for prime minister, but now he was beset with probing reporters from America, Canada, and Great Britain. Lester was calling for a judicial inquiry, and support for it was growing every day. Vere junior was facing political ruin.

Then Vere junior went on a two-pronged offensive. First, he importuned his father to save him; second, he retained the services of a pack of lawyers. The prime minister was rarely seen in public in the summer of 1990, but when he did make an appearance, Vere junior was always at his right hand. He had breakfast with his father every Saturday morning at the prime minister's residence, and he left his car parked in the front yard, where everyone could see it. Vere junior missed no opportunity to show in public just how close he was to the Father of the Nation. The first thing the six lawyers he hired did was to counsel him not to talk to reporters, to lie low and ride out the storm. Reporters representing some of the most prestigious newspapers in the world were turned away from Vere junior's door. In contrast, Lester provided them with information and said it was his solemn duty as foreign minister to see that this issue was fully explored.

One afternoon I drove about a mile northeast of St. John's to where Vere junior lives in a house once owned by V. C. Bird before he took over Moody-Stuart's old residence. Vere junior answered my knock on the door. He wore brown slacks, was barefoot, and had on no shirt. A pair of reading glasses rode on the tip of his nose.

"I'm not giving interviews," he said in a peremptory fashion. "Upon the advice of my attorneys, I cannot talk about my present ordeal." He turned away. I gathered that "present ordeal" was the euphemism used for the gun-smuggling charges.

"I don't want to talk about those allegations," I said.

Vere stopped and looked over his shoulder. His eyebrows knitted.

"I'm not interested in that," I said, and handed him a list of a half-dozen questions typed on a sheet of white paper. All the questions revolved around who would succeed the prime minister and take on the burden of leading Antigua into the twenty-first century. Softball questions.

Vere junior pushed open the screen door, accepted the paper, and studied the list. He nodded, smiled, then waved the list in the air. "This is all you want to talk about?" He was nonplussed.

"That's all."

Vere junior stared over his glasses, a half-smile of disbelief tugging at his mouth. He was not convinced.

"I won't ask a single question about the gunrunning," I said. "If I do, you can always throw me out."

Vere junior again scanned the list. Again he stared at me over his glasses. He tugged at his chin. Still again his eyes returned to the list. He opened the door. "Come in," he said.

I stepped from the bright sunshine into a dim room. On the left a middle-aged man stared at me with cold eyes. Five women ranging from their early twenties to middle age stood around the room regarding me in a hostile fashion. The cold-eyed man was introduced by Vere junior as the editor of his newspaper, and the women he collectively introduced as "my family." Two computers and a printer sat atop a table. A collection of sophisticated ham radio equipment was on another table. Vere junior said the computers were to produce his newspaper. "Also, I am giving some thought to writing about my present ordeal."

Vere junior said the ham radio was one of his few hobbies. On Antigua, his call sign is "VP1AG," and from England it is "G3ZLY." A black-and-white television set was turned on.

Vere junior sat in a Naugahyde reclining chair and turned

his attention to the television. He was in the middle of an afternoon cowboy movie, featuring former football player Jim Brown, who was somewhere south of the Mexican border with Raquel Welch and Burt Reynolds. The movie was vaguely familiar.

The living room windows were open, but the room was very warm. Vere junior idly scratched the gray hair on his chest as he peered over his glasses to watch Jim Brown leaping about the screen. At a commercial break I noticed the title of the movie was *100 Rifles,* and suddenly I remembered the plot: Burt Reynolds was a gun smuggler and Jim Brown was a cop. Brown was chasing Reynolds through Mexico.

The conversation with Vere junior quickly focused on his plans for becoming prime minister. His response was different from Lester's. He displayed none of the same gusto when the subject arose. At first I thought Vere junior was being coy. But it was more than that. He is intensely loyal to his father and did not want to talk about running for what almost everyone on Antigua sees as the office of V. C. Bird. Vere junior was delighted that I knew he had breakfast with his father every Saturday. He said that as long as his father was alive, it would be premature for him to talk of his own political plans. He did volunteer that his constituency is so loyal and so devoted that he won his last election by a greater majority than even the prime minister enjoyed.

The conversation was desultory. Vere junior rarely looked at me. His eyes were locked on Jim Brown. Occasionally his face lit up, and a broad smile creased his boyish face. After a while, when it became clear that I was not going to ask him about his "present ordeal," he began to loosen up. His favorite topic, and the only one that drew his attention away from the television, was talking about his strong relationship with his constituents.

St. John's Rural South is Vere junior's political base. This constituency of some four thousand people is immediately south of St. John's.

"I can be seen many days, most days, going door to door in my constituency," Vere junior said. "Shaking hands. Talking. I'm very frank. Every month I give money to sixty or one hundred people. I give money to them every month—money, refrigerators, vacuum cleaners, television sets. I know most people there. They call me Vere. They all know me. I serve everybody, even those who I know are not my supporters, and sometimes I turn them into supporters."

Now he was intense and animated. "I am popular throughout the island. I am known as a man of my word. I walk free. I have never been booed. I get no heckling. No boos. All the other politicians are booed at parades."

Does his popularity mean he will be the next prime minister?

Vere junior smiled an open guileless smile. He shrugged and, almost reluctantly, answered. "If I am elected, I will work closely with the United States of America. Only half a glance shows we are under U.S. influence. One cannot ignore the influence of the U.S. here. It is more than that of Britain or Canada. Almost all the television is from America, all the news we see on CNN is from America, our magazines are from America, most tourists are from America. We can't escape the influence of America and Americans."

Then Vere junior, in one of the sudden wanderings that mark his conversation, had an idea. A true and spontaneous picture of him and his political strength could be seen at a beach picnic he was giving the next day for his constituents. "You are invited," he said magnanimously. I decided to leave before he changed his mind.

He walked me to the door, occasionally glancing over his shoulder at Jim Brown and Raquel Welch, and told me how to find the beach on the western side of the island. As I walked down the steps, Vere junior laughed. "I am going against the advice of six lawyers in talking to you," he said.

I laughed and thanked him. But I did not tell him Jim Brown catches the gun smuggler.

The place that Antiguans say is the only spot where the queen of England has ever gone for a public swim is called Royal Beach. It is one of the few undeveloped stretches of sand remaining on the Caribbean side of Antigua, and to get there, one drives down the coastal road from St. John's, turns right at an unmarked dirt road, and bounces along for about a mile. Down the hill on the left the enormous marina at Jolly Bay was being dredged. Up the hill on the right was Antigua's leper colony. The road wends through a cassy thicket. Then it rounds a bend and suddenly there's a small, idyllic, crescent-shaped beach of indescribable beauty. Several yards from shore the white, gin-clear waters merge with deepening pale green waters, and then, a few hundred yards farther out, with the intense rich blue of deep water that stretches toward the horizon.

This remote location is unknown to tourists but quite popular with Antiguans. Under the coconut trees are the remains of a half-dozen picnic fires. Countless beer bottles and cans and stacks of refuse are scattered along the road and among the trees. Occasionally a large dump truck filled with sand growled its way around the corner and turned toward the main road.

I sat under a coconut tree and watched people arrive. Each family brought its own food and drink. Many people wore new white T-shirts that said

VOTE VERE
YOU KNOW HE CARES

The guests spread out sheets and lay down to nap until the picnic started. A few children played in the shallow water. More would have been there, but two young men were racing horses up and down the sand, thoroughly intimidating anyone who wanted to wade into the sea.

A van lurched down the dirt road and pulled close to the high tide line. Two middle-aged men opened the rear doors and pulled out a set of enormous speakers, each about four feet tall and perhaps two feet wide. Such speakers are standard issue for Antiguan politicians. The accompanying generator was so large that four men were required to carry it high up the beach and place it under the trees. A long extension cord was run from the generator to the speakers, and more wires were connected to a radio in the rear of the van. The generator began to emit a ponderous *chuunk-chuunk-chuunk-chuunk* that echoed through the air. The radio was tuned to a calypso station and the volume cranked up until the generator could not be heard. The calypso music was deafening.

When Vere junior came on the scene, about forty people were waiting. Vere junior alighted from the car wearing a tiny red bikini and a red knit shirt—ALP-approved beachwear—and flashed a brilliant smile. Arm waving and great enthusiasm from women in the crowd greeted him. "He is our father," one said.

The radio was so loud that I was not sure I had heard her correctly. I leaned closer and asked how many of those present were children of Vere junior. She laughed and said he was not their natural father but "all of us consider him our father."

Vere junior made the rounds, shaking hands, leaning down, shouting in order to be heard over the earth-thumping bass of the speakers. Then he walked under the trees, surrounded by the half-dozen women whom I met the day before in his home. The cold-eyed man who edited *The Sentinel* watched. Vere junior needed to talk, he had to explain himself to someone from America. Not speaking to all the reporters who had knocked on his door was frustrating, but now he could unburden himself.

As he and I sat on a blue tarp under the trees, Vere junior looked at one of the women in his party, held up two fingers, and motioned for her to bring us food. The music was so loud that Vere junior and I had to sit facing each other, side by side, mouth to ear. Vere junior, like his brothers and his father, is well over six feet tall, and when he sat, he sort of folded up like a gawky tropical bird, an image heightened by his graying hair and red bathing suit. And for one who has the reputation of being a mean-spirited and vindictive man, he was remarkably charming and solicitous.

Another dump truck filled to overflowing with beach sand rumbled past. Vere smiled at the driver and waved. Our food arrived, and Vere looked down at a heaping plate of barbecued chicken, ribs, red beans and rice, macaroni-and-cheese pie, candied baked potatoes, fungi, and fried dumplings. He pointed at the food, then leaned close and said, "This is good, but I am a salt fish and fungi man."

Fungi, a combination of cornmeal and boiled okra, is a subsistence food, a tasteless mass of carbohydrate that English sugar planters fed to slaves. Along with salt fish, it remains a staple of the Antiguan diet and is available in many island restaurants.

Vere junior noticed my quizzical expression and said, "I am a simple humble person. I have no great sophistication. I am one with the people." He shooed a few insects away from his plate. "I don't drink or smoke. Never have."

The mountain of food atop his plate was ignored. I knew

that the only subject on his mind was the forbidden topic of gunrunning, and I wondered if he would approach it.

"I am the eldest son in my family and I have a very paternal instinct. In my younger days, when my father was married to politics rather than to our home, I looked after my brothers. I slept in the same bed with Lester for many years. At political meetings as far back as the seventies, Lester listened to a man who wanted us all to march into the prime minister's office and harass him until he died. I walked out and told my father. Ever since, Lester has seen me as a stumbling block in his plans."

Vere junior pushed around the food on his plate. "My father is not well. His knees cause him a great deal of pain. We have a cane for him, a walking stick, but he doesn't like to use it. I tell him that your American president Franklin Roosevelt used a cane, but he doesn't like it." Vere junior's voice changed when he talked of his father. I heard respect and veneration there. But when he talked of Lester his voice became angry. "Lester is impatient for our father to die. He wants the job. My brother Lester is tearing down everything my father built." He added what people on Antigua have known for years: "Lester was seen as the obvious successor of the prime minister until about nineteen eighty-five or -six. My father brought us up as one, so it was disturbing when Lester began to turn on me, first during the airport business and then again during this present ordeal of mine. Now people are so tired of the Birds, they might toss us all out. They might elect anyone, anyone but a Bird."

Vere junior paused, and then in his soft, almost diffident voice, continued. "On that airport business, I got all the blame and the censure, but it was Lester who made all the money. His company, Antigua Aggregates, Limited, had the contract to supply all the runway resurfacing material. Mitsubishi had a contract to supply new vehicles at the airport, but Lester canceled that contract and awarded it to a car dealership on Antigua, a dealership in which he has holdings." He shook his head and darted off on another subject. "Lester has a problem with his weight. He went to a Miami fat farm once, but it did not work."

At the sound of a car he looked up, waved, and turned on a politician's quick smile. He told me how, when Lester was in college and wanted to drop out, it was he, the older brother, who convinced Lester to finish his education. And then when the Vietnam War escalated, Lester, as a United States citizen, would have been drafted had not the prime minister interceded. "It took all the savvy of the prime minister to get him into law school in London so he would not have to go to war."

Vere junior paused, looked around at his constituents, smiled, and picked at his food. He took a bite of fungi. Then came another abrupt change of subject. "I've been through an ordeal for about five years," he said. "I've never been booed or heckled. I've gotten a lot of affection and a lot of prayers. I do believe in God. A lot of people are praying for me."

Another bite of fungi and another conversational leap. "Did you know your IRS is investigating Lester? He does his banking in the Bahamas, but he has extensive holdings in America. The IRS doesn't want to do anything, because it might embarrass this government." He shook his head as if in great sadness.

"I have broken no Antiguan law," he said abruptly, and I knew he was talking of the gunrunning allegations. "I have broken *no* law. And that is the only finding the commission of inquiry can arrive at."

I cautiously mentioned that Roger Gamble at the American embassy had said the same thing. Vere junior was immensely pleased.

"On two occasions I have accused Lester in Cabinet of giving material to Tim Hector," Vere junior said. "He never responded. My wife and children are in the U.S., and they hear all of this on the radio." He shook his head again.

"My brother is tearing our family apart. It reminds me of Macbeth:

> I am in blood
> Stepp'd in so far that, should I wade no more,
> Returning were as tedious as go o'er."

24

Assassins and a Government Minister

By early summer of 1990, demands for an investigation into the gunrunning affair had grown to the point that Prime Minister Bird had no choice: he had to call for an inquiry. Louis Blom-Cooper, a British jurist who had investigated government corruption in the Turks and Caicos Islands, was chairman of the inquiry when it convened in St. John's in midsummer. And within the next few weeks, everything the people of Antigua had speculated about for months was revealed. According to testimony at the inquiry, it happened this way.

On Saturday, April 22, 1989, a nondescript cargo vessel named *Else TH* approached St. John's and anchored in the roadstead. The *Else TH* was a Danish ship chartered out of Haifa, Israel, by an Israeli company. Nothing about the vessel attracted attention, and there was nothing to indicate she was carrying arms and ammunition; there was no red flag, the international signal for a vessel carrying dangerous goods, and at night there was no red masthead light. The ship's captain went ashore and took a room at the Castle Harbour/Flamingo hotel. Early Monday morning he returned to the *Else TH*, eased the vessel into the harbor, and tied up at the deepwater pier. A container case addressed to the "Quartermaster-General, High Street, St. John's" was lifted from the deck to the dock.

The *Else TH* upped anchor and cleared the harbor. While leaving, it passed the *Seapoint*, a Panamanian cargo vessel that tied up at the same dock from which the *Else TH* had departed. A cargo of Wolmanized lumber was discharged from the *Seapoint*, and then the container case left on the dock by the *Else*

TH was hoisted aboard. The container case had sat unexamined on the dock for about seven hours.

The *Seapoint* cast off its lines, eased from the harbor, and steamed southwest across the great blue expanse of the Caribbean Sea. Somewhere off Colombia's Guajira Peninsula the *Seapoint* delivered the cargo it had picked up in St. John's to a waiting yacht, took on another cargo, and continued on a southwesterly course through the Panama Canal and then up the Pacific coast. Several days later it was boarded by Mexican officials, who seized almost four tons of cocaine bound for San Diego.

It was not the cocaine that was to make the *Seapoint* infamous; rather, it was the cargo picked up in Antigua and off-loaded in Colombia. That cargo consisted of automatic weapons and 200,000 rounds of ammunition. The weapons went to Rodríguez Gacha, one of the top members of the Medellín drug cartel.

On December 16, 1989, Colombian security forces raided Gacha's ranch, and the cartel leader and many of his men were killed. Afterwards the security forces discovered a cache of automatic rifles there. Research showed that a gun from the cache had been used to assassinate a Colombian presidential candidate. The assassination had been a pivotal event in Colombia, as it showed the world the power of the cartel. And when an automatic rifle from the same batch as the assassination rifle was found, Colombian authorities were unyielding in their determination to discover the provenance of the weapons. The rifles were traced to Israel, which produced an end-user certificate showing the guns had been shipped to Antigua. An end-user certificate is a document signed by weapons buyers that attests the weapons are for them and will not be transferred to a third party without authorization from the seller. This information was enough for Colombia. Ponderous diplomatic machinery was set into motion.

On April 5, 1990, Foreign Minister Lester Bird received an official communiqué from the government of Colombia demanding to know how weapons purchased for Antigua had wound up in the hands of narco-terrorists. The end-user certificate had been signed by Vere Bird, Jr., as "Minister of Defense." A shaken Lester immediately called his older brother and said, "You are being accused of shipping arms to the drug cartel in Colombia. Do you know anything about it?"

"I don't know of any arms at all," Vere junior responded.

But the wall of secrecy had been breached. And over the next few months the greatest scandal in the history of the country would unfold. At the heart of the affair were Vere junior and bankrupt melon king Maurice Sarfati.

In the fall of 1988 Sarfati told Vere junior that he knew some people who wanted to open a training school for security agents and gave him several brochures about a company called Spearhead, Ltd., which was owned and operated by Yair Klein, a former colonel in the Israeli army and a man of considerable experience in commanding tactical combat groups. In November 1988, Klein came to Antigua to talk with Vere junior and with Colonel Clyde Walker, commander of the Antigua and Barbuda Defense Force. With Klein was Pinchas Shachar, a former brigadier general in the Israeli army who then was a Miami representative of Israel Military Industries (IMI), the commercial branch of the Israeli military.

At the time, the Medellín drug cartel had declared war on the Colombian government, raising and equipping private armies to conduct a campaign of terror. Judges, journalists, soldiers, police, as well as a presidential candidate, had been gunned down. Though it was not publicly known, the private armies of the cartel were hired and trained in large part by Spearhead, Ltd. What Sarfati represented to Vere junior as a school for security agents was in fact a school that trained terrorists and assassins.

When Klein and Shachar came to Antigua to meet with Vere junior, they said the school would be an arm of the Antigua and Barbuda Defense Force. Additional brochures stated that students at the school would be trained in techniques of assault and assassination. Students would need guns and ammunition, both of which would be provided by Shachar. Colonel Walker drove the two Israelis around the island and showed them the ideal spot for the training school—Crabbs Peninsula, which had remained a fenced and secure Defense Force area since the time of Space Research Corporation. Several days later the details for the terrorist school and the importation of weapons were worked out. Although all national defense responsibilities belong to the prime minister, Vere junior would give himself the title of minister of national defense and order the weapons from IMI through Sarfati, whom he appointed as official agent of the Antiguan government in the contract with IMI. And Jeff Hawley, the longtime bagman for the Birds, would play the role of the quartermaster general—an outmoded and nonexistent rank—of the Defense Force.

All of this ignored a basic issue: Since Grenada, weapons for Antigua and other Caribbean states had been supplied exclusively by the United States under an agreement called the Military Assistance Program. No weapons could be shipped to Antigua without the express knowledge and consent of the prime minister.

Lester Bird had no connection with the terrorist school. It appears that Vere junior mentioned it to him en passant as the two men were about to enter a Cabinet meeting and that Lester suggested that Vere junior not bring the issue of the training school before the Cabinet. There had been various newspaper stories about Israel helping South Africa build an atomic bomb, and for Antigua to have any connection with Israel could prove damaging to the ALP in the general election scheduled for March 9. Vere junior agreed and told his brother he would drop the idea.

(Lester's argument against Israel and South Africa shows what can only be described as a situational ethics at work. After all, Lester had been involved in sending artillery to South Africa. As for the Israelis, Sarfati had been on the island for several years in connection with the melon farm, and, in fact, remained a special envoy of the Antiguan government.)

Later, Vere junior sought to implicate Lester, saying his younger brother had agreed to the training school if the travel arrangements of all participants were booked through Peter Pan, Lester's travel agency. But this was a desperation move by Vere junior, for Peter Pan was not operational until 1990.

The prime minister may have been given a cursory overview of the school, but there is no indication he knew that guns would be shipped to Antigua.

That Vere junior could implement his plan without the knowledge of the Cabinet reveals much about how the government of Antigua works. Vere junior and Colonel Walker, with the connivance of subordinates in the Customs department, carried out the details. They were able to do so because part two of the Defense Act of 1981, calling for the creation of a National Security Council, was never implemented. This meant Vere junior could make arrangements with Israeli arms dealers without being hindered by a statutory body whose duty it was to oversee such activity.

The weapons were on the high seas, en route from Haifa to St. John's, when newspaper stories in America revealed that the drug cartel assassins in Colombia were being trained by Yair Klein and Spearhead, Ltd. There was great concern by Maurice Sarfati, Yair Klein, Pinchas Shachar, and probably Rodríguez Gacha, that the Antiguans would figure out the true nature of the school. Plans were quickly made to divert the weapons from Antigua to Colombia.

Vere junior continued to play a pivotal role in events. The guns bound for Antigua were invoiced at $353,700. But $381,500 was paid to IMI—a difference of $27,800. Vere junior almost certainly got part of this amount. Experts later estimated that the price in Colombia for a weapons shipment of this sort would be about $2 million, which meant that, even after expenses, there was a profit of more than $1 million. Again, it is likely that Vere junior got part of this amount.

The news flashed around the world that the son of the prime minister of Antigua, a man who also was a minister of government, had planned to open a school for assassins and was moonlighting as a gunrunner to the Medellín cartel. Vere junior denied everything. Not until virtually every person on Antigua knew of the gunrunning allegations through Tim Hector's paper or from listening to the powerful radio station in nearby Montserrat did *The Nation* and *The Worker's Voice* publish their versions of the story.

Lester Bird was even more aggressive than Tim Hector in getting out the word about Vere junior, seeing the scandal as a chance to forever eliminate his brother as a successor to their father. Lester bent himself to the task with a campaign as thorough as it was relentless.

Makeda Mikael, the "Iron Lady of Antigua," was put in charge of publishing a new newspaper—*On Line*. The paper contained a column by Lester entitled *Do the Right Thing*. One of Lester's first columns trumpeted that all Antiguans "expressed shame that their country is connected to so sordid an affair." A blizzard of press releases poured from Mikael's office. Lester even slashed away at the prime minister, who had ordered that no news of the allegations against his oldest son be broadcast. In one of his columns Lester said, "Indeed, a few persons in high authority actually censored the media. . . ." In another column, Lester wrote that there had been many attempts to cover up the gunrunning scandal, that Antigua was in a state of crisis, and that it was his duty as foreign minister to speak out. And then, anticipating those who would say he was trying to use his brother's political problems to vault into the office of prime minister, Lester published a column claiming he did not want the job of prime minister handed to him on a platter, that he wanted to run for the job. He warned that tourists would not come to a country where a minister of government was running guns to Colombian drug smugglers, and he proposed that Vere junior resign from his ministerial duties until the issue was resolved. But Vere junior refused to do so, and was present at every Cabinet meeting.

Lester hired Lawrence Barcella as a special agent of the Antiguan government to investigate the gunrunning affair. Barcella, a former federal prosecutor and a member of the Washington, D.C., law firm of Washington, Perito and Dubuc, was the man who had tracked down rogue CIA agent Ed Wilson. Barcella was sent to Israel to secure the crucial end-user certificate.

Lester also asked Interpol to become involved. He took, in his words, the "unusual step" of briefing U.S. and British officials on what, in a diplomatic sense, was a matter for the Antiguan government, asking the U.S. chargé d'affaires to issue a statement condemning the gunrunning. To ministers of foreign affairs throughout the Caribbean, Lester sent a six-page confidential memorandum encouraging them to speak out on the issue and to put pressure on his father. He ended the memo by saying, "I am deeply conscious that this is a most unusual memorandum and its urgings are unique in the history of the Caribbean community." He meant that Caribbean countries usually have no official position on internal matters of another country. Lester publicly and repeatedly called for his father to establish a judicial inquiry to investigate the gun-smuggling allegations and to ask Vere junior to resign.

But Prime Minister Bird remained loyal to his firstborn son. He said Vere junior had committed no wrongdoing. He would not force his son to resign, and he would not call for a judicial inquiry. When the governments of Colombia and Israel publicly accused Antigua of supplying weapons to the Medellín cartel, the prime minister ignored the accusations and would not respond to official inquiries from those governments. Instead he appeared on his son's cable television system and, in a statement with no basis in fact, claimed that reports from Interpol and from the United States proved Vere junior was not involved in the gunrunning deal.

But the prime minister was feeling the pressure. Vere junior was allowed to "go on leave" from his ministerial duties.

Tim Hector continued to publish stories about "Vere 'Gunrunner' Bird." Hector suspected there had been other shipments of weapons to Colombia and that this was the only one to have been detected.

Lester told a meeting of schoolchildren that "the good repute of Antigua and Barbuda has been sullied by irresponsible and unacceptable actions by a few people in significant positions in our country." Antiguans had "to face a barrage of accusations that the country is a cesspool of corruption; that iniquity is almost the order of the day; and that behind the facade of rapid development, there is an ugly picture of backbiting, political bickering and self-interest. . . . We deny ourselves a wealth of talent and experience simply because of old fashioned politics." In a copy of the speech that Vere junior mailed to me, he wrote in the margin, "Unrealistic. Pious Hypocracy" (*sic*).

Then Lester announced he would attend no Cabinet meetings until the prime minister called for a judicial inquiry. For several months much of the business of government ground to a halt as Lester Bird, deputy prime minister, minister of foreign affairs, minister of tourism and economic development, refused to attend Cabinet meetings.

On May 16 the prime minister caved in and agreed to the judicial inquiry. On the day the judicial inquiry was announced, Vere junior resigned as a minister of government.

Vere junior quickly assembled a team of five lawyers to represent him. They came from Antigua, Barbados, St. Kitts, and Dominica. But still needing a star lawyer to head the defense team, he approached Fenton Ramsahoye, a Guyanese lawyer with an outstanding reputation in Antigua, a reputation that had come from representing V. C. Bird's political opponents. The Guyanese advocate did not want to take Vere junior's case, and he sought to discourage Vere junior by saying his fee would be $400,000. In cash. In advance. Vere junior never blinked. He agreed.

A few weeks later Prime Minister Bird told the Cabinet that the government of Antigua should pay his son's legal fees. "Where Vere Bird to get the money to pay for these lawyers?" he asked in his rough dialect. Members of the Cabinet, perhaps thinking of how much money Vere junior had allegedly made from the airport resurfacing project, from the desalinization project, from Maurice Sarfati's melon farm, and from the arms deal, did not respond.

"Vere Bird's legal fees going to cost him over one million dollars," the prime minister said. The old man paused, looked down, and repeated, "One million."

(It remains unclear today whether the government paid the legal fees. The Bird government borrows money from local businessmen and has numerous convoluted dealings with the business community in which large amounts of cash are exchanged. Tim Hector says the legal fee was hidden inside these transactions.)

The inquiry began July 16. Blom-Cooper wanted to hear witnesses in St. John's and then, in order to explore fully the international scope of the allegations, go to London and Tel Aviv. Ramsahoye's first victory was a declaratory judgment preventing the inquiry from sitting anywhere other than Antigua.

During the hearing, Vere junior denied any complicity in the arms deal and lashed out at everyone around him, including his secretary, a middle-aged woman who had served him for years. He said he had been duped by the Israelis, that the signature on the end-user certificate was a forgery.

One of the more unusual aspects of the hearings was the failure of the United States government to cooperate in the inquiry, even though narcotics trafficking had become the prime U.S. interest in the Caribbean and even though this was a clear example of a foreign official smuggling weapons to the Medellín cartel. When Blom-Cooper formally requested the U.S. Senate to provide him with bank records in Miami, the Senate, which then had a committee conducting hearings on arms trafficking, refused.

Blom-Cooper was disturbed by the intransigence of the United States. In his final report, he wrote that the gunrunning conspiracy "was hatched in Miami," and that "given the much-publicized 'war on drugs' waged against the Colombian cartels by successive American administrations, one would expect that this conspiracy to arm the Medellín drug cartel would have engaged the early and intensive scrutiny of American authorities . . . all the more so because the funds to purchase the weapons were transmitted through an American bank, Manufacturers Hanover Trust, to the New York branch of Bank Hapoalim, bankers to both Brig.-Gen. Shachar and Israel Military Industries (IMI)."

Other than the signature on the end-user certificate, the most important evidence was the source of the money that had been used to buy the guns. Lawrence Barcella asked a Senate committee to open U.S. banking books and reveal the origin of funds used to finance the Antiguan arms transaction. Once again, the Senate refused.

Blom-Cooper did not like this. "I find it wholly unacceptable that banks in America, whose services were used to facilitate what can without exaggeration be described as a crime against humanity, should be permitted through the inaction of the American authorities to hide evidence of that crime behind the cloak of confidentiality," he said.

Because the judicial inquiry was not a trial, the findings had no legal significance and the recommendations little weight. Nevertheless, they were awaited with great anticipation, and the prime minister said he would make the report public. But he was concerned that before he could do so, Tim Hector would publish the findings in *Outlet.*

Hector had been sued so many times by the government that, as a defense measure, he often printed copies of official government documents to substantiate his stories, particularly extremely sensitive ones. Blom-Cooper, back in London, sent only six copies of his report to Antigua—five to the Prime Minister and one to the governor-general. (Lester was furious that he did not receive one.) The prime minister secretly ordered that each copy of the report be coded so that whoever leaked a copy to Tim Hector could be identified. Just as the prime minister feared, in the next issue of *Outlet* Antiguans learned the details of Blom-Cooper's findings. Hector also learned of the coded reports, and when he published a page from the report, the code revealed that his documents had come from the prime minister's office.

Even though the prime minister had said he would make the Blom-Cooper report public, it, like the findings regarding the airport-resurfacing project, was never officially released. (Opposition members obtained a copy that was later printed in book form and sold in Antigua.)

The U.S. State Department, in a reference to the judicial inquiry, said government radio and television on Antigua "engaged in deliberate disinformation, lifting certain statements from the testimony and repeating them out of context to make them seem more favorable to the possibly implicated officials. Under extreme public pressure, the Government agreed to broadcast the hearings in their entirety, but began editing the testimony, reportedly for length, especially during the critical final week. This culminated in the deletion of the entire final day's testimony."

Blom-Cooper's report was scathing in its denunciation of what he called "unbridled corruption" in Antigua. And he was unstinting in his comments about Vere junior: "I entertain no doubt that Mr. Vere Bird Jr. was paid by, or at least with, money emanating from Senor Rodriguez Gacha, for the services rendered to the arms transshipment." And of Vere junior's cross-examination, he said, "I found his answers to questions evasive, irrelevant, or plain lies." Vere junior's behavior showed him to be a "thoroughly unprincipled man. Together with his mendacity and his behavior during this Inquiry, there is no room left to doubt that he was a conspirator in the plot to import guns and ammunition from Israel to Antigua for the use of a military training school to train mercenaries for illegal forces in Colombia."

Maurice Sarfati's appointment as a special envoy of the Antiguan government by a minister, and not by the governor-general as the law required, was not only invalid, it was "another instance of the failure of government to observe the rule of law." And the Antiguan government's failure to implement both the Defense Act of 1981 and the position of government ombudsman as called for by the constitution were paradigms "of the triumph of political power over the process of democratic government."

Blom-Cooper recommended that Vere junior never again hold ministerial appointment on Antigua and that Colonel Walker be immediately discharged. And he held out the hope that the report from the judicial inquiry would be used as the basis for legal proceedings against those involved in the gunrunning.

But in every quarter, the fallout from the report was minimal. As with every other scandal made public on Antigua, nothing happened that would prevent a similar occurrence in the future.

Blom-Cooper showed great naïveté when he wrote, "There can be little doubt that the findings of this report will be a severe blow to Mr. Vere Bird Jr. personally and to his father, the Prime Minister. I am not unaware of the unswerving support which the father has bestowed on his elder son throughout these trying times. Still more, Mr. Vere Bird Jr. may yet face further inquiries; as and when his bank accounts have been thoroughly examined, he may have to face civil proceedings for the recovery of any ill-gotten gains. It is quite possible, however, that he will become both politically and socially an outcast in Antigua and even in neighboring Caribbean countries. All of these consequences that may befall Mr. Vere Bird Jr. are more than ample to satisfy a public demand for punishment."

The truth is that Vere junior suffered, at most, a temporary embarrassment. The loyalty Vere junior engenders in his constituents is such that he can be elected to office for as long as he chooses to run. Today Vere junior is his father's closest and most influential adviser, his spokesman and his strong right arm. While he has no portfolio and is not a member of the Cabinet, he is the second most powerful man on Antigua. No further inquiry was made into his financial affairs, nor did any civil proceedings follow the judicial inquiry.

As for Colonel Walker, he was allowed to resign with full pay. The prime minister could not afford to be too harsh with the colonel; through Colonel Walker's good offices, Cutie Francis imports the goods for her boutique duty-free. The Antigua and Barbuda Defense Force continued to receive classified briefings and intelligence information on narcotics and defense matters from the U.S. military.

As for Lester, he miscalculated badly. He was so vocal and so vehement in his opposition to his brother that his carefully orchestrated campaign backfired. On Antigua, one's family is of paramount importance. To sling so much mud on one's brother is considered bad form. Lester suffered a serious political setback in his campaign to succeed his father, and he knows it.

Lawrence Barcella will not discuss the exact amount of money his law firm billed the government of Antigua for its work during the investigation other than to say it was "a significant amount." Whatever the amount, the Bird government, client number 65928.0014, did not pay its bill; and not long afterwards the firm went out of business. The Antiguan government's default was, according to Barcella, a "contributing factor."

In October 1990, shortly after the Blom-Cooper report was published, the Antiguan Chamber of Commerce called for the resignation of the entire government. A pastoral letter signed by the leaders of Antigua's largest churches said Antigua was in a "crisis born of greed and selfishness" and that "a pall of disillusionment and despondency hangs over the nation." Again, the prime minister took notice that several of the church leaders were from Jamaica and rumbled about having them deported. Again he accused the Reverend Neville Brodie of trying to destabilize his government.

I wanted to talk about the gunrunning scandal with Roger Gamble, who had been quite candid in our conversations, but other than his earlier statement that Vere junior had broken no laws and would receive no punishment, Gamble would only say, "That is strictly a matter for the governments involved—Colombia, Israel, and Antigua—to resolve." He would not be drawn into a conversation on U.S. policy deliberations.

At no time before, during, or after the judicial hearings did any State Department official issue a public comment on what it meant to the United States when a minister of a government friendly to America was found to be involved in setting up a school for assassins and in running guns to the Medellín cartel.

One State Department official privately stated the reason was simple: no one really cared. The Caribbean is so far down the list of State Department priorities that there is virtually no interest in what happens there. This official also said the only news that ever comes out of Antigua is bad news, and "we wouldn't care if the place just went away."

Another State Department official had a different scenario. The official pointed out that Vere junior has a green card and can live and work in America anytime he chooses. The State Department feared that, if U.S. banks had revealed the source of the money that financed the weapons deal or if the State Department publicly criticized Vere junior for his role in the gun smuggling, the prime minister's oldest son might have fled to America. Because the State Department did not want him living in America, the U.S. government withheld crucial evidence and remained silent.

Since Grenada, America has been the most powerful voice in the Caribbean. Yet America not only gave its tacit approval to Vere junior's gun-smuggling activities but it also was indirectly responsible for his political survival and his increased power in the Antiguan government.

Like his father before him, Vere junior has become a dependent of the United States government.

25

Giant Malt

Roger Gamble was musing about who would succeed Prime Minister Vere Cornwall Bird and, as usual, Lester Bird's name was at the top of the list. "He is by far the most qualified man to run this government," Gamble said. "He is articulate. He could go to a formal dinner at the White House and not embarrass Antigua." Gamble paused. "But Vere junior is the old man's favorite. The inquiry on the gunrunning almost certainly will implicate him. But Vere junior has broken no Antiguan law. In a legal sense, all he did was impersonate a minister of defense, a nonexistent office. The perception is harmful, but the old man would never allow Vere junior to go to jail. Now, if the old man dies in office and there is a secret vote, someone else, a third person such as John St. Luce, might have a chance at the job. But if it is in public, the third person will never have a chance; Lester will wheel and deal St. Luce out of existence. The old man has the power to put Lester in the job. He could do it now. The old man is a political animal. He will go straight down the family members and see who will work out. If it is Lester, promises and accommodations will have to be made for Vere junior."

"What sort of promises and accommodations?"

Gamble smiled and shrugged. "Promises that Lester will not prosecute him. And some accommodation, if not in the Cabinet, where he will be left alone."

As I left for an appointment at Lester's office, Gamble offered a bit of advice: "Ask him about the Deep Bay Project. Donald Trump tried to buy it, but they turned him down and they won't talk to us about the negotiations. And you might ask him about his citizenship. He is a U.S. citizen who holds a high position in a foreign country. We understand he tells people he has renounced his U.S. citizenship."

The best way to make sure Lester will be present for a meeting is to go through his administrative assistant, Makeda Mikael. Mikael is a Kittician whose skills as a businesswoman—she once owned a travel agency—made her a natural for Lester's staff when he was minister of tourism. This bold and brainy woman who calls herself "The Iron Lady of Antigua" is a controversial figure and the subject of many stories, the most intriguing of which is that when she was a young woman she went through a period as a Rastafarian and lived high in the Antiguan hills in a village called One Love. It is said that she rode naked through the hills on a donkey.

Mikael's loyalty to Lester is unbending. Acting as his agent she would confront the Devil. She was so protective of Lester's interests in Cabinet that other ministers, led by Vere junior, forced Lester to take her off the government payroll, whereupon Lester appointed her assistant secretary and a director of the Deep Bay Development Company, a title that belies her true power as Lester's alter ego. She is the person who guards his door and who whispers in his ear. When I met Mikael, her office was adjacent to Lester's office at Heritage Quay. On her desk were several telephones and Lester's private fax machine. On the wall was a framed bit of calligraphy, a quote from Langston Hughes: "Go slow, I hear— / . . . Don't demonstrate! Wait! / While they lock the gate." It is from this office that Mikael vetted various visitors. One group of American businessmen did not get past her because they were dressed too casually. "Lester is a minister of government, the deputy prime minister of this country," she said. "Visitors should be dressed appropriately."

Even though I had met Lester in 1982 and had talked with him at various times over the telephone, and even though I had run into him atop Shirley Heights a few days earlier and he had asked me to make an appointment with Mikael, she decided that before I could interview him again, she and I needed to talk. "Outside writers tend to disparage and criticize Antigua," she said. "And I need to know where you're coming from." She decided the perfect place for us to talk was at a reception being held that afternoon at the Museum of Antigua and Barbuda. The reception was to celebrate the opening of a traveling display featuring replicas of the Crown jewels and a display of coronation regalia. "I don't usually go to these queen things," she said. "But this will give us a chance to talk."

It was late in the afternoon of a very hot day when I met Mikael at the museum, and we began drinking wine. Neither of us had had lunch, and the wine quickly took effect. During the speeches a number of glowing comments were made about the crown, the queen, and Great Britain. Fatigue and wine, combined with a usually subdued distaste for monarchs, prompted me to turn to Mikael and make an irreverent comment about the queen. Instantly embarrassed, I began to apologize. She brushed aside my apology and stared at me intently, a smile of approval on her face. "Now I understand you," she said exultantly. "I know where you're coming from. You like the underdog."

I did not know how she made this leap of logic. Nor did I want to lose the sudden and entirely unexpected camaraderie. So I shrugged and took another drink. My unfortunate comment had sliced through the barrier between us, and she now saw me as a kindred spirit rather than as a threat to Lester. The tight mask of self-control she had worn all evening slipped away as the two of us giggled and tried to outdo each other in our comments about England and the replicas of the Crown jewels. Our remarks escalated. Mikael made a remark about "these bloody replicas" as a representative of the British High Commission approached. He overheard her. Being British, he wanted to avoid a confrontation with the personal aide of the deputy prime minister, so he smiled tightly, nodded, spun on his heel and walked away. Mikael seized my arm and nodded toward the man. "That's the walk of a British civil servant," she said loudly. "He's an utter fart. He walks as if he has a stick up his ass."

"To hell with the queen," said I.

We laughed uproariously and retreated to a corner, where we continued to drink. After a while our conversation, as ultimately does almost every conversation on Antigua, turned to

Prime Minister Bird, his sons, and the question of succession.

"If the prime minister were anyone but Lester's father, Lester would have walked in and taken over," Mikael confided. "He would have taken it away from him. The prime minister is an old man living in another time. He has no foreign experience. The country is falling apart. Lester is fifty-one. You might say he is losing some of his best years waiting for the old man to die."

I stared in astonishment. Without thinking, I said, "If you thought you've had problems with the press in the past, if you have Lester take the government away from the prime minister, the world press would give you more heat than you can imagine."

Mikael shrugged. Her gaze was flat and unblinking. "Yes," she said. "But nothing we couldn't handle." It was clear that this was an option that had been discussed many times.

"Are you serious? You would really do that? What about Vere junior?"

Mikael snorted in disgust. "I wouldn't drink his soup," she said—an Antiguan expression of dismissal. "You can rule him out totally. The private sector would close this island down if Vere junior was prime minister. Investors would not put up with him. He is a doomsday machine for the Labour party."

"I've heard it said that the Birds run Antigua as if it were a private company."

"And why not?" she said crisply. "We are about the size of a major American company. Why should not a man run it like a business?" I looked at my drink. Had she deliberately chosen to misunderstand? A sardonic smile appeared on Mikael's face. "You've got to understand that this island is only one hundred and eight square miles."

"Why is Lester not willing to wait? After all, his father is an old man who is not going to live forever."

Mikael shook her head. "Lester laughs that he is the longest-serving deputy prime minister in the history of the Commonwealth, that he should be in the *Guinness Book of World Records*. He is in his best and most productive years. The old man is frail. This is a rapidly changing world. The old man is uneducated and has no global understanding. And Vere junior is robbing his father of the historical acclaim he so richly deserves."

Now Mikael was becoming a bit nervous about the direction of the conversation. "Tell me," I said, changing the topic, "were you once a Rastafarian? Is it true that you rode a donkey naked through the hills?"

"Yes. I was a Rastafarian for a while. But I never rode naked through the hills." She paused and weighed me with her eyes, wondering if she should say what was on the tip of her tongue. As usual, she charged ahead. "You could never become a Rastafarian," she said. "You aren't the right color."

Mikael and I talked again the next day at lunch. She invited me to a reception honoring the Chinese, who had built a bridge on the west side of the island. And finally she decided it was okay for me to meet with Lester. When I came to her office, she took me to a room that contained a stack of large boxes. The boxes contained hundreds of red caps emblazoned with white letters—ALP colors—that said either LESTER LUV ANTIGUA or ANTIGUA LUV LESTER. "Wear one of these," she said. "He will like that." I put on a hat that said ANTIGUA LUV LESTER.

Lester was in a small conference room in the suite of offices he then had over the Gucci store at Heritage Quay. He was in the middle of a meeting with a government minister and a young Canadian business consultant. He glanced up from a stack of papers, smiled and nodded in approval at my cap, then looked at his watch. He wanted our talk to be a short one. He took the initiative by asking, "Did you see my father the other day? I saw you at his office."

"No, he had a bit of a conflict," I said. Lester was as bold as he was disingenuous. I realized why he was called "Giant Malt" as a boy.

We talked about the gunrunning affair, the ill health of his father, and the question of succession. "Will you be elected prime minister?" I asked.

Lester responded as if he were campaigning. He threw his arms wide and raised his voice as if to reach the last person in the last row at an outdoor political rally. "In a democracy, one can never be absolute. As for my qualifications, I have been in office since 1976 representing this country in all manner of affairs. I have supervised tourism and economic development during our most productive period. My track record shows I am as qualified as anyone in Antigua. The only argument against me is that the Birds have been in office too long. I accept that. But if my name were not Bird, it would be clear that I was the best candidate. And I do take some offense that—simply because my name is Bird—my contributions go by the board."

"What about the question of dynasty? Some have compared the Birds of Antigua to the Duvaliers of Haiti. Is that a valid comparison?"

Lester grimaced in impatience. Like a seasoned politician, he ignored the question he did not like—the comparison with the Duvaliers—and spoke to the dynasty issue. "This is not the only dynasty. Michael Manley is the son of the previous prime minister of Jamaica. And you have the Kennedy family in the U.S."

The meeting with Lester was difficult. He constantly glanced at his watch and this gave me a sense of urgency. The minister of government who sat to his left laughed and ridiculed almost every question I asked. The young Canadian business consultant slumped in his chair and stared straight ahead.

Vere junior was very much on Lester's mind, perhaps because the world's press had been beating a path to Antigua in recent months to talk about the gunrunning business. He had a quiver full of comments about his older brother. "I was chairman of the party from 1976 until now," Lester said. "Vere was not in Cabinet until 1984—eight years after I was supervising the economy of the country."

"So how does Vere junior continue to be elected? And with the greatest majority of any elected official in the country?"

"It is rooted in the trust toward the prime minister. My father led the nation from the colonial time forward. I came in the party at the lowest ebb. I paid my dues. I did not come in on the wings of the prime minister."

"What will be the long-term effect of the gunrunning scandal?"

Lester shrugged. "Tourism is a volatile and mercurial industry. We are concerned about this whole area, that this is a bad signal in the marketplace. We are so concerned, in fact, that this year we will begin advertising on American television for the first time."

"Why is Antigua the only country in the eastern Caribbean not to sign the Tax Information Exchange Agreement, an agreement to open bank accounts and trade information regarding drug smugglers and money launderers?"

"While we don't wish to be a haven for money launderers, we believe those agreements must be geared to the idiosyncrasies of each individual island."

I waited. But that was all he was going to say on the issue.

"How will Antigua handle its enormous debt load?"

"We believe we must borrow money to provide a catalyst for development." Lester shrugged. "Half the debt is from fluctuations in foreign currency. Thirty-five percent of the debt has been rescheduled, rolled over, and we are trying to reschedule the remainder." He pointed a finger at me. "You must remember the cruise ship market here is growing faster than the hotel business."

"Back to the succession question. Do you expect your brother to run against you?"

"Perhaps. There may be competition from my brother. But at the end of the day I will have more support at the convention. I have no intention of sitting in a back room like your Tammany Hall and saying, 'You have this many votes. I have that many plus one.' I must have a mandate. It will take a mandate to lead the country out of the trauma caused by a member of my family. And I believe I can get a mandate from the party convention."

Lester stared at me for a moment. "People say the Birds have been in office too long. But the U.S. should understand we are a friendly government. We recognize the colossus to the north, and we know we are a microcountry. But what we don't want is to be a lackey of the U.S."

I reminded Lester that even though he talked of a special relationship with the United States, he had a long history of opposing U.S. interests. He refused to turn over Robert Vesco. He opposed installation of the VOA antenna. He refused to sign the Tax Information Exchange Agreement. He opposed keeping Antiguan troops in Grenada, and he condemned the United States for "militarizing" the Caribbean. I asked him to take those issues one at the time and respond. Vesco first.

It was very difficult for Lester to control his anger. Almost never is he confronted and asked to explain himself, especially in matters regarding the United States. The minister who sat on his left snorted in anger. "Do like V. C. Bird does when these people come down," the minister said sharply. "Ignore him. Don't answer."

But Lester plowed ahead. "I should hope that the U.S. will harbor no resentment because of Vesco," he said slowly. "We were young in the game then. If we had to make that decision again, we would not do it." He leaned forward. "Do you know the real reason Robert Vesco came to Antigua?"

I waited.

"He was exploring the feasibility of low-income housing for Antiguans."

Lester sat back satisfied. "As for the VOA, we believe VOA was a cover for the CIA. I've told you why we don't sign the tax agreement. And it is a fact that the U.S. is militarizing the Caribbean. That has been true since Grenada."

Despite comments on U.S. militarization, mention of the bond between Antigua and the United States strikes a responsive chord with Lester. "You must remember that Antigua has a special relationship with the U.S.," he said. "Therefore, the U.S. should help us with the infrastructure. You should fix our roads. You should put a sewer system in the country. We can't continue to have open sewers in the streets."

Lester stood up, leaning over the table toward me, and waved his big arms. "We are not just a beach," he exclaimed. "We are a country, a people. We cry. We bleed."

Some unseen signal passed and Mikael pulled on my arm. The interview was over. Out in the hall I said there was much more I wanted to discuss, and I mentioned the Deep Bay project and said I wanted to know why Lester denied his U.S. citizenship.

"Come back tomorrow and we will see."

The next day Mikael and I were in her office. It was not clear if I would be allowed to see Lester, and she was discussing the issues I had raised the previous day. I said that records at the U.S. embassy show Lester is a U.S. citizen and that he petitioned the State Department to grant citizenship to his "four legitimate children" in America. She dismissed this by saying Lester had renounced his U.S. citizenship, and then she turned to Deep Bay and Donald Trump.

"Trump flew down on his jet," she said. "He had his yacht down here. He was impressed with Antigua and how safe the island is. He thought he had found the Caribbean hideaway he had been looking for. He offered us one dollar for the hotel and said he would pick up the loan. I was part of the negotiating team. It was a great gamble."

I told Mikael that Trump's offer seemed to be a good one. After all, the projected cost of the hotel had been about $49 million and fluctuations in the money market had pushed the cost to almost $100 million. The hotel, then appraised at about $40 million, was not generating enough revenue to retire the loan. The project was an enormous drain on Antigua's burdened treasury.

The suggestion that Lester might have erred in not accepting Trump's offer opened the gate. "Trump wanted seventy-five percent of the hotel," Mikael said. "He would put his name on it, guarantee high occupancy, use a helicopter to ferry guests from the airport. And he wanted a special customs facility for his guests. He said our twenty-five percent ownership under him would be worth more than our one hundred percent ownership without him. We turned him down."

I looked up as the door flew open. Lester stood there with his eyes blazing in anger. "I understand you think we should have sold the Royal Antiguan Hotel for one dollar to Donald Trump," he said. He was almost shouting. "Well I don't care if it was Donald Trump or Jesus Christ, I would not accept such an arrangement." He raised his hands high in the air. "I will not be Trumpized," he said. "Trump was just another investor."

I was baffled. Mikael and I had been talking in a normal conversational tone, certainly not loud enough to be overheard outside her office. How did he know what we were talking about?

"And you ask about my being a U.S. citizen," Lester continued. "Several years ago I renounced my citizenship. It was at a political speech in 1976. This rock is my home." His voice boomed throughout the office. "When I go to America and people see I was born in the U.S. but have an Antiguan passport, they say to me, 'Why do you want to live in Antigua?' And I just smile."

He waved in dismissal. "I expected more than this from someone from a developed country," he said. He began to back out of the office. But he had a parting shot. "There are many signs of progress on Antigua," he said. "But if—when—I become prime minister, the best is yet to come. All the improvements, all the progress will be as nothing." He smiled a great beatific smile. "You ain't seen nothing yet." And he closed the door.

A few minutes later I left and drove up the hill toward the embassy. The question of Lester's citizenship stuck in my mind. The idea of a U.S. citizen being deputy prime minister of a foreign country was intriguing, especially when he stood a good chance of becoming the next prime minister.

At the embassy, Gamble asked a consular officer to bring up Lester's records. "We have nothing at all that indicates he renounced his U.S. citizenship," the consular officer said. "In fact, he fought to maintain it."

How?

The consular officer said the question first came up in 1981, when the State Department could not make a decision on whether Lester had lived long enough in the United States to satisfy residency requirements that would allow him to pass along his citizenship to his children. The question was never one of whether Lester was a citizen. Apparently the issue languished undecided until April 25, 1988, when, according to an "operations memorandum" in Lester's file, he appeared at the embassy and asked to "transfer his citizenship to his four legitimate children." When the consular officer said the residency requirements had not been satisfied, Lester said embassy records were wrong and demanded that his citizenship be transferred to his children. It was done

"The U.S. government caved in?"

The consular officer shrugged, pursed his lips, and stared at the folder. "He is a senior minister of a government friendly to the United States."

I turned to Gamble. "Lester says he renounced his citizenship. He said he did it at a political rally."

Gamble snorted. "Well, goddamn. He might as well stand in the middle of the goddamn ocean and say, 'I renounce.' I don't care what he says to you, or what he says at a speech, our records show that Lester Bird is a U.S. citizen."

"Does he pay income taxes?"

The consular officer snapped the folder shut and looked at Gamble. Gamble stared at the floor for a long moment. "That's an interesting question," he said.

26

Playing Warri with God

In the summer of 1991, the mental hospital on Antigua was so understaffed that inmates were stationed at the front gate to admit visitors. At Holberton Hospital there was a chronic shortage of essential supplies such as the reagents used to test blood and urine. Drugs often were borrowed from a hospital on St. Kitts, and several times the Montserrat police rushed emergency medical supplies to Antigua. At the Fiennes Institute, the government home for the poor and the indigent, men regularly came through a hole in the fence to rape female patients. One retarded woman was raped almost nightly for months.

The inability of the Bird government to care for the sick and the infirm was a searing metaphor for the increasing disintegration of almost every aspect of Antiguan life. Freebooting predacity became so common that the Antiguan Chamber of Commerce, the last organization one would expect to go public in such matters, published a series of surprisingly blunt newsletters in 1991 and 1992. One such letter said government avarice and thievery had sifted down to the private sector and that Antigua was beset with crime; that "major embezzlements" had been reported from airline offices, banks, and stores. Some employees had been caught stealing money at two or three jobs, according to the chamber. A feeling existed that one could not be held accountable for crime. After all, Antigua had gone through an inquiry into the airport resurfacing scandal, another inquiry on the melon farm scandal, and a third inquiry into the gun-smuggling allegations, and no punishment had been meted out to the principal figures involved. Vere junior remained one of the most powerful men on Antigua. The atmosphere of corruption "permeated the minds of smaller individuals," according to the chamber. The newsletter ended by saying, "If these practices continue, if drastic measures are not imposed, if strong stands are not taken, if culprits escape the weight of the law, our society will continue to deteriorate rapidly, and tomorrow will find very few who could cast the first stone."

The Antigua Christian Council of Churches issued a pastoral letter saying the country was in "deep troubled water" caused by the "lack of accountability and the presence of gross dishonesty in the public sector. A pall of disillusionment and despondency hangs over the nation." The prime minister remembered from his own experience how an association with God can be translated into political power—that's why an Antiguan law forbids clerics to hold elective office—so he attacked the Reverend Orland Lindsay, who, as the Anglican archbishop of the West Indies, was the ranking cleric on Antigua. Bird said Lindsay, a Jamaican, was vexed because Antigua was "making progress" and that the cleric held a grudge against "Antigua man." And Bird reminded his listeners that he had delivered them from a time when the land was covered with "cattle, horse, and donkey mess," a time when they had been forced to eat cockles and widdy widdy bushes and drink pond water.

But the Christian Council was not deterred. The clerics asked the government to call on Scotland Yard to assist local police in investigating numerous firebombings. Vere junior's newspaper responded with outrage at this "offense" to local police.

To outsiders, the signs of Antigua's descent were everywhere. Americans living on the island grew tired of their letters being opened by Antiguan postal workers, and many of them cultivated friends at one of the U.S. military bases and had their mail routed through the military mail system.

British Airways served notice that in 1992 it would end its exclusivity arrangement with Antigua and Barbuda Airways, the shell company established by Vere junior when he was minister of aviation. Much of Europe was about to be united in an economic consortium, one facet of which would be airline deregulation. In addition, British Airways did not like the adverse publicity the arrangement with ABA was generating, especially when load factors on the London–Antigua route made it unafraid of competition—it could fly at almost 100 percent occupancy without paying Vere junior's company $280,000 each year and without giving away a hundred free seats to Antiguan officials. Nevertheless, when aviation charter companies from the United Kingdom wanted to fly to Antigua—a business that the Chamber of Commerce said would bring the country about $7 million annually, most of it during the summer tourism slump—the Antiguan government refused. Charters were allowed from the United States, Canada, and Europe. But the arrangement with British Airways allowed no competition on the London route. When BWIA asked for permission to fly to Heathrow, the Antiguan government refused. Not until the summer of 1992, in the face of overwhelming pressure from the business community, were charters from the United Kingdom allowed and BWIA given permission to fly to Heathrow.

At the Ramada Renaissance, the official hotel of Antigua, occupancy was down and crime was up. A series of muggings involving American women stationed at the Navy base took place almost at the front door of the hotel. At a restaurant almost next door to the Ramada Renaissance, cars were regularly broken into and expensive items stolen.

The commanding officer at the Navy base was stopped on suspicion of driving under the influence of alcohol. In a bellicose fashion he announced to the police that he was commanding officer of the Navy base and should not be ticketed. He called an Antiguan a "goddamn nigger." Within days he was shipped out and replaced by Lieutenant Commander Tim Quitter, a smooth and urbane officer with two master's degrees in international affairs.

U.S. chargé d'affaires Bryant Salter was a man looked up to and admired by many Antiguans, but he had almost no credibility at the State Department. Salter, who golfed several times each week with Lester Bird, was playing in a tournament to benefit local police when his official embassy car was broken into and his diplomatic passport and briefcase were stolen. He said there were no classified papers or any documents in the briefcase that might prove embarrassing to America. State Department officials were told that Bryant Salter was involved in several Antiguan real estate investments with Lester Bird. But

Salter had been investigated twice. Even though no charges were filed, no one wanted to go after him again.

That he was allowed to continue as the senior State Department representative in Antigua is indicative of America's attitude toward the island. That a series of incompetent appointees were named ambassador to Barbados—where they represented America to numerous countries in the eastern Caribbean—is indicative of America's attitude toward the region. Unless another Maurice Bishop springs into Caribbean prominence, or unless the Birds become mixed up in a bloody battle that involves U.S. citizens, nothing will change.

At V. C. Bird International Airport the runway surface was deteriorating. American Airlines, Antigua's economic lifeline, was demanding repairs. During the 1991–92 season, America was in a recession and Antigua's tourism business dropped more than 25 percent. The hotel at Mill Reef—the ultimate "upmarket" destination—had a 47 percent drop in reservations. The Bird government of Antigua was so near financial collapse that it closed its tourism office in Germany, while tourism offices in London, Toronto, Washington, and New York tottered on the edge of collapse. For-sale signs hung on a half-dozen hotels in Antigua. But yet, when a European newspaper criticized the unreasonably high costs on Antigua, the director general of tourism, Yvonne Maginley, said, "The more I look at places like Cancún, the more I am happy that we are up-market, because there is no point in having thousands of people come to your country if they have no spending power." The prime minister went on government radio and said not enough people were coming to "my island," and those who were coming were not spending enough money.

Looming ever larger as a threat to tourism was Cuba, which was building three thousand new hotel rooms a year in the early 1990s.

Robert L. Crandall, president of American Airlines, addressed the Caribbean Hotel Association in San Juan, and gave a dozen or so ministers of tourism a taste of the new reality. He spoke from the standpoint of a man whose company "owns" the all-important U.S.–Caribbean routes. He reminded those present that tourism in the Caribbean accounts for a higher percentage of gross domestic product than in any other region in the world and that, while one would expect local people to do everything possible to encourage tourism, "the reality is frequently indifference—and sometimes even obstructionism." He pointed out that one reason the Caribbean is losing market share to Hawaii and Mexico is because Caribbean hotels are outdated and offer poor services. Tourists do not want to go to islands where there are dirty beaches, crime, drugs, and rude local people. Shape up and become professional or risk losing U.S. tourists was his message.

Afterwards, Crandall offered to meet individually with various tourism ministers so he could discuss the problems on their particular island. Dr. Rodney Williams, who had replaced Lester Bird as Antigua's minister of tourism, used his private audience to gripe that, while he was American Airline's designated physician in Antigua, he did not have free first-class tickets on the airline. Crandall, outraged, tossed Williams out of the room.

In 1991, Lester Bird, on a matter of "principle," resigned from government. He explained that he wanted the full implementation of the Blom-Cooper report (a polite way of saying Vere junior should be out of government), an investigation into the questionable issuance of more than EC$4 million in promissory notes, legal measures to stop the increasing governmental corruption, and the opening up of government radio and television to members of the opposition. Lester convinced three other ministers to resign with him. The prime minister assumed the portfolio of finance minister and filled the vacancies left by Lester and his friends. His annual budget presentation lasted about five minutes. Lester said no budget can exist until its full details have been presented to Parliament, that the government was "in the midst of a constitutional crisis," and that the prime minister should resign. In reply, the prime minister went on government television and reminded Antiguans of how, until he became the leader of the country, they had been eating widdy widdy bushes and drinking pond water, and that the country had been covered with "cattle and horse and donkey mess."

Lester took to the streets, marching with Tim Hector in a protest against the ALP—the party of which he was chairman. He was photographed under a banner that proclaimed the government—in which he had held various crucial portfolios and been deputy prime minister—was corrupt. Lester attacked his father, his brother, his trade union, his political party, and his government.

But Lester missed the power that goes with being a minister of government. Several months later he met with his father and asked to be allowed to come back into government. When the prime minister relented, Lester issued a statement saying he had left on principle and was returning on principle. After being given a new junior portfolio as minister of planning, Lester stood up in Parliament and said his father should be declared a national hero. In his new ministerial quarters at Heritage Quay, Lester may be the only minister of government in the Caribbean whose offices are in a hotel.

John St. Luce, the former minister of finance who had resigned with Lester, returned to government as minister of information. He, too, opened a new suite of offices and pledged that *The Nation* and government broadcast media would become more open and more available to opposition political leaders.

When the Cabinet members, none of whom knew about Lester and John St. Luce coming back into government until it was a done deal, complained to the prime minister, he told them it was *his* government and *his* Cabinet, and he would do as he pleased. When one minister protested, the prime minister angrily turned on him and said, "You just shut up, boy." A few days later the prime minister, upon hearing that several ministers were threatening to go public in their accusations against him, reminded them he had the power to dissolve Parliament and call an election. In the ninety days between the dissolution of Parliament and the election, he would be the sole governing authority; and the ministers would not be allowed on television or radio while his own field of candidates would be given unlimited air time. He also indicated that if his government fell, they all might go to jail, so they had better stay loyal. Armed with this new and better understanding of politics, the ministers reaffirmed their loyalty to the Father of the Nation.

In Antigua, if someone dies who has not regularly attended church, the body goes from the funeral home to the cemetery. It is, as they say locally, "not churched." This practice, known as a "straight flight," is thought to endanger the soul of the recently departed, and the threat of a "straight flight" is one way local clerics make sure the members of their flock stay in the fold. By denying disloyal politicians the heaven of television time and threatening them with jail, V. C. Bird has perfected the secular version of "straight flight."

After Cutie Francis heard that Lester was back in government she exploded in anger. She complained that "V"—as she calls the prime minister—"did this deal behind my back," and she fought for days to have Lester tossed back on the street. But Cutie had lost her power base. She had been publicly accused of having an affair with Dr. Rodney Williams, the man who had succeeded Lester as minister of tourism and the man she supported for Lester's old job as deputy prime minister. (She bought Dr. Williams a ring costing $32,000, but it was not enough to hold his loyalty. He was caught in a compromising situation with another woman, and he and Cutie had a tumultuous parting.) About the same time, Lester and Vere junior decided that Cutie was the cause of all the prime minister's problems. When they threatened to physically throw her out of the prime minister's house, she quickly packed up and moved to New York. Antigua's era of *Fotzepolitik* had ended. A few days later, Vere junior moved in with his father.

In 1991, another scandal about the sale of Antiguan passports erupted. The obvious duplicity of Antiguan officials in the matter was so brazen that people bearing a passport from this tiny Caribbean country became suspect around the world; they were questioned at length and their bona fides were at doubt solely because immigration authorities knew an Antiguan passport could be bought by anyone—no matter his criminal background—for a few dollars.

The BBC broadcast a television series called *Redemption Song* that chronicled the state of British colonies in the years after independence. The segment about Antigua concluded it was almost as poor as Haiti. The Bird government was criticized for the country's primitive electrical and telephone systems and narrow, potholed roads. The documentary forecast a bleak destiny for Antigua. The prime minister, in speaking of the BBC program at a public meeting, became so angry that he lost his balance and knocked over the podium.

Scotland Yard came to Antigua to investigate another scandal. Expensive cars were being stolen in London, hoisted aboard freighters, and taken to Antigua, where they were sold at bargain-basement prices. A number of Antiguan officials were driving the cars.

Within weeks after the disintegration of the Soviet Union a team of U.S. workers showed up on Antigua and dismantled the VOA transmitter. The reason for the radio station, fighting communism and preventing another Grenada, was gone. In perhaps the greatest irony of all, the collapse meant that the State Department suddenly needed embassies in the Soviet republics and the Baltics. Severe budget restraints meant existing U.S. embassies would have to close. High on the list were Grenada and Antigua. Eastern Europe was far more important than the eastern Caribbean. The Grenada embassy was downsized, the first step toward being closed, and the Antigua embassy was cut from six Americans and twenty Antiguans to three Americans and twelve Antiguans. Then the consular function was removed and Bryant Salter and his administrative officer were the only two Americans remaining.

Tim Hector broke the story that the consular office was closing. Several days later the embassy counted more than six thousand Antiguans lined up for visas. In less than a month, the U.S. embassy issued more than ten thousand visas. Tim Hector was too embarrassed to write the story. "It was the only time in my life I ever applied self-censorship," he told me. In recent years twenty thousand Antiguans had been issued American visas. Another ten thousand in the past month meant that half the Antiguan population wanted out.

While the U.S. embassy was downsizing as a step toward closing, the U.S. military presence held firm. The Navy facility remains open because of the extraordinary freedom America's underwater warriors have in training with explosives and in assaulting beaches. The Air Force station stays entrenched for three reasons. First, if the Air Force was forced to use Navy vessels to monitor missile launches, it would result in a split command. Interservice rivalry is too strong for that. Second, the Air Force likes having a solo operation in Antigua. Self-interest is a strong motivator. Third—and this applies also to the Navy base—to close the station would be too loud a declaration that U.S. interests in the Caribbean are lessening. The

United States looks at the Caribbean the way a street gang looks at a remote block in its turf: it may be neither necessary nor useful, but to abandon it would be seen as weakness.

Since the mid-1980s, America's primary objective in Antigua has been to increase cooperation against narcotics traffickers and money launderers. The best vehicle for this was the Tax Information Exchange Agreement, which Lester refused to sign. In 1991 Bryant Salter offered the Bird government $150,000 in State Department funds if Antigua would sign the agreement. The Bird government finally relented, and Antigua joined the battle to identify Caribbean money launderers. A few weeks later the Castle Harbour/Flamingo hotel suddenly closed.

In the weeks leading up to November 1, 1991—the tenth anniversary of Antiguan independence—the airwaves of Antigua were filled with rousing calypso songs. Many dealt with the themes of freedom or slavery or colonialism. During the celebrations, a first-time visitor to Antigua would never have known that Antigua had cast off slavery a full generation before the United States did, or that the country had been independent for a decade.

(When Prime Minister Bird was told that Minister of Information John St. Luce offered airtime to calypso singers who were not supporters of the ALP, the prime minister publicly humiliated St. Luce by ordering that the calypsonians not be allowed to sing on government television.)

No chiefs of state from neighboring Caribbean islands attended the tenth anniversary of independence. Antigua had become a pariah among Caribbean governments and a virtual outcast in the Organization of Eastern Caribbean States. On Independence Day, the prime minister was driven onto the parade field. He stepped out, walked a few feet to his chair, sat through perhaps twenty minutes of ceremonies, and was driven away without making a speech to his people.

A severe drought seized Antigua that fall, and some hotels were paying $40,000 per month for fresh water to be barged in from Dominica. The desalinization plant continued pumping fresh water back into the sea. For six days a week, the water pipes in many Antiguan homes were dry.

Early in 1992 the prime minister, for the first time in his years of public service, was publicly accused of personal wrongdoing. The eighty-two-year-old leader was caught stealing money from the government. Hector revealed that Prime Minister Bird approved the issuance of a $25,000 government check to a woman named Carla Samuel, ostensibly to pay for medical treatment in America. Parliament records were doctored to show the check had been approved by Parliament when, in fact, it had been issued unilaterally by the prime minister. No one in the Cabinet complained that official minutes had been tampered with, and the money wound up in the prime minister's personal bank account. The resulting furor reached such proportions that the Christian Council of Churches asked the prime minister for an explanation. He said he had been advised by his lawyers not to discuss the situation.

Hector began referring to the prime minister as "Vere 'Carla' Bird." The opposition embarked upon a protracted process of attempting to charge the prime minister with embezzlement, a chore they found extremely difficult both because of the aura surrounding Papa Bird and because the prime minister had appointed the officials who would have to bring the charges.

And then, on February 27, 1992, for what Hector said was a first in the history of a Commonwealth nation, the opening day of Parliament and the "throne speech" were picketed by hundreds of Antiguans. The opening, the biggest government event of the year, is steeped in the symbolism of the British empire; and the throne speech, delivered by the governor-general, is equivalent to a State of the Union Address by a U.S. president. The picketing was seen as a political and personal insult to the prime minister. He responded to this precedent-setting event with another precedent: he sent armed police to confront the demonstrators. With no warning, the police fired rubber bullets and tear gas canisters into the crowd. The crowd fled down the hill, crossed Queen Elizabeth Highway, and moved another hundred yards onto the grounds of a Catholic cathedral. The police pursued them, even firing tear gas on the cathedral grounds. More than two dozen demonstrators were arrested and charged with various offenses. Hector filled several issues of *Outlet* with news of what he called "Terror at Parliament Square."

The Chamber of Commerce wrote the governor-general that

its members deplored "very strongly the indiscriminate and unnecessary use of tear gas by the police to disperse what appeared to be a lawful and peaceful demonstration." The chamber claimed the demonstrators were gassed simply because they wanted an explanation of the $25,000 check. A few weeks later, after the Antiguan bar association agreed to represent the demonstrators free of charge, the charges were dropped. But the uproar continued. In Parliament, the speaker of the house, a longtime supporter of the prime minister, refused to allow opposition leader Baldwin Spencer to discuss the $25,000, thereby violating a fundamental principle of parliamentary democracy. He also made biting personal remarks against Spencer, seeking to provoke him so that the sergeant at arms could be called upon to eject him from the chamber.

The UNDP, the ACLM, and the PLM, the three long-feuding opposition political parties in Antigua, cast aside their considerable differences and decided to merge into a new party to fight the Bird government. The first national strike in the history of Antigua was called. It was only for one day, but the degree of cooperation was such that the country was indeed shut down for the day. One of the largest demonstrations in the history of Antigua, a crowd estimated at considerably more than ten thousand, paraded to show their support for the strike and the new political party. The bust of V. C. Bird that stands at the edge of the harbor was splashed and streaked with white paint.

When the annual convention of the Antigua Labour party approached, the supporters of V. C. Bird were everywhere. But now their red shirts, red ties, red belts, red trousers, red socks, and red shoes made them figures of derision—they were ridiculed as "red asses." The prime minister said that if the party picked a new leader he would step aside. Lester and John St. Luce, both of whom had earlier resigned from government and whose financial backing came respectively from Bruce Rappaport and from the Hadeed family, were the candidates. They spent the sort of money that usually is spent in a general election. The prime minister did as Roger Gamble had predicted. Realizing that Vere junior could not be the new leader, he campaigned for Lester. He got in his car and rode all over the island. It was an imperial sort of campaigning; he stopped at homes, summoned residents to his car, and asked them to vote for his son.

Lester's campaign showed just how far removed from reality a foreign minister can become. Historically, foreign ministers are rarely successful at becoming leaders of their countries. Lester issued a brochure showing him and Vere junior walking down the street. The caption read: "Take away the contribution of the Birds to Antigua and what do you have?" The arrogance of the statement so angered Antiguans that many began saying, "We got to manners Lester."

Vere junior campaigned for St. Luce. Lester played on the antipathy some Antiguans feel for Vere junior by saying St. Luce had promised Vere junior a senior ministerial post in return for his support.

When the 300 delegates voted, the results defied statistical probability. Lester and St. Luce had split the votes—150 each. Because the party had been unable to elect a new leader, the old leader remained: V. C. Bird was still in charge.

St. Luce looked upon the vote as a victory. I talked to him not long after the campaign and he was elated. "Considering the power of the Bird name, what I did was one hell of an accomplishment," he said. For him, the vote was pro–St. Luce rather than anti–V. C. Bird.

The country was in turmoil and bent on a course that engendered only more confusion. Edward Henry from the Museum of Antigua and Barbuda, the man who knows more about the environment than any other person in Antigua, had hoped to go to the Earth Summit in Rio de Janeiro that summer. But Dr. Rodney Williams, as the minister of economic development, did not pick him to be part of the delegation. Dr. Williams had little personal loyalty to the prime minister—after all, he had cuckolded V. C. Bird in his own home. But Dr. Williams did have political loyalty, a trait the prime minister prized above all others. Dr. Williams made a speech in the empty meeting room at Rio and said, "Today, environmental degradation is no longer acceptable." The conference "must conclude with a binding pledge by all nations to sharply curtail our environmentally harmful activities. . . . We thus dare to demand that the developed countries desist from conducting business as usual, for our existence is at stake." He also loosed a panegyric for V. C.

Bird. When the prime minister ordered ABS television to broadcast the speech, the tape of Dr. Williams standing before a podium was mixed with tapes showing a wildly applauding audience in Rio. It played well in Antigua.

A few weeks later Dr. Williams immersed Antigua in yet another international scandal. An Italian whom Dr. Williams had allowed special investment concessions was charged with tax evasion in Italy. But since the Italian was Antigua's consul in Rome, his diplomatic status prevented his government from prosecuting him.

Then came talk that Bruce Rappaport and Lester Bird were involved in an enormous $2.6 billion project for which Rappaport had been given permission to tear down the oil refinery and move it inside the national park on the south side of Antigua. All of Antigua was abuzz with how Rappaport was trying to buy property stretching from the present site of the refinery down to the fashionable beaches on the northwest corner of the island. Here he would build the biggest all-inclusive tourism complex ever constructed on Antigua.

Soon, an Antiguan calypso singer had a song that included the line, "I want to be around when the caged bird sings." One night his house, which was part of a large parcel of land needed for Rappaport's giant complex, burned to the ground, and it was said that he should not have embarrassed the Birds.

About this time the Haitian refugee situation became front-page news. The U.S. Navy base at Guantánamo Bay in Cuba was crowded with thousands of Haitians, and the State Department quietly and urgently appealed to countries throughout the Caribbean and in Central and South America to accept the Haitians. Most countries replied with a flat "no." One or two countries accepted a token number—a dozen or so people. Then the Bird government agreed to take the refugees if the United States would pay off a substantial portion of the country's foreign debt and if the consular function of the U.S. embassy would be reopened. By then, the Antiguan option was not necessary, because U.S. policy toward the Haitians changed.

All of these rumblings and portents reminded me of a conversation with Bryant Salter. We were in his office at the embassy and I sat in the same chair I had sat in during a decade of conversations with almost every chargé who had served in Antigua. I wondered aloud, since there was so much known about the Birds, what they might be doing that was not yet known, what might bubble up a few years later. Salter dismissed such speculation. He boiled Antigua down to what he saw as the distilled essence of the country. He said, "I would focus on people. But not government people. They are not part of the real story of Antigua. The real story here is that if people see you stopped by the side of the road, stopped because your car has broken down, they will pick you up and take you to where you were going. People here have a very positive attitude toward tourists."

He paused and looked at me. He smiled. But his eyes had the same cold thousand-yard-stare that Makeda Mikael's eyes had when she told me I was the wrong color to be a Rastafarian. Then he added, "You've got to drink ginger beer and eat fungi to really understand Antigua."

Epilogue

The tidal wave devours the shore,
There are no islands anymore.

—Edna St. Vincent Millay

All the grand old men are gone now. Bustamante, Manley, Adams, Burnham, Barrow, and all the others are retired or dead. Only V. C. Bird remains. He has been a national leader longer than anyone else in the Caribbean, longer even than Castro; and he is one of the few heads of state who have been in a position of power since before World War II. Honors have come his way—the airport named for him and a stamp minted in his honor—and honors have been denied him. He is one of the few grand old men of the Caribbean who has not been knighted by the British government.

Historians will see the reign of V. C. Bird as a time of lost opportunity. He committed many mistakes; but, in retrospect, one of the most crucial was abolishing personal income taxes. This caused Antiguans to believe Papa Bird and the ALP would take care of them and helped turn Antigua into a nation that expects handouts. Bird also failed to establish the needed moral tone for his nation. After the British departed and the fast-buck boys came calling, Bird and his sons did not have the backbone to resist.

None of this seems to have affected Bird. He marches to the drum of the trade unionist today as enthusiastically as he did that day in 1951, when he stood under the tamarind tree and confronted Moody-Stuart. He remains a man whose basic philosophy revolves around muscle and intimidation. He does not recognize that the trade union movement is a vestigial remnant of another time, and that developing a small island nation calls for more than threats and force. Nor does he recognize that Antigua is the last country in the Caribbean where government is a family business. He only knows that V. C. Bird and the widdy widdy bush reign supreme.

The scandals that began in 1978 and galloped unchecked through the 1980s and into the 1990s will continue in Antigua. This is a country whose infamy was nurtured and developed in the bosom of its relationship with America. But the day is coming when someone in the Antiguan government, most likely a man named Bird, will go too far; a crime or a scheme will be revealed that is of such amoral dimensions and such unholy implications that the U.S. government will be forced to turn its back on Antigua.

V. C. Bird is a tired old man whose physical and mental health are failing. And were it not for his extraordinary will to remain in control of his country, he might have died years ago. But even V. C. Bird cannot live forever. One day he will join all the other grand old men of the Caribbean. And afterwards there will never again be an Antiguan leader with the same almost absolute power. It is doubtful that any future politician can again reach so deep into the Antiguan psyche and mix the volatile ingredients of slavery, colonialism, and freedom, leaven them with pond water, and stir them with widdy widdy bushes. The next prime minister will be forced to confront reality; he will have to deal with the leavings of V. C. Bird.

Today the Caribbean is caught in a terrible dilemma. It is one of the most unstable, constitutionally diverse, and economically fragmented regions of the world. As Eric Williams said, "A too long history of colonialism seems to have crippled Caribbean self-confidence and Caribbean self-reliance, and a vicious circle has been set up: psychological dependence leads to an ever-growing economic and cultural dependence on the outside world. Fragmentation is intensified in the process. And the greater degree of dependence and fragmentation further reduces local self-confidence."

Some Caribbean countries are among the poorest in the world. They are all former colonies of European powers and face essentially the same combination of opportunity and risk—the same tourism marketing strategies, the same external pressures—and they hear the same siren song of growth, modernization, and progress.

The people of the Caribbean are fleeing in great numbers to America, Canada, or England, but they never quite fit in. When they go back and visit their respective countries, their experiences enable them to see with fresh eyes the harsh reality there. And they feel as dislocated at home as they do overseas, rootless and sad. European countries have joined together in a common market. The United States, Canada, and Mexico have negotiated a free-trade arrangement. New Zealand and Australia are talking of trade and economic arrangements in Southeast Asia. But Caribbean countries, which need to join forces more than any other place on earth, dissipate their energies and their economies by going their individual ways, by fighting with neighbors, by being insular and parochial, by being victims of their own politics, and by having political leaders who prefer to be big fish in little ponds. But perhaps these countries can do nothing else. A generation ago their people were colonial subjects. Freedom and independence remain new to them, and nationalism is all-important. Joining forces with other countries means a loss of national identity and a return to the condition they fought so long to overcome.

Eric Williams wrote that of all the formidable contributions sugar made to Caribbean psychology, the most enduring is that it "engendered and nurtured an intercolonial rivalry, an isolationist outlook, a provincialism that is almost a disease. . . ."

However, even if the Caribbean had a shared currency and even if there were a free movement of investment funds, and even if the countries were united in a common market, it would remain an almost insignificant economy among the common markets of the world. And, as Dr. Kennedy Simmonds, the prime minister of St. Kitts and Nevis, has said, "No political rhetoric about colonialism or the heritage of slavery and indentureship will change the fact."

The insular little islands of the region are anachronisms, tiny nations literally lost in the great blue Caribbean.

Lester Bird knows this. Speaking from prepared remarks at a Caribbean Community meeting, Lester said, "No crisis in the

Caribbean gives cause for alarm; no ideological alliance poses problems for others. Thus, we are ignored. Yet our economic foundations remain fragile, and the potential for fragmentation looms large. As the attention of some donors turns away from our development needs, our economies are threatened with reversal, and with all the political and social consequences that entails."

Caribbean countries, once the wealthiest colonies in the world, have not fared well since independence. Tourism was the great hope of the region, yet the islands have become supplicants before more developed nations. Invariably, the donor thinks the money is too much and that too little is done, while the recipient feels the money is too little and the strings attached are too many. Caribbean nations look to America for financial aid but complain that the United States tries to impose its morality as part of every loan package. Many of these countries equate success not with personal accomplishment but with how much they can borrow. There is little effort to break this chain of dependency. In a cable to the State Department, one chargé d'affaires in Antigua wrote that Prime Minister Bird "emotionally defends" Antigua's indebtedness and "lashes out at the insensitivity and lack of understanding" of the United States. Bird told the chargé that Antigua would continue to restructure its debt and to seek more loans.

A case can be made that Antigua has never been truly free. Antiguans first were slaves and they suffered perhaps an even worse fate under the British colonial system. Then they came under the power of V. C. Bird, who keeps them restless and stirred up with constant references to the old days and with a yearning to be led into the promised land. The average Antiguan has as little influence in government now as he did under the colonial system. It long has been recognized that slavery is more than physical repression: it also creates ties of dependency. And it can be argued that V. C. Bird, by creating a mind-set of dependency among his people and by causing his country to depend on foreign banks, has perpetuated slavery.

The schools of Antigua today are little better than they were in colonial times. Now, as then, wealthy Antiguans send their children abroad for their high school or university education. One of the few times I ever heard an Antiguan use profanity was when Tim Hector and I were talking one day about education. We were sitting in his living room. "V. C. Bird has not built one goddamn school on this island," Hector said. "Every school here was built by the British, by the PLM, or by the Canadians."

"You must be exaggerating," I said. "As long as Mr. Bird has been in office, surely he built some schools."

Hector jumped up and paced about. As a former schoolteacher, he is deeply stirred by the subject of education. "Every country must have its myths," he said. "V. C. Bird is a myth. The man has publicly boasted that he has not read a book since he was a teenager. He has not built one school." He leaned toward me, held up a forefinger, and spoke slowly and with great emphasis: "Not . . . one . . . goddamn . . . school."

If the legacy of Great Britain is not one of which that country can be proud, neither is the still-forming legacy of America. The big-footed ineptitude of the United States needs only a few more years to reach the depths of British insensitivity.

There appears to be little change in store for the continuing sadness of Antigua. Vere Cornwall Bird lives in the old home of Alexander Moody-Stuart, but he is far more powerful and more oppressive than was the British sugar baron. He appears to want nothing so much as for the Bird dynasty to continue. But he, like the Caribbean, is in a terrible dilemma. His fiercely loyal firstborn son believes that when the U.S. pulls out of the Canal Zone in the latter part of the 1990s, Antigua will become an even greater Caribbean bastion of American influence and investment. Vere junior looks ahead to that day; and despite his many ordeals, he has more influence and more power than ever before. He has gathered about him men who will do whatever it takes to hold onto that power, a flying squad of loyalists who are suspected of setting a series of fires that have caused unease and fear, the same technique his father used throughout his political career. No one has been arrested in connection with what obviously is arson. There is fear that the police are becoming government agents rather than officers of the law. Those loyal to Vere junior are also thought to be armed with weapons borrowed from the Defense Force. Some Antiguans think Vere junior is capable of orchestrating events to make it appear the country is in a state of emergency, thereby enabling the prime minister to suspend the government and lock up his political opponents before Vere junior steps into his job.

The prime minister's dilemma, as Makeda Mikael pointed out, is that the business community of Antigua would rise up in rebellion if V. C. Bird attempted to hand over his office to his oldest son. All over St. John's are double-barreled reminders of Vere junior's past, graffiti that says: "I am against gunrunning. Don't pay any cable TV bills."

Lester, the man who had it all, might seem a tragic figure after his flip-flopping in and out of government under the banner of principle. With his ministerial office in a waterfront hotel and his junior portfolio, he appears out of the mainstream of Antiguan politics. Nevertheless, he remains a strong candidate for prime minister.

The new political party that may successfully challenge the long-omnipotent ALP would not accept Lester Bird as a member, so he must stay with the ALP. But what appears a weakness may in fact be a hidden strength, for if the new party self-destructs, which is possible, and if the prime minister dies in the next few years, which is likely, Lester could become leader of the ALP. And as the leader of the ruling party, he automatically becomes prime minister.

Because the Birds have been so powerful for so many years, no truly talented opposition leaders have emerged. Antiguan politics has not yet revealed a man with the intellect, experience, and magnetism to equal Lester Bird's. However, John St. Luce has been the beneficiary of the "No More Birds" movement within the ALP, and he is becoming less intimidated by Lester. But opposition leader Baldwin Spencer, when asked by the BBC what changes he might make if he became prime minister, could only stutter and say nothing. Among U.S. embassy personnel Spencer is famous for a preelection comment: "We are going to have trouble canvassing because we don't have money to pay our volunteers." Hilbourne Frank of Barbuda is too closely aligned with the Barbudan separatist movement to become party leader. Dr. Ivor Heath had the ability but not the support, and has withdrawn from politics. Tim Hector is too emotional and volatile; and his political following, which is considerably smaller than his journalistic following, is far too insignificant for him to become prime minister.

But in the early 1990s, Hector became the darling of the island cocktail-party circuit. He was even invited to the homes of wealthy whites on Antigua and asked for his opinion on every subject under the sun. The old business that had nagged him for years, the charge of being a Communist, no longer seemed relevant. Communism was dead. And people listened when he said, "I have fought many battles for freedom of the press, and freedom of the press is the antithesis of what communism stands for."

Hector's youthful revolutionary fires became, in his middle age, faint embers. Today he seeks to revise the history of which he once was so proud. Instead of wanting credit for forming the ACLM, he calls himself "one of the early members." As a top official of the United Progressive Party (UPP), the new amalgamated political party that seems certain to win some seats in the 1994 general election, Hector would like the job of foreign minister if a new government is formed. He has even gone to Bryant Salter and asked what would be the reaction of the United States if he held that post. Would the United States deal with a leftist politician who had traveled to Cuba and to Libya and who had been virulent in his criticism of the United States for more than a decade? Had he been so leftist in his political rhetoric that his appointment might cause a resurgence of the feared Grenada Syndrome? "I am not a fool," Hector said to me. "I realize that one travel advisory from America could wipe out tourism here in a week."

"I don't want your reaction," he told Salter. "I want the official reaction of the U.S. government." So Salter sent a cable of inquiry to the State Department.

"The State Department said it would be no problem," Hector told me, pleased that he had passed muster in Washington.

"But what about *Outlet?*" I asked him. "What about your career as a newspaperman? If you became a minister in a new government, will you continue to publish *Outlet?* Can you, as a minister, continue to publish the newspaper?"

Hector smiled. And I wasn't sure if he had simply not considered the issue or if he was amused by my näiveté. He thought for a moment before replying that he had long wanted to make *Outlet* a regional newspaper that would "publish alternative news that will cause the leaders to react."

"Does that mean you want to be remembered as a newspaperman rather than a politician?"

Hector laughed. "I want to be remembered as a human being," he said.

There is little chance that an unspotted man will arise from nowhere and, by sheer force of character, emerge as a new political leader.

Lester, if not the best choice, is perhaps the only choice. One way or another, he is almost certain to become the next prime minister. If that happens, America will embrace him. The IRS investigation has already been dropped; but even if the investigation had been pursued, nothing would have been gained by discrediting Lester. Had he been pushed hard enough, he would have renounced his U.S. citizenship and attacked the great colossus to the north for picking on the leader of such a small and insignificant island.

For such a small country, the miasma of corruption emanating from Antigua has spread far and wide: to America, Canada, and Africa with Space Research; to France with the airport financing; and to Israel and Colombia with the arms smuggling.

At this writing, there appears little hope for change. To reclaim Antigua would call for sacrifices that neither the Antiguan people nor their leaders are willing to make. They will not turn back. They have watched CNN and they want the world. They saw Antigua featured in a segment of *Lifestyles of the Rich and Famous* and they believed what they saw.

In considering Antigua's future, the words of Jamaica Kincaid should be heard once again. In her trenchant book *A Small Place*, she says, "Is the Antigua I see before me, self-ruled, a worse place than what it was when it was dominated by the bad-minded English and all the bad-minded things they brought with them? How did Antigua get to such a state that I would have to ask myself this? For the answer on every Antiguan's lips to the question 'What is going on here now?' is 'The government is corrupt. Them are thief, them are big thief.' "

As I left Antigua for the last time and over my shoulder the island became a pale green blur in the midst of a rich blue sea, my thoughts went back to Shirley Heights and to the boisterous and popular party held there each Sunday.

So many cars and vans and taxis and tour buses park along the road that latecomers often must trek half a mile up the steep road to the peak. Hundreds of people gather here. Their happy talk fights with the noise of a steel band that pounds out rhythmic calypso songs. Chickens are barbecued by the flock, ribs cooked by the herd, and beer consumed by the barrel as tourists dance the loose, abandoned dance of those enjoying an idyllic Caribbean vacation.

The view from Shirley Heights is the most impressive in all Antigua. To the south is almost 180 degrees of Caribbean Sea and numerous picture-book half-moon harbors. To the northwest, below the heights, are English Harbour, Nelson's Dockyard, and Falmouth Harbour. Luxury yachts from around the world lie at anchor, bobbing gently with their fine bows pointed into the prevailing easterlies. Beyond is Boggy Peak and the jagged tops of hills etched against the cerulean sky. Brilliant bursts of poinciana explode from the hillsides. To the east, the land slopes down past the ruins of numerous sugar mills, ubiquitous reminders that Antigua once was among the most valuable real etsate in the world.

This heart-stopping view is one reason tourists almost universally fall in love with Antigua.

Lester Bird occasionally drops in at the party atop Shirley Heights. I saw him there wearing chartreuse nylon shorts, a yellow T-shirt, and a red hat upon which was written ANTIGUA LUV LESTER. Few tourists recognized the big man; their eyes were drawn to the beautiful young woman at his side. He left early and walked a few paces to where his dark BMW was parked on the fringes of the party, far closer than any other vehicle. The Birds of Antigua always roost in the highest branches.

Guests from the cruise ships mingled with guests from the hotels. They danced with young Antiguans. The conversation was a raucous babble. Weaving in and out among the tourists were hucksters carrying gym bags jammed with tapes whose music was pirated from Caribbean radio stations. The tapes were for sale. The primary sales tool was a demonstration. The hucksters stood close to a prospect, patted his foot, and sang in the prospect's ear.

Yachties, men who can be identified by their tanned leathery skin, sun-bleached hair, and the shorts and shirts with proper tags and decals, were at the party, accompanied by much younger women of startling beauty. A few clean-cut and well-tanned young men were in attendance, men whose serious demeanor and hard eyes showed they were not tourists, but rather some of America's toughest young warriors in training at the Navy base.

Various American women were also there, including the hairy-legged Birkenstock-sandal-wearing types common on Caribbean islands. Like flotsam washed above the high tide line, they stay awhile and then they disappear as quickly as they came.

Hour after hour the steel band played its throbbing, pounding, pulsating rhythm. Partygoers who began by wiggling their shoulders or tapping their feet and snapping their fingers, found that, almost without being able to control themselves, they were standing up and abandoning themselves to the music.

Blue smoke rose from dozens of distant fires. The smoke, borne on the ever-present easterlies, brought the odor of burning garbage wafting over the crowd. As the afternoon wore on, the number of fires and the amount of smoke increased.

About twilight an airliner filled with fuel and passengers flew overhead. Climbing out of V. C. Bird International Airport nine miles to the north, it was flying so low over the mountain that one could almost see sunburned faces in the windows. But there was no sound of its engines. The steel band was too loud. And the aircraft, like a closeup in a silent movie, slowly disappeared over the horizon.

A Rastaman in a blousy black cat suit danced through the crowd on an herb-powered trip to the ethereal realms. The tourists watched him and smiled, their heads nodding and keeping time with his dancing as he twisted and turned and rolled his eyes.

As the sun went down, some of the younger partygoers eased out to the edges of the firelight, where they kissed and fondled each other. By now the steel band no longer was pausing between songs. Each time you thought the music was about to end, the band segued into another number and the loud, mesmeric pounding continued. The people atop the mountain were in a near-trance as their bodies throbbed and twitched to primitive rhythms. The deep bass of the drums was relentless. A palpable musk hung in the air.

A few guests left the party early, but atop the mountain the tourists remained clumped together, dancing, drinking, and laughing far into the evening. The party atop Shirley Heights was everything and more of what they expected of their Caribbean vacation. No one seemed to notice the east wind and the unmistakable and pervasive odor of garbage.

Selected Bibliography

Adams, James Truslow. *Empire on the Seven Seas: The British Empire, 1784–1939.* New York: Charles Scribner's Sons, 1940.

Aflak, Alan. *A Little Bit of Paradise.* Limited Hertford: Hansib Publishing, 1988.

Antigua and Barbuda Independence. Official independence magazine published by Ministry of Foreign Affairs, Government of Antigua and Barbuda, 1981.

Aspinall, Algernon E. *The Pocket Guide to the West Indies.* London: Duckworth, 1910.

Augier, F. R. *The Making of the West Indies.* Trinidad: Longman Caribbean, 1960.

Blom-Cooper, Louis. *Guns for Antigua: Report of the Commission of Inquiry into the Circumstances Surrounding the Shipment of Arms from Israel to Antigua and Transhipment on 24 April 1989 En Route to Colombia.* London: Duckworth, 1990.

Blome, Richard. *The Present State of His Majesties Isles and Territories in America.* London: H. Clark, 1687.

Burke, Edmund and Burke, William. *An Account of the European Settlements in America.* 2 vols. 6th edition. London: Printed for J. Dodsley, 1777.

Burns, Alan. *Colonial Civil Servant.* London: George Allen & Unwin, 1949.

Caribbean Countries: Economic Situation, Regional Issues, and Capital Flows. Washington: World Bank, 1988.

Caribbean Conservation Association. *Environmental Agenda for the*

1990s: A Synthesis of the Eastern Caribbean Country Environmental Profile Series. St. Thomas: Caribbean Conservation Association and the Island Resources Foundation, 1991.

Coram, Robert. "Ancient Rights." *The New Yorker,* Feb. 6, 1989; pp. 76–94.

Dyde, Brian. *Antigua and Barbuda: The Heart of the Caribbean.* London: Macmillan, 1986.

Edwards, Bryan. *The History, Civil and Commercial, of the British Colonies in the West Indies.* 2 vols. Dublin: Luke White, 1793.

Fortis, Paul de, ed. *The Kingdom of Redonda, 1865–1990.* London: Aylesford Press, 1991.

Gaspar, David. *Bondmen & Rebels: A Study of Master-Slave Relationships in Antigua.* Baltimore: Johns Hopkins University Press, 1985.

Increasing the International Competitiveness of Exports from Caribbean Countries. Washington: World Bank, 1989.

Kincaid, Jamaica. *A Small Place.* New York: Penguin, 1988.

Lamb, David. *The Africans.* New York: Vintage Books, 1987.

[Lanaghan, Mrs.] *Antigua and the Antiguans: A Full Account of the Colony and Its Inhabitants from the Time of the Caribs to the Present Day, Interspersed with Anecdotes and Legends.* 2 vols. London: Saunders and Otley, 1844.

Littleton, Edward. *The Groans of the Plantations: or, A True Account of Their Grievous and Extreme Sufferings by the Heavy Impositions Upon Sugar, and Other Hardships.* London: M. Clark, 1689.

Lowes, Susan. *Time and Motion in the Formation of the Middle Class in Antigua, 1834–1940.* A paper written for the Teachers College at Columbia University. N.D.

McCabe, Carol. "The Caribbean Heritage." *Islands,* April 1992.

McKinnen, Daniel. *A Tour Through the British West Indies, in the Years 1802 and 1803.* London: Printed for J. White by R. Taylor, Black-Horse Court, 1804.

Morison, Samuel Eliot. *Admiral of the Ocean Sea.* New York: Little, Brown, 1941.

Morse, A. Reynolds. *The Quest for Redonda.* Cleveland: Reynolds Morse Foundation, 1979.

Nicholson, Desmond V. *Antigua, Barbuda, and Redonda: A Historical Sketch.* St. John's, Antigua: Museum of Antigua & Barbuda, 1992.

Nicholson, Desmond V. *The Story of English Harbour.* St. John's, Antigua: Museum of Antigua & Barbuda, 1991.

North American and the West-Indian Gazetteer. London: Printed for G. Robinson, 1776.

Oldmixon, John. *The British Empire in America, Containing the History of the Discovery, Settlement, Progress and Present State of All the British Colonies, On the Continent and Islands of America.* London: Printed for John Nicholson, 1708.

Oliver, Vere Langford. *The History of the Island of Antigua, One of the Leeward Caribees in the West Indies, from the First Settlement in 1635 to the Present Time.* London: Mitchell and Hughes, 1894–1899.

O'Shaughnessy, Hugh. *Grenada: An Eyewitness Account of the U.S. Invasion and the Caribbean History That Provoked It.* New York: Dodd, Mead, 1984.

Pastor, Robert A. *Whirlpool: U.S. Foreign Policy Toward Latin America and the Caribbean.* Princeton: Princeton University Press, 1992.

Pitts, Denis. "The Dotty Dynasty of Redonda." *Sunday Express Magazine.* London. September 23, 1984.

Raynal, Abbie. *A Philosophical and Political History of the Settlements and Trade of the Europeans in the East and West Indies.* London: W. Strahan, 1783.

"Redonda and Its Phosphates." *Popular Science.* Vol. 46, November 1894.

Restructuring and Debt in the Caribbean: Selected Papers of the Second Conference of Caribbean Economists. Special Issue of *Caribbean Studies,* Z4, Jan.–June 1991.

Richards, Novelle. *The Struggle and the Conquest.* Part I, St. John's, Antigua: Benjies-Antigua, 1964.

Richards, Novelle. *The Struggle and the Conquest.* Part II. St. John's, Antigua: Benjies-Antigua, 1981.

Rochefort, Charles de. *The History of the Caribby-Islands.* Translated by John Davies. Printed by J.M. for Thomas Dring, 1666.

Scotland, James. *Antigua Free Press.* July 31, 1834.

Smith, Keithlyn B. and Smith, Fernando C. *To Shoot Hard Labour.* Ontario: Edan's Publishers, 1986.

Steele, Ian K. *The English Atlantic 1675–1740.* New York: Oxford University Press, 1986.

Thome, Jas. A. and Kimball, J. Horace. *Emancipation in the West Indies: A Six Months' Tour in Antigua, Barbadoes, and Jamaica in the Year 1837.* New York: American Anti-Slavery Society, 1838.

Thompson, John. "Selling Sand by the Seashore." *Islands.* July-August 1990.

Tuchman, Barbara W. *The First Salute.* New York: Ballantine Books, 1988.

Watkins, Frederick Henry. *Handbook of the Leeward Islands.* London: West India Committee, 1924.

Williams, Eric. *From Columbus to Castro: The History of the Caribbean, 1492–1969.* New York: Vintage Books, 1984.

Wouk, Herman. *Don't Stop the Carnival.* New York: Doubleday, 1965.

Wynne-Tyson, Jon. *So Say Banana Bird.* London: Pythian Books, 1984.

Index